Money at Interest: The Farm Mortgage on the Middle Border

Robert E. Bieder

MONEY AT INTEREST

The Farm Mortgage on the Middle Border

ALLAN G. BOGUE

A BISON BOOK

UNIVERSITY OF NEBRASKA PRESS · LINCOLN

Manufactured in the United States of America

First Bison Book printing March, 1969

Bison Book edition reprinted by arrangement with Cornell University Press

To PAUL WALLACE GATES

PREFACE

IN THIS book I have tried to explore one aspect of the western farm credit problem during the late nineteenth century—the use of the land mortgage. This monograph is not a history of farm credit in the middle west during the years of the "agrarian crusade." Chattel credit and the efforts of western states to regulate the relations between debtor and creditor, for example, are treated but incidentally. Nor do I claim to have said the last word in description of farmland mortgage credit on the middle border. By detailed analysis of representative business manuscripts and county records I have sought to show the operation of the mortgage business in that region. But my research has been concentrated mainly in four states and my sources are limited in number. I regard my conclusions therefore as tentative rather than final.

During the course of this study I have become indebted to a considerable number of historians, professional and amateur, who assisted me in a variety of ways. So deep is my obligation to some that I must make specific acknowledgment. My primary debt is recognized in the dedication; this book grew out of a seminar conducted by Paul Wallace Gates, who has continued to show lively interest in the subject. Some years ago James C. Malin of the University of Kansas saved the papers of J. B. Watkins from destruction. Later, through his efforts, I obtained financial assistance which enabled me to use this excellent collection of business records and at the same time to benefit from his vast knowledge of agriculture in general and the plains country in particular. With my needs in mind, Edith M. Fox, curator of the Collection of Regional History at Cornell University, painstakingly gathered together an excellent collection of the business manuscripts of New York investors. At the University of Western Ontario, Professor Fred Landon was instrumental in obtaining a Fred Ashplant Travelling Fellowship for me, while James J. Talman, chief librarian, generously arranged my schedule as assistant librarian so that I could spend a considerable amount of time in writing. My debts to Nyle Miller and his staff at the Kansas State Historical Society, Topeka, and to James C. Olson and his helpers in the Nebraska State Historical Society, Lincoln, differ only in degree from those owing to a long list of librarians and document custodians in both the northeastern states and the middle west. Margaret Beattie Bogue has been a constant source of encouragement, clerical assistance, and professional advice.

Some of the material in this book has previously appeared in articles published in *Agricultural History*, the *Kansas Historical Quarterly*, *Nebraska History*, and the *Bulletin of the Business Historical Society* and is reproduced here by permission of the editors of those periodicals.

I wish to express my thanks for the financial assistance in meeting the costs of publication, provided by the fund established by Miss Mary F. Hall in honor of the New York State Society of the Daughters of the American Revolution and supplemented by the Graduate College of the State University of Iowa.

ALLAN G. BOGUE

State University of Iowa
March 1, 1955

CONTENTS

INTRODUCTION

AS YET our understanding of the role of land credit along the middle border has been perverted by the hysteria of the Populist era. The professional historian has cherished the charges which the agrarian radicals made against the moneylender and the mortgage,[1] while the novelist has equated the mortgage with catastrophe and the moneyman with heartless, grasping avarice.[2]

Why did the settler who established himself in Kansas or Nebraska between 1854 and 1900 have need of capital? Until 1862 of course he generally had to pay $1.25 per acre for land obtained from the federal government, but in that year the homestead act was passed, allowing 160 acres of land to settlers who paid minor fees and performed settlement duties that included occupancy of the land for five years. Henceforth the term "free land" was to be used in promiscuous fashion. Actually the act did not throw the plains states into the hands of eager

[1] For example, see John D. Hicks, *The Populist Revolt* (Minneapolis, 1931), pp. 20–24, 89–90, 95.

[2] Hamlin Garland, "Under the Lion's Paw," *Main Travelled Roads* (London, 1892), pp. 217–240; Willa Cather, *My Antonia* (Boston, 1946); Mari Sandoz, *Capital City* (Boston, 1939).

settlers for the mere taking.[3] In Nebraska, for example, some 10,690,990 acres of the 48,636,800 acres of the state were claimed by four railroads and the state government. These agencies disposed of their holdings as profitably as possible, with the exception of certain school lands which are still leased by the state. Aside from the state and railroad land, individuals had obtained 3,695,792 acres from the federal government as early as 1870 under the terms of the pre-emption act of 1841, by cash sale or through the operation of the military bounty acts.[4] By 1870, therefore, almost a third of the state had been allotted without recourse to the homestead law. The settler who obtained his land from this third had to pay more than nominal fees.

But even if he homesteaded, the western pioneer still had need for capital. Clarence H. Danhof has investigated the cost of bringing forty acres of prairie land into production in Illinois during the 1850's. It was his conclusion that the task would require a minimum expenditure of $1,000, aside from the purchase price of the land.[5] There is no reason to believe that farm-making costs diminished after settlement crossed the Missouri. The geographer classifies eastern Kansas and Nebraska as prairie country, much akin to Illinois. As settlement moved into the plains country of central and western Kansas and Nebraska, the "cash capital costs" of settlement probably rose.[6]

In Illinois the timber for buildings and fences was usually available on the settler's holding or along some nearby stream bed which could be easily pillaged. The major cost was that of labor, and the settler supplied most of that himself. In the plains country there were few log or frame houses built of timber grown on the settler's own property. Despite the prevalence of the sod house and of the dugout in the fiction of the plains country, settlers hastened to buy lumber with which to build frame buildings as soon as possible.[7] To solve the problem of fenc-

[3] Paul Wallace Gates, "The Homestead Law in an Incongruous Land System," *American Historical Review*, XLI (July 1936), 652–681.

[4] Commissioner of General Land Office, Annual Report, 1870, pp. 504–507; Addison E. Sheldon, *Land Systems and Land Policies in Nebraska* (Lincoln, 1936), pp. 2–93, 360.

[5] Clarence H. Danhof, "Farm-making Costs and the 'Safety Valve': 1850–60," *Journal of Political Economy*, XLIX (June 1941), pp. 317–359.

[6] The following five paragraphs owe much to James C. Malin, *Winter Wheat in the Golden Belt of Kansas* (Lawrence, 1944), pp. 102–137.

[7] James C. Malin, *The Grassland of North America; Prolegomena to its History* (Lawrence, 1947), p. 268.

ing his holdings the settler of the plains country had to resort to hedge or wire fencing. It is true that a herd law might bind residents to keep their livestock from raiding the unfenced crops of their neighbors, but such laws were not universally applied or enforced.[8] No farmer could regard his acres as improved or safe from marauding livestock until they had been surrounded by a fence.

In Illinois the settler could generally obtain his water from a nearby spring or stream, or, at the worst, from a shallow well. Deeper and more costly wells became necessary as the plains country was invaded. Fuel became a problem as well. The buffalo chip, hay, or even grain might serve temporarily, but the only satisfactory substitute for wood was coal. This had to be purchased at the nearest railway station.

More machinery was also needed. James C. Malin has argued that large horse-drawn machines were essential in the subhumid climate of the plains country. Only by their use could soil be worked while its moisture content was adequate. Yield per acre was lower and the possibility of crop failure greater than in humid climates. It was advisable, therefore, to farm more acres less intensively in terms of human labor by using machinery.[9]

Finally, the variable climate of the plains country might bring crop failures in successive years. A larger cash reserve therefore was essential for the settler in the plains country than had been necessary for his predecessor in the more humid climates to the east.

In the fall of 1885 Orange Judd, the editor of the *Prairie Farmer*, toured portions of Dakota Territory, Kansas, and Nebraska. On the basis of his observations he made various estimates of the cost of farm making in the plains country. He claimed that $500 would "buy a good span of working horses, first rate farm wagon, plows, harness, seeder etc. almost anywhere in the West," and added that on the average the cost of the dwellings first used on government land did not exceed $250.[10]

To the cost of machinery and buildings the settler was forced to add the cost of fencing his land and digging a well. Since breaking sod usually required the use of more than one yoke of oxen or team of

[8] See for example, Nebraska, *Laws, 1870–71*, pp. 120–122. Counties might, by petition of a majority of the electors, confirmed by a majority vote at the next election, suspend action of the law.

[9] Malin, *Winter Wheat*, p. 104.

[10] *Prairie Farmer*, Dec. 12, 1885, p. 812; see also, Oct. 17, 1885, p. 678; Oct. 24, 1885, p. 701; Nov. 7, 1885, p. 732; Nov. 21, 1885, p. 764; Dec. 5, 1885, pp. 796–97.

horses this operation also might require the outlay of capital. In 1879 a hardheaded New Englander calculated the cost of fencing a quarter section in Kansas with two strands of Glidden barbed wire at $200.[11] Hedge fences cost as much or more.[12] The price of wire, it is true, fell sharply after 1880,[13] but according to Professor Fred A. Shannon a mile of barbed wire fence in the range country cost $136 in 1900.[14] It required two miles of fence to enclose a quarter section of farmland. The cost of wells naturally varied from place to place, but the relatively inexpensive drivewell of the 1870's and 1880's cost $2.00 per foot without the controversial royalty.[15] The cash cost of breaking sod between 1868 and the 1890's varied from $1.50 to $3.50 per acre in various sections of the northern plains.[16] The western settler who homesteaded 160 acres of land, bought his farming equipment, erected farm buildings of a sort, hired someone to break forty acres of prairie, fenced it, and finally drove a forty-foot well, had incurred cash costs of almost $1,000. In addition he had to support his family and himself for at least a year before he could expect the farm to provide the income with which to purchase household supplies.

Writing in *Forum* a few years after Judd's journey, Professor Rodney Welch estimated that a minimum of $1,000 was needed by the western homesteader if he were to bring his land into production, not to mention support himself during the first years of light crops. Arthur F. Bentley quoted this figure approvingly during the early 1890's when he wrote *The Condition of the Western Farmer as Illustrated by the Economic History of a Nebraska Township*.[17] Without doubt, $1,000 stood as the

[11] C. M. Hawkes, New Haven, Conn., to J. B. Vance, Alfred, Maine, Dec. 7, 1879. In Hawkes Papers, Archives of Kansas State Historical Society, Topeka, Kans.

[12] *Kansas Farmer*, Nov. 1868, pp. 1 and 7, Jan. 1871, p. 6, Mar. 25, 1874, p. 91; Fremont *Tribune*, Oct. 10, 1867.

[13] Walter P. Webb, *The Great Plains* (New York, 1931), p. 310.

[14] Fred A. Shannon, *The Farmer's Last Frontier; Agriculture, 1860–1897* (New York, 1945), p. 207.

[15] Earl W. Hayter, "The Western Farmers and the Drivewell Patent Controversy," *Agricultural History*, XVI (Jan. 1942), 16–28, 20, fn.23.

[16] *Kansas Farmer*, Nov. 1868, pp. 1, 7; Larned *Chronoscope*, May 29, 1880; *Prairie Farmer*, Oct. 17, 1885, pp. 6–8; Harold E. Briggs, *Frontiers of the Northwest; A History of the Upper Missouri Valley* (New York, 1940), p. 515; M. J. Dart, Lawrence, Kans., to W. C. Holder, Newton, Kans., Apr. 3, 1878, A. L. Stanton, Lawrence, Kans., to P. A. Hallowell, Belleville, Kans., Mar. 4, 1892, J. B. Watkins Papers, Library, University of Kansas, Lawrence, Kans.

[17] Arthur F. Bentley, *The Condition of the Western Farmer as Illustrated by the*

minimum figure needed by a settler in the form of cash, or perhaps partly of equipment, before he could hope to bring a homestead into production in Kansas or Nebraska during the 1870's or 1880's.

How many of those who helped to unroll the carpet of settlement across the plains country during the years between 1854 and 1900 actually possessed adequate capital with which to establish themselves? One veteran student of western history has written of an area in central Kansas, "Most new settlers came with scarcely enough capital to meet expenses until the first crop should have matured." [18] Such being the case, many pioneers found it necessary to obtain additional funds during the first years of settlement. If they were situated close to a western town and were lucky enough to possess a special trade or skill, they might work for wages as Howard Ruede did in Kansas or obtain jobs in the construction crews of the transcontinental railroads.[19] Others might scrape along at a bare subsistence level until they obtained title to their lands and then mortgage them to buy additional improvements. Thus entered the moneylender. But this picture is too simple. He found other clients as well. For speculators of both large and small degree were eager to use the funds of others to carry their holdings until they could sell them. In short order, too, began the transfer of land from one farmer to another and from one generation to the next, which also required the aid of the moneymen.

In this study an attempt is made to disregard what the Populist, or his radical predecessor, claimed, as well as the arguments of rivals from the established parties, and to deal with basic questions. What proportion of the original settlers used their land as security for loans? Why did these farmers borrow? What was the source of their funds? Who negotiated loans and what were their methods of business? How successful were the lenders in realizing returns on their capital? How successful were the borrowers in utilizing borrowed funds and eventually repaying them? What was the legal framework in which borrower and lender operated? These are far-reaching questions and more work must be

Economic History of a Nebraska Township (Johns Hopkins University Studies in Historical and Political Science, 11th ser., nos. vii, viii; Baltimore, 1893), p. 28, quoting from Rodney Welch, "Horace Greeley's Cure for Poverty," *Forum*, VIII (Jan. 1890), 586–593.

[18] Malin, *Winter Wheat*, p. 106.

[19] Howard Ruede, *Sod-house Days; Letters from a Kansas Homesteader, 1877–78*, edited by John Ise (New York, 1937).

done before they can be answered positively. The collection of sample studies which follows, however, does provide evidence on all of these problems. This evidence in turn may be used to evaluate the arguments and demands of the agrarian radicals during the last quarter of the nineteenth century.

The answers to the questions posed here may be sought through different approaches. In this essay there are three main lines of attack. The story of the mortgage investments of a New York family over a period of some fifty years serves as an introduction to the problems of eastern investors who loaned extensively in the western states. One study sketches the career of an important western mortgage broker. In the final section an effort is made to show the use of land credit in a Nebraska and a Kansas township during the years before 1900.

PART I

THE EASTERN INVESTOR

John and Ira Davenport of Bath, New York

THE eastern investors who purchased mortgages, written on land in the western states between 1854 and 1900, differed considerably in economic status. Large corporations like the insurance companies of Hartford, Connecticut, were investing millions of dollars in farm mortgages by the early 1870's.[1] There were individuals or family groups who controlled large amounts of capital. An ever-increasing number of investors of smaller stature—ministers, teachers, and other professional people—invested their savings in western mortgages during the 1870's and 1880's. The study given here describes the investments of a family group which were administered by John and Ira Davenport of Bath, New York.

It is not argued that the problems faced by the Davenports and their method of lending funds were typical among those who

[1] See Connecticut, *Annual Report of the Insurance Commissioner, 1875* and *1876,* for a description of the mortgage investments of the Hartford companies; also "Western Loans for Life Insurance Companies," *Spectator,* XX (Mar. 1878), 140–141.

invested money in mortgages on western farmland. Controlling the allocation of several hundred thousand dollars annually, the Davenport brothers undoubtedly influenced the activity and policy of their agents to a greater extent than did the small investors who loaned funds during the 1880's through farm mortgage companies. Nor were their problems the same as those encountered by the insurance companies, which loaned millions of dollars annually. Whether large or small, however, investors operated in a common framework of federal and state laws and faced similar difficulties in obtaining responsible agents and working out adequate methods of supervision. That a large investor might solve his problems differently than a small investor cannot be argued. But the study of the lending activities of the Davenport brothers, who stood midway between the small investor and the large corporate investor, should serve as an introduction to the problems faced by investors in western farm mortgages during the last half of the nineteenth century.

I

ILLINOIS

JOHN and Ira Davenport built their business careers on the foundation provided by their father. Ira Davenport, Sr., was born in Columbia County, New York, in 1795 and clerked in his father's store until he attained his majority.[1] Then he set out for himself, laboriously transporting a stock of goods into the semiwilderness of Steuben County. Davenport was to do well in the mercantile business, and as he prospered some of his profits were diverted into other avenues of investment. By the 1830's he was speculating in the raw lands of Illinois and had probably already made intimate acquaintance with the tax title business as well. By the 1850's he was lending funds to the farmers of Michigan through the agency of his son-in-law, J. W. Waterman, as was his brother Charles Davenport of Savona, New York.[2]

In the late 1850's Ira Davenport, Sr., and James Adsit of Chicago

[1] For brief notes on Ira Davenport see Millard F. Roberts, *Historical Gazeteer, Steuben County, New York* (Syracuse, 1891), pp. 161–162, 365.

[2] John Davenport to J. W. Waterman, Detroit, Mich., Feb. 7, 1871, in the Davenport Collection, Collection of Regional History, Cornell University, Ithaca, N.Y. Unless otherwise stated all other correspondence cited may be found in this collection.

dissolved a partnership which held title to a considerable acreage of land in Illinois. In the process, Adsit tendered a series of notes to Davenport that were payable in the bank currency of Illinois. Instead of transferring Adsit's payments home, Davenport began in 1859 to lend them on the security of improved farms in central Illinois. To establish the lending business in Illinois, Davenport sent his eldest son, John, to take up residence at Pekin, the county seat of Tazewell County. For his time and effort young Davenport received any commissions which he could collect above the 10-per-cent interest called for in the notes and mortgages. To the eastern lad, fresh from college, the lending business represented a radically different way of life, entailing trips to the west in all manner of weather and residence in Pekin, where he found society unsophisticated at best. But business ran smoothly for some years. By 1863 the county officers of Tazewell County estimated that John Davenport had loaned more than $250,000 in the counties of Logan, Mason, and Tazewell on behalf of his father, his uncle, and a cousin.

In 1863 the assessor of Tazewell County assessed the mortgages which were outstanding, arguing that John Davenport was a local resident and that the mortgages under his control as the agent of eastern investors were taxable as personal property. Young Davenport obtained an injunction which prevented the collection of the tax, and a writ of error was obtained by the board of supervisors of the county. Early in 1866 the case reached the supreme court of Illinois. Could John Davenport be considered a resident of Illinois and the funds at his command be taxed by the state? When the court answered affirmatively, the state auditor was authorized by the legislature to compromise the sum at issue, and the Davenport family paid at least $4,000. Unquestionably, too, John Davenport paid heavily in pride when his brother, Ira, and two brothers-in-law arrived in Illinois to make the compromise settlement.[3]

After the disastrous decision of the Illinois supreme court, John Davenport withdrew his residence from Pekin and the legal fiction was preserved that Ira Davenport, Sr., had no agent in Illinois. Actually, business was carried on much as before. Borrowers made their applica-

[3] Illinois, *Public Laws, 1867,* p. 165. The original assessment was $1,450 per annum, but an act of Feb. 28, 1867, authorized the state auditor of Illinois to compromise the claims against John Davenport.

tions to the private banking firm of George Greigg and Company at Pekin, which forwarded them to Bath. On advice from Davenport, Greigg negotiated loans for the New York capitalist.[4]

On the death of Ira Davenport, Sr., in 1868, John and Ira Davenport became executors of the estate, worth some $1,000,000. They each received one-fifth of the residue after certain bequests had been satisfied.[5] One sister had already died, and to the brothers fell the responsibility of administering the considerable inheritance of her children until they came of age. Charles Davenport also died, a few years after the death of his brother, and the brothers became executors of his estate, which also numbered minors among the heirs. In addition to these trusts, John and Ira Davenport were to supervise the investment of the funds belonging to the Davenport Home for Female Orphans in Bath, New York, which their father had established and endowed. Several female relatives entrusted investment funds to them for varying periods of time. From these sources and on their own account John and Ira Davenport loaned almost $5,500,000 between 1868 and 1904, when Ira, the surviving brother, died.[6] Most of the ledgers and correspondence bearing on this business have been preserved, and they serve as the major source for this study.

Farmers in Michigan, Illinois, Iowa, Kansas, and Nebraska borrowed funds from the Davenports on the security of their farm lands. Since the local agents in Michigan were relatives of the New Yorkers and there was visiting back and forth, the correspondence on the details of the lending business in Michigan is less revealing than that of the other states. Our attention, therefore, will be centered on the loan business of John and Ira Davenport in Illinois, Iowa, Kansas, and Nebraska.

The Davenports lent the bulk of their funds in Illinois through two agents. When Ira Davenport, Sr., died, George Greigg continued to serve his sons as he had their father. S. A. Foley was the second important agent of the Davenport brothers in Illinois. An attorney of Lincoln, the county seat of Logan County, Foley may not have represented Ira Davenport, Sr. He was, however, acting for the sons as early

[4] This account of the establishment of the loan business in Illinois is based mainly on *Board of Supervisors of Tazewell County et al.* vs. *John Davenport, Illinois Reports*, XL, 190–209, and John Davenport to J. W. Waterman, Feb. 7, 1871.

[5] Steuben Co. Surrogate Court, Record of Wills, X, 262–264, also Folder A-2767.

[6] Statistics are based on an analysis of the loan registers of the Davenports in the Davenport Collection.

as 1869.[7] Thomas Hoblitt, a private banker of Canton, Illinois, also negotiated some loans for the Davenport brothers in the 1870's but his activities were of a minor nature.

For the most part the agents were encouraged to negotiate loans in their own counties only. In December 1869 Ira Davenport apologized to Foley because a loan had been made to a Logan County farmer through Greigg and Company. He pointed out that the man had relatives in Pekin with whom the Davenports had dealt and he had therefore logically applied to Greigg. Ira Davenport assured Foley that neither he nor his brother desired to have any conflict between their agents and that the loan had occurred only by accident. He added, "As Mr. Greigg has been our friend from the Commencement I do not now wish to withdraw from making the loan, but I regard it as an exceptional case and also that you should be properly so informed of the way it occurred." [8]

On occasion loans were accepted from other counties than Tazewell and Logan. Tempted by the higher rates available in Mason County, the Davenports allowed Greigg to negotiate a number of loans there in the early 1870's. But when Foley suggested in 1873 that he be allowed to enter Pike County, John Davenport refused him permission, writing that there were insufficient funds available to expand their Illinois territory and that he doubted the wisdom of going into Pike County, since it was in the military tract where titles would undoubtedly be in some confusion.[9]

During the 1870's the Davenports came to depend increasingly on Foley. The loans which Greigg transacted in Mason County had turned out badly. In 1873 he uncovered a case of embezzlement among his employees which shook the confidence of the Davenports.[10] But more important was the character of Foley. The lawyer from Lincoln was a man of considerable ability, which his fellow citizens eventually recognized by electing him a judge of the district court. While he was working into the lending business in the early 1870's he may well have forwarded payments to the Davenports before the mortgagors tendered them to him. John Davenport wrote in February 1871, "You certainly

[7] For a sketch of Foley see Interstate Publishing Company, *History of Logan County, Illinois* (Chicago, 1886), pp. 309–310.

[8] Ira Davenport to S. A. Foley, Dec. 29, 1869.

[9] John and Ira Davenport to S. A. Foley, July 1, 1873.

[10] Ira Davenport to George Greigg and Co., Nov. 25, 1873.

Table 1. Loans made under the supervision of John and Ira Davenport in Illinois.

Year	No.	Amount	Prevailing rate—%	Foreclosed or deeded
1868	29	$45,650	10	—
1869	66	93,360	10	—
1870	103	159,100	10	4
1871	75	109,500	10	1
1872	78	143,050	10	—
1873	51	112,250	10	—
1874	63	103,500	10	3
1875	82	160,957	10	6
1876	89	137,470	10	3
1877	61	70,125	10	2
1878	70	118,596	10	—
1879	73	165,785	8	1
1880	91	161,826	8	—
1881	81	173,723	7	—
1882	89	200,624	7	—
1883	69	198,159	7	—
1884	50	90,222	7	—
1885	39	91,298	7	—
1886	28	39,197	7	—
1887	20	41,351	7	—
1888	26	51,796	7	—
1889	15	28,170	7	—
1890	2	15,000	6	—
1891	6	13,840	6.5	—
1892	3	4,600	6.5	—
1893	7	34,000	6.5	—
1894	5	6,891	6.5	—
1895	5	9,677	6.5	—
1896	1	100	—	—
1898	1	3,000	—	—
1902	1	500	6	—
Total	1,379	$2,583,317		20

keep your men up to promptness. For farmers Logan men are very prompt. I am inclined to think you paid up for them if they dont come up to time—I hope you will continue to keep them up to the promptness they have shown."[11]

Occasionally the Davenports directed friends to their western agents, although the results were not always completely happy. A Mr. Windsor journeyed west on his own initiative and arranged to lend funds through George Greigg, who agreed to split commissions with his new client. But when Greigg failed to invest his funds rapidly enough, Windsor asked the Davenports for the name of another western agent. The brothers referred him to Foley but specified that in return they would expect to share the commission which the agent obtained from the borrowers. In accord with their instructions Foley began to allot half of the commission on Windsor's loans to the Davenports. Soon, however, Windsor became discontented and argued that he should be getting the same proportion of the commissions from Foley that he was obtaining from Greigg and Company. John Davenport wrote, "It would seem proper he should but as our recommendation stated the interest we had and as our knowledge was the result of years of business we are entitled to the part comm. at least."[12] He agreed regretfully to relinquish the share of the commissions which he and his brother had been receiving.

The lending business of the Davenports was organized as simply as possible. To either Greigg, Foley, or Hoblitt, farmers who were desirous of obtaining a loan submitted applications and an abstract showing the chain of title to their property. These were forwarded to Bath along with the agent's critical appraisal of both borrower and security, based on a full and careful examination of all details having to do with each loan. If the Davenports approved of a loan, the western agent drafted a note and mortgage and sent them east for signature. On their return they were duly recorded at the office of the register of deeds and the funds paid to the borrower. At times the step of sending applications for approval was omitted and the agents acted under general instructions to negotiate loans up to a certain stated amount. The Davenports, however, retained the right to reject a loan at any time before the papers were duly signed and recorded.

Funds were sent to the west by checks drawn on the account of the

[11] John and Ira Davenport to S. A. Foley, Feb. 4, 1871.
[12] John Davenport to S. A. Foley, June 21, 1873.

Davenports at the National Bank of Commerce in New York. Much of the time the western agents were allowed to hold the payments of principal and interest and to reinvest them in approved loans. Both Foley and Greigg maintained several accounts. In the early 1870's Greigg was maintaining one account for John and Ira Davenport in their capacity as executors of the estate of their father and separate accounts for John and Ira as individuals. When loans were made for the estate the Davenports' portion of the commission was credited to either John or Ira. When loans were made in the name of one of the brothers the commission was credited to the account of the other brother.[13] Thus, the Davenports believed, no one could accuse them of obtaining more than the legal rate of 10 per cent on any loan and thereby committing the crime of usury. By 1872 Foley was handling various accounts for the Davenports. He was lending the endowment funds of the Davenport Home for Female Orphans and funds belonging to the estates of both Charles Davenport and Ira Davenport. He was maintaining at least one separate account for the brothers. Greigg and Foley were expected by the mid 1870's to render reports at the end of each month on the balance in the various accounts.[14]

At Bath, William S. Burns kept the accounts of the Davenport brothers. His most important records were the loan registers. A small leather-bound ledger contained all of the loans made by the Davenports in any one state. When such a ledger was opened, a single loan was entered at the top of each page until all of the loans in the state were recorded. An entry of this type included the name of the borrower, the amount of the loan, and the terms of repayment. A small symbol revealed the account for which the loan had been made. As interest payments were received from the western agents they were recorded below the original entry. When the term of the loan expired and the principal was repaid, the loan was closed out and a line drawn below the entry. Burns then entered a new loan on the page. Only one live loan, therefore, stood on a page at any one time. Where a loan was closed out by foreclosure, Burns inserted a note, "transferred to land book." From the loan registers came the material used by Burns in balancing the individual accounts kept for each source of funds.

[13] John Davenport to George Greigg and Co., Dec. 3, 1869.

[14] John and Ira Davenport to George Greigg and Co., Mar. 12, 1872, to S. A. Foley, Feb. 19, 1877.

The Davenports specified that loans should never exceed one-third of the valuation of the security.[15] In 1869 Ira Davenport noted that a loan to a farmer of Illinois was for $5,000 and averaged $16 per acre. Davenport did not order Greigg to refuse the loan but cautioned, "This is a large loan and Smith should be a prudent money making man himself as well as the security should be perfect to get so much. I wish to be entirely satisfied of this—there is more call for money now than receipt."[16]

In the early 1870's loans were usually negotiated for a shorter period of time than eventually became common in the western farm mortgage business. In November 1871 George Greigg inquired if he might lend funds for a period of five years. Ira Davenport could see little advantage in substituting five-year loans for the two-year loans which the brothers were then making, but he gave Greigg permission to make loans for the longer period if he could obtain suitable security.[17] Greigg's effort to lengthen the term of the loan may have been an indication that the rate was showing signs of falling. When the interest rate was rising, short-term loans were obviously more advantageous to the lender. Then, too, since the Davenports charged a bonus or commission for extending loans, the short-term loan produced more frequent borrowers. Mortgagors were permitted to repay part of the principal on two-year loans at the end of the first year. As three- and five-year loans became common in the late 1870's, a part of the principal was usually made payable during the term of the loan.

In 1882 Foley analyzed the motives which led the mortgagors to borrow funds. He believed that many of the farmers to whom the Davenports loaned money in the 1860's and 1870's were borrowing to tide themselves over a period of bad times or were stocking and equipping their farms. But by 1882 almost all of the loans were made to finance the purchase of land. He discerned a difference also in the racial origins of the debtors. Originally they had been mainly of American stock, but by the late 1870's many were of German origin. These men had been buying out the native Americans throughout central Illinois and had turned to the Davenports to finance their purchases.[18]

[15] Ira Davenport to S. A. Foley, Aug. 27, 1870.
[16] Ira Davenport to George Greigg and Co., Dec. 21, 1869.
[17] *Ibid.*, Nov. 29, 1871.
[18] S. A. Foley to John and Ira Davenport, Mar. 7, 1883.

In Illinois, until 1872, the Davenports had used either a simple mortgage or one which included a power of sale. This power of sale delegated a party who was specified in the body of the mortgage to sell the land with no further formality than advertisement if the debtor became delinquent. In 1872 the Davenports shifted to use of the trust deed. Generically the trust deed is a form of mortgage and was treated in identical fashion to the simple mortgage under the law of some states. Under the terms of a trust deed the title to land which stood as security for a debt was vested in a third party who, as trustee, sold the land if the terms of the loan were broken. As in the mortgage containing the power of sale, no recourse was made to the courts. The courts of Illinois held that a mortgagee could not buy property at foreclosure when the sale was held under the terms of a sale mortgage. At a trustee's sale, however, the creditor could buy the property. Since there were seldom disinterested individuals willing to bid enough to extinguish the claim of mortgagees at foreclosure sale, it was of great convenience to them if they could obtain title and hold the security until a buyer was found.[19] Such legal advantage prompted the Davenports to use the trust deed in Illinois from 1872 onward.[20]

Only on one condition would the Davenports accept other than a first mortgage. When one of their debtors wished to borrow additional money and his property stood as adequate security, they were sometimes willing to accept a second mortgage on property to which they already held first claim. Never did they consent to accept a lien which stood inferior to that of another investor.

At least once during the early 1870's Foley asked whether or not the Davenports would buy assigned mortgages or city bonds. Ira replied, "Both may be good but they don't come in our regular system, as you say."[21] As rates tumbled at the end of the 1870's, the Davenports retrenched on this ultimatum and allowed Foley to buy assigned mortgages in an effort to obtain a higher yield.

John Davenport had been a resident in Illinois for some years and Ira, as well, was fully versed in the peculiarities of that state. Frequent trips kept them aware of the condition of the farmers of Illinois. In the 1860's and 1870's at least the brothers took a close interest in the mortgagors. If they were behind on payments, the Davenports inquired the

[19] Ira Davenport to S. A. Foley, Aug. 13, 1872.

[20] *Ibid.*, Sept. 5, 1872.

[21] *Ibid.*, Aug. 3, 1870.

reason for such delinquency and granted extensions if there was a legitimate reason, such as the failure of a corn crop or an outbreak of hog cholera. In October 1869 John Davenport wrote to George Greigg of one delinquent: "Dont you think we better foreclose on this mortgage? Dont want to sell him out if he has had bad luck or been unfortunate." [22] A couple of months later John Davenport lectured a mortgagor who had paid up after long delay: "Am glad you have at last paid up & got free of debt you have had a long time but have at last got out—now dont go & mortgage your homestead again, keep a house over your head clear & free from all." [23] When in 1870 John Davenport sent to George Greigg a list of sixty-nine loans which he wished to have collected as part of the preliminary settlement of his father's estate, he specified that they should not be collected so rapidly as to distress the debtors.[24]

On the other hand, the Davenports expected a return on their money and did not hesitate to compound interest. An agent of Hoblitt's wrote, "You must not be angry with me when I tell you you are too clever folks for any man to make loans for, that is, you let your interest lap too much. . . . You cannot collect interest on back interest here unless they are a mind to pay it." [25]

At times the initial proceedings in foreclosure were brought to stimulate the mortgagor into paying past-due interest or principal. In 1870 the Davenports' secretary suggested that advertising the farm of an Illinois farmer for sale might encourage him to meet his back payments.[26] In 1874 the same reason was given when it was decided to begin proceedings against another delinquent.[27]

In 1871 John Davenport, while defending his record from the criticism of his brother-in-law, argued that he had not lost a dollar through bad debts.[28] There had been some sales at foreclosure, he admitted, but these had been requested by the parties owning the land. Of the 1,380 loans made between 1868 and 1900, some nineteen went to foreclosure and one piece of property was deeded over to the brothers by the borrower. On four of the foreclosures a settlement was apparently

[22] John Davenport to George Greigg and Co., Oct. 15, 1869.
[23] John Davenport to Thomas Huxtable, Deer Creek, Ill., Dec. 20, 1869.
[24] John Davenport to George Greigg and Co., Jan. 29, 1870.
[25] Amos Babcock, Canton, Ill., to John Davenport, Mar. 27, 1879.
[26] James Burns to George Greigg and Co., Nov. 29, 1870.
[27] *Ibid.*, Sept. 9, 1874. [28] John Davenport to J. W. Waterman, Feb. 7, 1871.

made before the land was taken by the Davenports or other individuals bid in the land. The property lay in Mason, Fulton, Logan, Tazewell, and Peoria Counties, comprising in all some 2,652 acres. Eleven farms, totaling 2,181 acres, were taken in Mason County.[29] In 1870, enticed by the promise of interest at 15 per cent, the Davenports allowed George Greigg to extend his lending into Mason County. But Greigg trusted his local agent in Mason County too fully, and excessive amounts were loaned on infertile farms. As Foley summed the situation up later: "If there are any honest men, I believe Mr. G. to be one of them, but there can be no reasonable defense for these loans as made & some of them were not obtained in good faith & the borrowers left the lands at once." [30]

Table 1 gives the rates of interest returned by the mortgage papers held by the Davenport brothers. Until 1879 the legal maximum rate of interest in Illinois was 10 per cent per annum, but in that year it was lowered to 8 per cent. Until 1873 all of the mortgage paper obtained by the Davenports in Illinois was drawn at 10 per cent per annum. From 1874 to 1878 a few mortgages were taken on which the notes returned 8 or 9 per cent, but for the most part the rate stood at the legal maximum. Eight per cent predominated on the mortgages negotiated in 1879 but it was possible to hold that rate for only two years. In 1880, 7- and 6-per-cent paper began to make its appearance. From 1883 to 1887 notes were drawn at 7 per cent, but in 1888 the first loan returning 6½ per cent appeared. For the most part the few mortgages negotiated during the 1890's bore the latter rate, but 6-per-cent paper was also present.

The commission complicates the problem of discovering the exact return on capital invested in farm mortgages. In the early 1870's both the Davenports and their western agents obtained a commission from the borrower above the rate shown on the notes. As the rate of interest fell, so did commissions, until the Davenports ceased to stipulate that they should receive a portion of the commission. To complicate matters further, the commission to the agent, after the mid 1870's, was subtracted from the rate stated in the note and mortgage. At the end of the decade, also, an amount of mortgage paper was bought at a discount which was not shown in the Davenport records. The references to in-

29 Acreages are taken from the Land Book marked Fannie Davenport Ledger.
30 S. A. Foley to Ira Davenport, Nov. 9, 1888.

terest and commissions which appear in the correspondence of the Davenports and their agents add flesh to the statistical skeleton of Table 1.

In January 1870 George Greigg suggested that he could obtain a straight 15 per cent on loans made for one year in Mason County. John Davenport admitted that money was tight in both east and west, but he wondered if men who were willing to pay 15 per cent were not offering inferior security. He pointed out that there were at least three other loan agents in Pekin, including the agent of the Aetna Mutual Life Insurance Company, and cautioned:

> I hope *these other parties* are not taking the *cream* of loans & throwing the poor ones on us—I want to be more than ever careful now as to securities—so many are applying—Mason County applicants will bear the closest kind of examination as to men land & location & titles—I see no indication of poor loans—only I am nervous—applicants all want too large loans. . . . Would suggest that when you increase the rate [of interest] you make for *one year* —you will see why—We dont want lands as our whole course in dealing with farmers has shown—still we want to keep on the inside of the track. . . . By making loans run one year we have things in our hands more—[31]

Davenport was afraid that increasing the rate of interest might damage the reputation for leniency which his family had built up over the years in central Illinois, but he concluded that the higher rate was justified because there was more risk and trouble involved in lending on Mason County security, and he agreed to Greigg's proposal. In fact, he was so interested in the interest rate that he borrowed $5,000 in the east for use in Mason County. To Greigg he wrote, "Notes for men situated as we are are bad bits of chirography to have out—still we can manage some and not run much of a risk."[32] Davenport's profit on this transaction arose from the difference in the interest rate east and west and the portion of the commission which he obtained. In all probability George Greigg charged a commission for himself equal to the 5-per-cent fee above 10 per cent which Davenport obtained. But the usual commission obtained at this time in other counties was undoubtedly less.

Until 1876 the Davenports obtained a portion of the commission realized above the 10 per cent usually contracted for in the mortgage and

[31] John Davenport to George Greigg and Co., Jan. 22, 1870.
[32] *Ibid.*, Jan. 29, 1870; see also *ibid.*, Jan. 27, 1870.

note. In 1876 and 1877 the Davenports temporarily checked their lending operations until they had finished paying for lands purchased in eastern Nebraska from the Union Pacific Railroad Company.[33] To compensate Foley for the loss of business, Ira Davenport proposed to forego the portion of the commission which had formerly been credited to the brothers. He wrote:

> Concerning Coms It is apparent that they are growing smaller, and it is questionable whether the division we have heretofore made is any longer just. We want security & promptness & care & you want enough from the business to pay you for your trouble & as you say in some cases you may have for the sake of getting a good loan, to put up with very little coms— We think you are entitled from this time on to whatever coms you are able to get upon the regular loans.[34]

From late 1876 to December 1, 1878, Foley made a series of loans at 10 per cent without any compensation whatever. These were five-year loans maturing in 1881–1882 and 1883. By 1881 the current rate of interest in Illinois was well below 10 per cent, and the Davenports rewarded Foley for his sacrifice by granting him the equivalent of a one-per-cent-per-year commission on the loans.[35]

By the late 1870's public sentiment in Illinois was generally in favor of dropping the legal maximum rate of interest from 10 to 8 per cent. Ira Davenport wrote in 1878, "I fully realize the cry that is being made upon interest. It is difficult to see what to do. Interest brought down cant be put back well but I dont have much faith in its being done by legislation. . . . It seems when int gets down to 8% that 7% Bonds are better—saving in expense, trouble, & interest upon unloaned balance worth 1% less." [36]

In 1879 the change was made [37] and Foley was later able to boast that he had made the five-year loans of 1876, 1877, and 1878 at 10 per cent in anticipation of just such a contingency.[38] It is doubtful whether the action of the legislature had any real effect upon the rate. It was tumbling downward in other western states no less than in Illinois.

[33] Ira Davenport to George Greigg and Co., May 5, 1876.
[34] John Davenport to S. A. Foley, May 12, 1876.
[35] S. A. Foley to Ira Davenport, Aug. 15, 1881.
[36] Ira Davenport to S. A. Foley, Oct. 30, 1878.
[37] Illinois, *Laws, 1879*, pp. 144–145.
[38] S. A. Foley to Ira Davenport, Nov. 17, 1882.

Legislative action merely confirmed economic fact. For the occasional individual whose bargaining position was extremely weak, however, the new law may well have proved a boon.

In March 1879 Ira Davenport again discussed the interest rate in Illinois: "The difficulty is to know whether 8% is going to be the normal int of Illinois. For the present it seems that and we must take the situation—perhaps in time it may raise. You will have probably to act upon a basis of 8% for the present in loans."[39] Davenport pointed out that in the past loans had been transacted in Illinois on valuations of $10.00 or $15.00 per acre whereas they were now standing at $30.00 to $75.00 per acre. He believed that when foreclosure became necessary the mortgagee ran a poorer chance of being able to recover his investment than had been the case when valuations had stood at a low figure while the actual value of the land was increasing rapidly. He emphasized that the valuation was now even more important than the interest rate in making loans. In the future neither he nor his brother would expect to obtain more than 8 per cent on the funds which they loaned in Illinois.

A few months later in 1879 John Davenport was contrasting the merits of 7-per-cent bonds with mortgages returning 8 per cent. "I suppose we must take 8% for the present, but it makes one look about for 7% bonds when it comes to that. I know you are careful & dont need any reminder to be but I must say in connection with taking 8% int—that the loans should be gilt edged," he confided in a letter to George Greigg.[40]

Despite Ira Davenport's hope that the interest rate might stabilize at 8 per cent, it continued to fall. By June 1880 Foley was enclosing clippings from the newspapers of central Illinois in his letters which showed that brokers in the area were offering funds at 7 per cent per annum. He wrote: "And gentlemen the question is now up for consideration. What shall we do, wait for 8% or go along take what loans I can get at that & if necessary to hunt up special investment, accept 7%—May be able by so doing to get 3% com & if I can will divide."[41] In order to evade temporarily the effect of the decline in rates, Foley began to buy completed mortgages at a discount as well as some personal and commercial paper. In June 1880 Foley summed up his ex-

[39] Ira Davenport to S. A. Foley, Mar. 24, 1879.

[40] John Davenport to George Greigg and Co., July 1, 1879.

[41] S. A. Foley to John and Ira Davenport, June 3, 1880.

perience: "So far we have had very good luck with purchased paper —and I have thought of going over to Petersburg & trying to buy some mortgage paper—In this way we could probably realize over 8%." [42]

But later in 1880 Foley was complaining of the difficulties which a falling rate brought to the mortgage agent. Lenders who had borrowed for five years at 10 per cent were clamoring for permission to pay off their loans or at least to be granted a reduction in the rate of interest which they were paying. It required much cajoling to keep debtors happy under such conditions.[43] Foley wrote of one borrower who, he said, "complains of me, because, he says I should not let him have it for so long a term—& that I knew interest was going down & all that— If I hold this loan to level up on the others it will not be a bad idea— the Aetna Life & some other large Ins Cos have reduced to 6% & get ½ com." [44]

This testimony does not support the reasoning of Herrick and Ingalls, who in a later period deplored the fact that mortgaging in the last quarter of the nineteenth century had not been of a long-term sort extending for periods of fifteen and twenty-five years.[45] Mortgagors were hardly eager to make long-term contracts in a period when the interest rate was dropping rapidly.

By 1881 Foley was displeased with the situation in Illinois and suggested that he be allowed to supervise the lending of funds in Kansas, where high rates might still be obtained. When the Davenports inquired if he had opportunities to loan funds in the spring of 1881, he replied, "You may send me 5,000 for Logan Co.—but I feel that our chances here are declining fast. I would like to get a hold in Sedgewick Co. [Kansas]." [46] A few months later Foley explained the way in which he had been obtaining commissions since 1880. He wrote, "If I could get 7% interest & ½ com or ⅓ com I made it or if I could get 8% & pay all expenses myself I did it, trying & taking that which would net 7% to Messrs D. and pay me best." [47]

[42] S. A. Foley to John and Ira Davenport, June 11, 1880.

[43] *Ibid.*, Oct. 11, 1880.

[44] *Ibid.*, Mar. 15, 1881; see also *ibid.*, Dec. 1, 1881.

[45] Myron T. Herrick and R. Ingalls, *How to Finance the Farmer, Private Enterprise—Not State Aid* (Cleveland, 1915), *passim.*

[46] S. A. Foley to John and Ira Davenport, Mar. 21, 1881.

[47] *Ibid.*, July 15, 1881.

In November 1882 Foley decided that the 10-per-cent rates on the five-year loans of 1876, 1877, and 1878 should be lowered for influential members of the farming community in order to keep their good will. Foley advised:

If we pinch now when our loans become due we will be paid & the influence of these men will tell against us. Of course, I will do just as you say, but it will be against us to do it. I arrange these matters quietly, and certainly think it is for our interest. . . . This . . . Evans has brought us loans of over 50,000 & has been our fast friend & had the bad judgement to *renew* at the *wrong time*—It was my policy . . . to renew all I could at 10% for 5 years & I did.[48]

Early in 1883 the Davenports were withdrawing funds from Foley's control as payments were made by the mortgagors. The policy was merely a temporary one, and Foley suggested that $25,000 should be obtained on the New York money market for use in renewing the good securities on which loans were maturing in the month of March. Foley desired that the money should be borrowed in part for sixty days and in part for four months. Interest on the new loans would be drawn at 7 per cent free of all charges, with the exception of those necessary to set the papers of the applicants in order. Foley assured the brothers, "I have held our field here at 7 net without Coms since Mch 1/82 and can hold it against comers at 6 & 6½ that may show up." [49]

In December 1883 Foley could see no indication that the interest rate was stabilizing. Further decline seemed to be in prospect. He suggested, therefore, that all of the short-term paper which could possibly be collected should be gathered and the funds reinvested in loans running for as many years as possible. "Just now I feel as if we ought to weed out short time paper & plant it for a long time," wrote Foley.[50]

In January 1884 Foley reported on his competition in Lincoln:

The banker loans at a fraction under 7% & the North Western [Mutual Insurance Company of Milwaukee] at 7% under 5000, over that 6%—The Conn Mutual [Insurance Company of Hartford] loans at 6½ net—A new dodge is to receive payments as offered before due . . . which I have re-

[48] *Ibid.*, Nov. 17, 1882; see also *ibid.*, June 29, 1882.

[49] S. A. Foley to Ira Davenport, Feb. 2, 1883; see also S. A. Foley to John Davenport, Feb. 2, 1883.

[50] *Ibid.*, Dec. 13, 1883.

fused to do, & that the lender must control. It is not the thing for if money gets plenty as it will one day then you would have a lot of idle stuff.[51]

In January 1885 John Davenport informed Foley that it was now time to call in the $380,000 belonging to the Waterman heirs which was loaned out in Illinois under his supervision. He suggested that Foley might now desire to act as agent for some other individual or corporation with funds to loan and complimented him on the job which he had done.[52]

By April 1889 Foley was well along with his task of withdrawing the Davenport funds. He reported that after he had received instructions to curtail loaning he had helped many to obtain money elsewhere. He concluded tactfully, "Many say to me, we prefer Davenport funds. Even here, your good name is at a premium." [53] Henceforth the loans negotiated by Foley for the Davenports were a mere trickle in comparison to the stream of credit which had been flowing through his hands in the late 1870's and early 1880's. The interest rate had continued to decline. Where, in 1881, Foley had been worrying whether or not he should cut back the rate on long-term loans bearing 10 per cent, he was now referring to a few payments of interest at 8 per cent as the "last run of shad." [54]

Foley's record seems to have been a remarkable one. The Davenports obtained almost no land by foreclosure through his agency. Apparently Foley took over some bad loans for himself.[55] Certainly he regretted the occasional loan. In December 1889 he noted, "I am glad to clean up the Wright loan, 6½ years old, 2 yrs interest paid, a bad record for me, wiped out. The next fellow that wants a loan in *June* will stand off until I take a second look at him. June loans and June bugs no good." [56]

When lending was curtailed in Illinois, the Davenports found other duties for Foley. Several troublesome cases of litigation which had arisen from the investments of the Davenports in other states were assigned to him. In Illinois the administration of the lands in Mason County was transferred to him.[57] These farms had been rented under

[51] *Ibid.*, Jan. 31, 1884. [52] John Davenport to S. A. Foley, Jan. 14, 1885.
[53] S. A. Foley to John and Ira Davenport, Mar. 5, 1889.
[54] S. A. Foley to James Burns, Apr. 13, 1889.
[55] S. A. Foley to Ira Davenport, Aug. 15, 1881.
[56] S. A. Foley to John and Ira Davenport, Dec. 9, 1889.
[57] Ira Davenport to S. A. Foley, Oct. 23, 1888.

the supervision of George Greigg since they had been acquired by foreclosure in the mid and late 1870's. When Greigg interpreted the transfer as criticism of his agency, Ira Davenport wrote to him:

> Never in all the years we have loaned in Ills or anywhere else has any such disaster attended . . . I think, too, you must admit we have waited long for the lands to bring back the money. We have had to be out the interest, as we have had to pay it to the parties whose money was loaned & worse yet, we have to make good the principal. It is this fact, with the fact that nothing like a similar experience has occurred in the 30 years loaning, that has made this situation a growing anxiety to me, and on each occasion as I have come home & looked into business, I have found this situation practically unchanged.[58]

Late in 1888 Foley began an active campaign to increase the income from the farms and to improve their appearance so that he might realize the highest possible prices for them.

The Davenports kept detailed records of the income from foreclosed land. Of the sixteen farms in Illinois which they were forced to take for resale all but one had been completely sold by the date of Ira Davenport's death in 1904. On the average, the brothers held the farms for thirteen and a half years and had by the date of sale invested an average of $4,622.82 in each piece of property. The average return on the investment per loan was 4.9 per cent, while the average return per dollar invested was 5.3 per cent.[59]

[58] Ira Davenport to George Greigg, Nov. 2, 1888; see also *ibid.*, Oct. 23, 1888.

[59] In the Davenport land book are to be found income and expenditure figures on the foreclosed farms including purchases of nails valued at 38 cents. The writer in calculating the rate of return assumed that the loan was converted into a purchase by the Davenports as soon as the interest became delinquent and from this point regarded the principal of the loan as the first payment on the property. Foreclosure costs, delinquent taxes, etc., represented subsequent payments against which interest had to be figured also. Simply by experimentation, the rate of interest was discovered, which, when applied to all the expenditures on behalf of the property before and after foreclosure, produced a total investment equal to the price for which the property was eventually sold. Where, as in Illinois, the real estate was rented or when portions were sold, revenue was deducted from the capital investment when it was received by the Davenports.

II

IOWA

IN 1868 John Davenport and his brother, Ira Davenport, loaned some $18,000 on the security of farms in eastern and central Iowa. The next year they increased the amount to $50,374, divided among fifty-three loans. During the thirteen years 1868–1880 they made 878 loans in Iowa, totaling $553,745, in addition to 140 loans, totaling $44,000, in the Territory of Dakota (see Table 2). By 1875 William S. Burns estimated that the brothers had $155,000 out on security in Iowa.[1] For the most part this security was farmland, although loans on town property or personal security crept into the total occasionally. With few exceptions these funds were loaned through John Weare, a banker of Cedar Rapids.

John Weare settled in Iowa during the early 1840's and conducted a profitable banking business in the land-office towns, where he financed the location of land for settlers and located lands for nonresident speculators.[2] One cannot be certain when Weare first became acquainted

[1] W. S. Burns to Charles Parkhurst, Cedar Rapids, Ia., Mar. 25, 1875.

[2] For a sketch of Weare see Western Historical Company, *The History of Linn County, Iowa* (Chicago, 1878), p. 680.

with the Davenport family. Ira Davenport, Sr., acquired an interest in the land grant given by the federal government to finance improvement of the Des Moines River, and he may well have come into contact with so important a business figure as Weare as a result. But Weare's second wife had family ties in Bath, New York, and perhaps it was this relationship which brought the Davenports and Weare together. At any rate, the Davenport brothers were entrusting money to him in 1868 and greatly accelerated the flow of funds into his hands during the next few years.

When the Davenports began to loan in Iowa, they loaned at a rate of 10-per-cent interest—the legal rate—and Weare demanded a 10-per-cent commission from borrowers in addition. Since the loans were written for one or two years only, borrowers were paying well over 10 per cent for their money. The 10-per-cent commission was split between Weare and the two Davenports. As in Illinois, when the loan was drawn in the name of one brother, the commission was credited to the other.[3] The division of the commission between Weare and the Davenports was not made immediately.[4] Instead, the commissions were segregated in a special commission account which Weare loaned out at the high rates obtainable for short-term funds.[5] The account stood in part as a contingency fund from which unexpected losses and charges which could not legitimately be levied against the borrower were deducted. The rates and arrangement were so attractive that John Davenport borrowed $4,000 from his brother-in-law in the east, specifying to Weare that it must be used for "a good loan [or loans] . . . that you know is good as wheat & no doubt—man prompt & all right."[6]

The general system followed by the Davenports in Iowa was much the same as that used in Illinois, although in Iowa the Davenports contributed to the salary of a clerk who made their accounts his special charge and at times made inspections of securities.[7] In the mid 1870's the Davenports obtained copies of the bond and coupon type of mortgage papers which the Corbin Banking Company was then popularizing among eastern investors. When they asked Weare if the documents were superior to those which he was using, he explained his system of

[3] John Davenport to John Weare, Dec. 11, 1869.
[4] *Ibid.*, Nov. 13, 1871. [5] *Ibid.*, Mar. 23, 1872.
[6] *Ibid.*, Jan. 18, 1870; also John Davenport to Sherman S. Rogers, Jan. 22, 1870.
[7] John Davenport to John Weare, Nov. 3, 1874.

Table 2. Loans made under the supervision of John and Ira Davenport in Iowa and Dakota Territory.

Year	No.	Amount	Prevailing rate—%	Foreclosed or deeded
		IOWA		
1868	19	$18,053	10	2
1869	53	50,374	10	—
1870	130	63,202	10	1
1871	105	72,344	10	6
1872	84	53,319	10	6
1873	48	37,737	10	13
1874	110	64,511	10	13
1875	113	54,127	10	15
1876	82	42,762	10	3
1877	58	32,027	10	5
1878	49	40,592	10	—
1879	19	11,801	10	1
1880	8	12,896	10	—
Total for Iowa	878	$553,745		65
		DAKOTA TERRITORY		
1878	18	$9,670	10	1
1879	74	21,763	10	4
1880	48	12,635	10	27
Total for Dakota Territory	140	$44,068		32
Gross total	1,018	$597,813		97

loaning in some detail. There were five basic papers: the application, the abstract of title, the mortgage, the notice of payment due, and the application for extension. He described his procedure:

First the party loaning makes his application. . . . As Lawyers would say, "He is now in Court," And I make it a point to become fully posted respecting the man. For What purpose he desires the Money, And his prospects of meeting the payments. If the party makes an inteligent [*sic*] Showing I then decide to make the loan, and require the abstract, . . . with full certificates respecting title & value of property, improvements etc etc. Next have the mortgage executed and *put on record before* paying over the money. . . . In all cases, I first pay off with proceeds all incumbrances, balances (if any) to the party. By this policy I have never been triped [*sic*] up on titles or has my papers failed to protect the interest they represent. . . . The form of notice . . . [is] sent to the party a month in advance of Note maturing which to render more expressive I have written, in this way I can change my letter as the case requires.[8]

Weare argued that the most important thing in drafting mortgage forms was to have them simple and free from legal loopholes. They should also, he believed, be of the kind to which the farmers of a district were accustomed. "To [*sic*] many papers are looked upon with suspicion and a man who begins to believe he is the owner of a good farm, & able to live under his own vim and true (and such are preferable to loan money to) will reluctantly submit to any system of papers he does not fully comprehend, or perhaps has never seen the like before."[9] He told the Davenports that if he was working up a clientele for mortgage investments in the east, the system of bond and coupons which was being introduced by the Corbin Banking Company and other mortgage brokers would no doubt find considerable favor, but he did not believe that such a system would either bring greater safety to the investor or insure prompter payments. He argued that farmers paid their debts when they obtained the money, or in other words, when they sold their crops. If crops were good and prices reasonable they would pay well. Otherwise it would be difficult to make collections. Weare clinched this argument. "I find we have to adopt the idea of the Irishman, who a little coined was shown to his roome [*sic*] and being asked why he did not retire his reply [was], he 'Would do so when the Bed came Round.' So with payments, we get the money as they come round."[10]

Weare believed that a clause in mortgage paper waiving appraisement was of little value in Iowa. Appraisement insured that land would not be sold at judicial sale for a sum less than two-thirds of its appraised value, but Weare claimed that a clause waiving the safeguard could

[8] John Weare to John Davenport, Jan. 30, 1875.
[9] *Ibid.*
[10] *Ibid.*

be easily evaded and only prejudiced the borrower against the lender. Weare preferred to pick a fine type of borrower rather than putting too much trust in clauses of this sort. He summed up:

> First, try to deal with men of substance both in a moral & pecuniary Sense and avoid any obligation which in your opinion there is doubt of the party paying. Except he makes sacrifices to do so. He soon gets restles [*sic*], Cross & perhaps Mulish, & if you finally get through with him he leaves you with unkind feelings, & anxious for an opportunity to place trigs under your wheels. It is important to have a community feel that you are doing them good, rather than an injury. As a Rule you have greater interest to be effected than those to whom you intrust [*sic*] your Money—Thus far I have succeeded in establishing a popular business. The people have confidence in the Stability & good intentions you entertain for their prosperity and you will not distress the unfortunate. Hence it is well established opinion among the people that while they are expected to pay for all they get at full rates, they are safe from any sharp practise, or *undue* advantage.[11]

By 1875 Weare was finding it difficult to lend money on as favorable terms as formerly and complained of parties "fowlering" him and undercutting his rates in the older counties of Linn, Benton, and Tama. As a result, with the encouragement of the Davenports, he began to consider extending his field of operations into the northwestern counties of Iowa in the winter of 1874–1875.[12]

When Weare decided to extend operations into the northwest of the state, he found it necessary to change his system of lending. When he had lent funds only in the immediate vicinity of Cedar Rapids, he could exercise complete supervision over all of the stages involved in making loans. In the western counties it would be necessary to build up a system of local agents. In the early months of 1875 he busied himself contacting agents in western Iowa and indoctrinating them in his way of doing business. He wrote:

> As you see, our new program opens a new field in which we are geting [*sic*] the first loans, and at our full rates. I hear of Eastern parties with funds to loan in Many Counties, Commission Six per cent, but most borrowers prefer our way of doing business. They Say, "If we do have to pay a little more coms we know as long as we keep matters straight & do the fair thing Weare will not distress us." [13]

[11] *Ibid.*

[12] John Weare to John and Ira Davenport, July 3, 1875.

[13] *Ibid.*, Apr. 7, 1875.

By June a flow of applications was coming to Weare's bank at Cedar Rapids, but he complained that the Davenports were limiting the supply of funds at his disposal. Since he had just got the new business under way, he argued that this was most discouraging.[14] But the Davenports had their reasons. At one point in 1875 some $6,000 stood idle upon Weare's books.[15] The natural reaction of the brothers was to limit the amount of money which they sent west to Iowa.

Weare's inability to lend funds immediately was understandable. When loans often took several months to complete, a high proportion of poor applications or unexpected repayments might well throw the demand for money and the supply at his disposal out of balance. But of all the agents with whom the Davenports dealt Weare was most prone to carry a considerable uninvested balance for several months and then to cry for more funds when demand eventually caught up to supply.

In August 1875 Weare was generally satisfied with the way in which his business was progressing, although he complained that the demand for money was light. He could see only happy results to come from the extended business. In western counties like Crawford and Plymouth land values were rising steadily and the country was settling up rapidly.

> This desirable State of Affairs [he wrote] renders it a Safe business to loan money on property at low valuation, and upon which rapid improvements are being made—This idea is becoming to [*sic*] generally understood, and is attracting the attention of capitalists, and I find them following after me as I advance in the new counties and in some places a sharp competition has been Started—Which of course I do not participate in much.[16]

Two weeks later Weare's optimism was rudely shattered. Weare had put the affairs of the Davenports in the special charge of his clerk and brother-in-law, Charles Parkhurst. In June or July 1875 a businessman of Algona, in Kossuth County, applied for an agency. After Weare had interrogated the man and received letters of recommendation from the Kossuth County Bank and the officers of the county, he accepted him as an agent. Applications began to come to Cedar Rapids in considerable volume from Algona. The abstracts, the certificates of appraisal, and the mortgage papers were filled out in extraordinarily good form.

[14] *Ibid.*, June 15, 1875.
[15] *Ibid.*, July 3, 1875, marginal note.
[16] *Ibid.*, Aug. 21, 1875.

It was Weare's custom to draw the mortgages in his office and send them to the local agent who obtained the signature of the borrower and recorded the indentures in the county records. When they were returned to Weare, he rechecked them and forwarded the money to the local agent. Several mortgages from Algona had been duly signed by the borrower and returned to Weare by August, and he was holding them until he could get more information on the value of farmland in Kossuth County. At this point he was warned that there was chicanery involved. Weare put a detective to work on the case and discovered that the applications submitted from Algona were forgeries. Further investigation revealed that the agent in Algona had been working under the direction of Parkhurst. The latter departed hurriedly while the investigation was under way, but he was captured in St. Paul.

Parkhurst, it was found, had already steered one group of forged papers through to completion, but the Algona scheme had just been put into operation when it was detected. When Parkhurst, however, succeeded in again escaping, the Davenports lost some $7,000 on the clerk's first venture in forgery.[17]

The embezzlement disrupted the new organization which Weare had set up. While his agents in Plymouth and Cherokee Counties held their applications, he worked out a new plan of operation. He believed it essential that he himself or someone whom he could trust absolutely should make a personal inspection of the applicant's security. To save traveling expenses he decided that he would allow the local agents to accumulate a supply of applications which he would inspect when the value had reached a figure that would make a trip worth while. If he approved an application, he would supervise the signing and recording himself and pay over the money to the borrower immediately.[18] By January 1876 John Weare reported that his new plan was fairly under way.[19]

While the Davenports complained at times that Weare held funds idle at Cedar Rapids, the shoe was occasionally on the other foot. When the Davenports withdrew large amounts of their own funds in 1876

[17] *Ibid.*, Aug. 27, 1875, Sept. 1, 1875, Sept. 10, 1875, Oct. 28, 1875; John and Ira Davenport to John Weare, Sept. 16, 1875.

[18] John Weare to John and Ira Davenport, Oct. 7, 1875, Dec. 29, 1875.

[19] *Ibid.*, Jan. 19, 1876, Jan. 25, 1876.

to pay out on land contracts, Weare found himself with an expanded field of operations and a diminished flow of money. He eventually allowed the Davenports to borrow funds from him to fill in until their extraordinary demands were met. He wrote: "The importance of maintaining our position with applicants for money and prevent others from getting our business is of No Small Consideration. Hence I have concluded to authorize you to draw on me for amount. . . . By this plan, I can manage to keep the business in tack." [20]

During the early 1870's the Davenports placed considerable trust in John Weare. He was not required to send applications east for approval and he was allowed to keep the mortgages and notes in Cedar Rapids.[21] In fact, Weare was more than a mere loan agent for the brothers but was actually their partner in developing at least one subdivision in Cedar Rapids.

The Davenport brothers subscribed to newspapers from the counties in which they were lending, in an attempt to keep abreast of events in the state, interlarded their letters with many questions about the state of the crops, the financial condition of the west, the incidence of grasshoppers, and requested other kinds of information which would allow them to evaluate more reasonably the state of their lending business. One of the brothers went west at least once a year, and sometimes the secretary, William Burns, was sent west to carry out a detailed loan-by-loan check.

The Davenports made no attempt to lend money at a lower rate of interest than did their competitors. Undoubtedly at times they were lending at a somewhat higher rate than were others. When interest payments lagged they approved of charging interest upon the past-due interest.[22] This was of course compounding interest—a practice which was not popular with the western borrowers. Yet, as in other states, they were not disinterested in the welfare of their borrowers and strove to avoid taking land by foreclosure.

In January 1877 Ira Davenport, who was the more punctilious of the brothers in business protocol, pointed out to Weare that it was necessary for him to raise a large sum of money, and enclosed a list of his loans which were coming due. He asked that these loans be col-

[20] *Ibid.*, June 8, 1876.
[21] John and Ira Davenport to John Weare, Mar. 25, 1875.
[22] John Davenport to John Weare, Nov. 17, 1870.

lected when they came due and no extensions be made if Weare believed that the debtor could raise the money. He qualified:

I understand there may be cases where peremptory coll means foreclosure & taking the lands & while if the loans have been made on proper margin such a course would be more profitable than loaning to me, I dont loan for that purpose & when cases come up where the borrower cannot pay & you are satisfied he can by giving another year, you can proceed as want to extend but *I only mean such cases* & I hope there won't be many.[23]

In May 1877 Weare argued that the reluctance of the Davenports to foreclose allowed them to obtain higher rates:

Money is offered on Real Estate Security in this State by Capitalists on long time, Eight per cent interest and five per cent Commission. . . . It is only from the fact where ever you have made loans the citizens have learned you have No other objects in view First your money with use. Second. Their prosperity, and the people throughout the State. They know you do not seek to get their homes. Hence they prefer to deal with you even though you charge them higher than others.[24]

At times John Davenport felt it necessary to curb Weare's business practices. He noted that one borrower had paid a commission of more than 10 per cent on his loan initially and advised Weare: "Would suggest since he pays interest promptly and times are hard that you *extend* his $150 note at ten percent. . . . I dont want to *interfere* with your plans—Would not in this *case* but by his account he has already paid a good *coms* & he pays his int promptly—& security is good." [25]

Excerpts from a letter written by John Davenport in December 1872 seem to mirror the attitude of the Davenports in the early 1870's:

I send list of all delinquents as our Books show—look it over make remarks & return it here—Notice several marked with an X—stir these up first . . . dont want to distress these men—use your discression [*sic*]. Those marked X investigate as they are large loans—int counts up fast in them—the little loans that are behind stir the men up but don't distress them. . . . Where a man has had bad luck in crops or sickness give him time—on large loans investigate cause of delay & see if security is good & not decreasing. We don't want to go into court until we have tried all means—Where a man

[23] Ira Davenport to John Weare, Jan. 6, 1877.

[24] John Weare to John Davenport, May 12, 1877; see also Davenport to Weare, May 3, 1877.

[25] John Davenport to John Weare, Dec. 18, 1878.

has 2 loans get int on the poorest secured one and give time on other—Don't expect you will work all up at once but let the men see we are after them & not disposed to push them where they have good reasons for non payment. . . . In all cases have an eye to Commissions—where a man is behind & feels discouraged throw off some coms especially if he paid a good com in start—Where it will do increase loan if it will square up back int. . . . It is to be expected in such a list of men as we have on our Books that some will be behind—these men we want to work off and take prompt ones in their place —We can have our pick of men now the demand for money is so great & especially when it is understood that we don't want land but the interest.[26]

With the exception of the Parkhurst affair the lending business of the Davenports in Iowa apparently proceeded to the satisfaction of the Davenport brothers during the first half of the decade of the 1870's. They were less well satisfied during the years after 1875. Late in 1877 the Davenports sent W. S. Burns to make a detailed inspection of all the mortgage loans in Iowa. Burns reported that some of the loans were in bad shape. Especially annoying to the Davenports was the case of J. E. Legore, who had managed to obtain, not one or two, but four loans from Weare. Burns considered Legore to be a shiftless fellow, although he was not without a certain type of enterprise, since he had managed to borrow $2,500 on the security of a farm worth no more than $2,800 in the estimation of the New Yorker. John Davenport pointed out that such a loan required considerable nursing.[27]

In reply to the strictures of the Davenports, Weare maintained that the securities were, on the whole, in sound condition despite the depression which held Iowa and the rest of the country in its grip. Not only were the mortgages good but they were increasing in strength, although

doubtless there are some (in view of the poverty of the past years) not in as good shape as we desire, and I submit to your own experience, that it is not strange in the thousands of persons I have loaned your funds to, that a few scalawags are found. Yet I do not know but a limted [*sic*] number and as these parties will be able to bring up their back interest, and from present prospects farming and good farms will advance I believe in one year from this time your now weak securities will have strengthened and prospects brightened . . . *especially in Iowa.*[28]

[26] *Ibid.*, Dec. 27, 1872.
[27] John and Ira Davenport to John Weare, Aug. 17, 1877.
[28] John Weare to John and Ira Davenport, Sept. 5, 1877.

As for Legore, Weare explained that he had been sick when this rascal had procured his last loan. Whereas Legore was to have merely consolidated previous borrowings, he had succeeded in getting an additional loan. The security, however, was in a district which thrifty Germans had been infiltrating over the past few years, and Weare believed that it could easily be sold for more than enough to pay the debts.

In February 1878 the Davenports' dissatisfaction at the way in which Weare was handling their affairs came out into the open. In a letter which was furiously underlined John Davenport charged that inquiry after inquiry had been submitted to Weare over various matters of business and that no reply had been received. Nor did Weare send in his reports by the fifth of each month, as expected. His tardiness delayed the reports which the brothers themselves were expected to submit to other members of their family.[29] By dispatching a mollifying letter and submitting the report of the month's business on time, Weare was temporarily able to bring the Davenports to a better state of mind.

To add to the other unsatisfactory aspects of their lending operations in Iowa, the Davenports found rates declining in the late 1870's no less than in Illinois. Increasingly Weare claimed that it was most difficult to maintain an interest rate of 10 per cent along with a commission of 10 per cent. In June, 1878 he wrote:

> At all the points where we have agents, as well as here we are meeting with Sharp Competition. There are plenty of funds offered at eight per cent and coms of three to five per cent. We have maintained rates to present period more on account of the confidence the people regard us [with] and the leniency you have manifested but for this feature of the business we would have long since been obliged to give place to others loaning at less rates. It now seems clear we cannot maintain our former rates of Commissions the expense to the borrower must in some way be lessened.[30]

Weare now offered to the Davenports all of the commission which he could obtain above 5 per cent plus half the bonuses for renewal as before.[31] Soon after the Davenports surrendered their share of the commissions completely.[32]

Until the mid 1870's Weare and the Davenports avoided foreclosures.

[29] John Davenport to John Weare, Feb. 9, 1878.

[30] John Weare to John and Ira Davenport, June 18, 1878, July 11, 1878.

[31] John Weare to John Davenport, July 26, 1878, Aug. 8, 1878.

[32] *Ibid.*, Oct. 23, 1884.

In the fall of 1875 Weare reported that the years of depression had left him with only four doubtful loans which he was about to foreclose.[33] But instead of improving, the economic condition of the Iowa farmers who owed money to the Davenports appeared to grow worse. In April 1880 Weare claimed that valuations in Iowa had been slipping downward during the four years in which he had been kept busy following up delinquents, negotiating sales, and remortgaging where loans could be secured in a more desirable form. At times foreclosure seemed to be the only alternative.[34] Although Weare had written, "I entertain a mortal horror of legal contests, as a rule you are the loser, even though you Win," [35] sixty-three of the 878 loans made in Iowa ended in foreclosure and another nine at least were taken into court. Weare was not prepared to admit that his earlier reluctance to bring foreclosure proceedings was a mistake. Of overdue loans which were settled without litigation in 1879 he wrote:

> If I had foreclosed these at maturity (as many are doing) we should probably have their farms in place of the money with an additional investment of cost attending the foreclosures. It is doubtful if these Eastern Insurance Cos succeed better in geting [*sic*] their money by this general foreclosure system they have adopted than by a more conservative policy. Their course has engendered a spirit of opposition and already usury is being established.[36]

Some of the debtors of the Davenports defended themselves by alleging usury. In November 1878 Weare reported that a mortgagor, James Henry, had used this defense. Despite the "usury dodge" the judgment was in favor of the Davenports. Weare added that some of the insurance companies, doing business in the state, had lost heavily in court actions. Usury had been proved against the Aetna Mutual Life Insurance Company of Hartford, Connecticut, for example. This corporation had been splitting the commission taken above the legal rate of interest with its agents. Weare was gratified that the system of the Davenports was not tainted with any such defect.[37]

Weare, however, was not certain that his business practices were completely pure. In December 1878 he cautioned John Davenport, after

[33] John Weare to Ira Davenport, Oct. 19, 1876.
[34] John Weare to John and Ira Davenport, Apr. 12, 1880.
[35] John Weare to John Davenport, June 16, 1876.
[36] *Ibid.*, Feb. 24, 1879.
[37] John Weare to John and Ira Davenport, Nov. 23, 1878, Jan. 21, 1879.

the latter had received inquiries on the Davenports' method of lending from farmers in western Iowa:

Suggest you observe *caution* in writing to parties respecting loans. It has been decided in our Supreme Court, that where the party Making the loan . . . charge[s] ten per cent per annum [and] in any way participate[s] in the Commission renders the transaction usurious. It is on this point a few of the parties I have sued made their fight but of course they failed to make their point as I do *not know* Ira in *any* commission transaction—I suspect these letters were dictated by some of the many Shysters out in that part of the State. These are times that men develop new characteristics even to taking all advantage that dishonesty can suggest.[38]

Despite Weare's protestations that the system of the Davenports was court proof, many of John Davenport's letters in the late 1870's caution the agent lest he taint the loans with usury. In June 1880 Weare wrote of a case then pending. The mortgagor, William Harper, had alleged usury in his defense and called for John Davenport's deposition. Weare believed that the action was merely one of delay, but to be careful he wrote out the deposition which John Davenport was to return to the interrogation of the court:

1. John Weare was in January, 1878, and prior thereto to my Banker at Cedar Rapids. I had told him, I would accept real Estate as Security and furnish money at ten percent interest per anum [*sic*] such instruction was by parol. John Weare, the First National Bank, W. W. Walker or either of them was not my agent in any other sense than expressed above.
2. John Weare as my Banker lends under a general instruction that I Would loan on real estate security for ten per cent per anum. The Notes and Mortgages taken connected with said loans are in the possession of Mr. Weare at Cedar Rapids—I have not paid or agreed to pay Mr. Weare or any other person any Compensation for making the loan. Mr. Weare has at various periods funds belonging to me.[39]

Weare's commission, according to the logic involved in this declaration, was paid to him for his services on behalf of the borrower. How the portion of the commission which went to the Davenports was rationalized is less certain. We have seen that when Ira Davenport lent money in Iowa, a portion of the commission on the loan was paid to John Davenport. Although the attempt to circumvent the statutes is

[38] John Weare to John Davenport, Dec. 21, 1878.
[39] John Weare to John and Ira Davenport, June 3, 1880.

obvious, the Davenport who loaned his money on mortgage security in Iowa was within the letter of the law when he swore that he obtained no portion of the commission. The correspondence of the Davenports does not show that the charge of usury was ever sustained in court, on any of the loans negotiated by Weare. The fear that usury might be proven, however, may well have contributed to Weare's antipathy to legal proceedings, and encouraged him in the policy, commended by John Davenport in 1879, of rewriting delinquent loans into new mortgages on which there could be no suspicion of usury.[40]

Most distressing of Weare's difficulties was the problem of the "Cameron claims." In 1878 Weare began to lend money in the Territory of Dakota. In October of that year his assistant, W. W. Walker, was investigating conditions in Sioux Falls, where a railroad terminated and where one of the territorial land offices was located. Weare wrote that the land district was rapidly filling up with an intelligent and thrifty population which would take all of the funds that the Davenports could spare at 10 per cent and a commission of 7 or 8 per cent. Loans would be made to pre-emptors who were in need of funds to buy their land from the federal government.[41] Only eighteen loans were made in the territory during 1878, but during 1879 Weare supervised the loan there of some $21,763 in seventy-four transactions.

In the summer of 1880 Walker was again in Sioux Falls, where he met a group of pre-emptors who were in need of loans. They had been gathered together through the agency of John D. Cameron, an attorney at Yankton, who had also drawn up the affidavits necessary to complete pre-emption entries. Walker paid $200 at the government land office for each settler in addition to the pre-emption fees. In total he loaned $250 on each 160 acres. Walker believed that the whole transaction was in accord with the law and the rules of the general land office. Although the pre-emptors did not have their patents, they did have their receipts from the land office before they signed the mortgage papers, and these they handed over to Walker.

When the first payment of interest on some twenty-seven of these loans fell due it was not paid. Investigation showed that the pre-emptors were not on the land, which for the most part lay in Beadle County in the James River Valley. In the meantime it was discovered that Cam-

[40] John Davenport to John Weare, Jan. 30, 1879.

[41] John Weare to John and Ira Davenport, Oct. 5, 1878, Oct. 16, 1878.

eron had forged the affidavits which the pre-emptors had presented to the land office. Federal officers charged Cameron with forgery in a case which reached the Supreme Court of the Territory of Dakota in October 1882. But the federal attorneys had brought the charges under an inappropriate section of the Federal Statutes and Cameron escaped more on a technicality than because he was innocent.[42] Undoubtedly Cameron had required his bogus entry men to deed their holdings to him, and had his activities not been detected, he would subsequently have recorded the deeds and been in a position to resell the land.

In December 1882 John Weare was sanguine of the outcome of the loans. At his request the Davenports had placed the case in the hands of Drummond and Bradford, counselors at law in Washington, and these attorneys were endeavoring to have a bill passed through Congress confirming the entries. If they were successful in obtaining passage of the bill, it would be a simple matter to acquire the land through foreclosure. If on the other hand, the entries were canceled, Weare believed that the money would be refunded to the Davenports, who had provided the entry men with their funds.[43]

In 1883 Weare was aggrieved at the tardiness with which Congress was acting. He wrote to John Davenport:

> The Attorneys in Washington who are managing the Dakota land matter have a bill before Congress which they hope to get throu [*sic*] this term, quieting the title. But Congress is waisting [*sic*] so much time for little or no purpose I doubt if it is reached this term. I cannot see how they can refuse to reconise [*sic*] the justice of the claim. The Government have their $200 for each Quarter Section and office fee of $12 for each entry.[44]

But Drummond and Bradford were unsuccessful in obtaining their desired bill from Congress. Meanwhile the borrowers' titles on at least half of the tracts were declared void when settlers contested the title of the pre-emptors to whom the Davenports had loaned funds. However, foreclosure suits were entrusted to William T. Love of Huron,

[42] *U.S.* vs. *Cameron, Northwestern Reporter,* XIII, 561; "Report of Special Agent William W. Burke to the Commissioner of the General Land Office," *Senate Executive Document, No. 61,* 47th Congress, 2d Session, Vol. III (1882–1883), 41–49. Cameron was also involved in a more famous scandal when he and three colleagues were indicted for forging Santa Fe scrip, Yankton *Press and Dakotan,* Oct. 30, 31, 1882; *U.S.* vs. *Cameron et al., Federal Reporter,* XV, 794.

[43] John Weare to John Davenport, Dec. 5, 1882, Dec. 13, 1882.

[44] *Ibid.,* Feb. 19, 1883.

Dakota Territory. This attorney contracted to foreclose the loans for $15.00 per case, only to revise his demands up to $25.00 per case once he had begun proceedings. When Love changed his residence and the cases were transferred to another lawyer, it was found that most of the original documents had been lost. Twenty-six mortgages were put into foreclosure, but six settlers obtained injunctions to prevent sale by advertisement, pleading that the mortgage claim should be disallowed because the title on which suit was brought had been voided by decision of the land office. Over the years these injunctions and the demurrers to the answer of Ira Davenport were fought through to the supreme court of South Dakota. Davenport's attorney argued that the cancellation of title was invalid because the procedure of contest had been defective.[45]

In 1890 S. A. Foley became western agent for Ira Davenport and he set himself to clear up the cases in South Dakota. Twenty tracts had been sold at foreclosure sale and bought in by Love, but that jurist had neglected to obtain deeds to the land. In 1894 the local attorney hired by Foley was endeavoring to obtain deeds and to institute suits for the possession of the tracts. But two years later he was still struggling to bring to a final decision the cases in which six settlers had challenged the chain of title upon which the Davenports based their claim to these Dakota lands. It proved impossible to close the matter satisfactorily, and by the date of his death in 1904 Ira Davenport had evidently charged off the Dakota lands to experience.

In 1880 the Davenports ceased lending funds in Iowa and Dakota. A series of minor catastrophes had attended Weare's agency from 1874 onward. The defalcation of Parkhurst, the suicide of an agent, and the loans on disputed titles in Dakota had all brought loss or promise of it. Many loans had been collected in Iowa only through foreclosure, and it was evident that others would have to be terminated in the same way. Weare's inability to get his reports in on time and the fact that unloaned balances often stood in his bank may well have contributed to their decision. If it did not occur to the brothers, Weare's business rivals

[45] John Davenport to John Weare, May 12, 1884, Oct. 11, 1884, June 13, 1885; John Weare to John Davenport, Mar. 31, 1884, Sept. 19, 1884, May 18, 1885, June 1, 1885, June 29, 1885, Sept. 29, 1885; W. T. Love, Huron, D.T., to Weare and Walker, Mar. 20, 1884, Nov. 29, 1884, to John Davenport, Nov. 7, 1889; W. R. Lynch to John Davenport, June 18, 1884, to J. J. Walker, 1894 (?), to S. A. Foley, Nov. 20, 1896; *Risdon* vs. *Davenport, South Dakota Reports,* IV, 555.

were very willing to suggest that such funds were being used to the banker's own advantage in the short-term field.[46] Finally, Weare was by this time an elderly man and much crippled with rheumatism. Since the amount of funds loaned in Illinois during the next few years rose sharply, the decision to curtail lending in Iowa was not dictated by lack of funds.

During the decade of the 1880's the outstanding loans were collected and the last stubborn cases of delinquency were put through the process of foreclosure. By the mid 1880's most of the loans had been closed out, and after another decade almost all of the foreclosed real estate had been resold. An analysis of the receipts and expenditures on thirty-eight foreclosed Iowa farms showed that on the average the farms were held for eight and one-half years and represented an investment of $1,335 at the date of sale. The average return per foreclosure was 10 per cent, but the average return on every dollar invested in foreclosed property was only 6.4 per cent.

Few loans were negotiated in Iowa by the Davenports calling for a return of less than 10 per cent. Admittedly the delays, incidental to reinvestment, would have prevented the Davenports from realizing the straight 10 per cent on money invested in loans which were successfully repaid. But assuming such a frictional loss of 1 per cent, or even of 2 per cent, it is obvious that there was little to be gained from foreclosing farm real estate if it could be avoided.

In any attempt to evaluate the lending business of the Davenports in Iowa it must be remembered that the commission account made a significant contribution to their returns. Amounting originally to 10 per cent of the face of the loans and then loaned on short term, the commissions and the interest returned on them, according to Weare's estimate, stood at close to $80,000 by late 1877. One half of this sum went to the Davenports.

[46] John and Ira Davenport to John Weare, June 10, 1878; see also John Weare to John Davenport, Sept. 5, 1879, marginal note and Abner Grover, Dow City, Ia., to Ira Davenport, Nov. 10, 1879.

III

KANSAS

THE experience of the Davenport brothers in Kansas differed somewhat from that which they met in Iowa and Illinois. In those states they obtained agents of high caliber who served them for many years. Between 1868 and 1893 at least a dozen agents handled aspects of their business affairs in Kansas. Between 1868 and 1903 the Davenports made 571 loans, totaling $342,919, in the state (see Table 3). This was the smallest amount of lending done by the brothers in any of the states discussed in this study, but at the same time it represented a substantial contribution to the credit needs of the farmers of Kansas.

Early in 1868 Ira Davenport visited southeastern Kansas, where he was attracted by the possibility of purchasing land in the portion of the Osage Indian Reservation which had been ceded to the federal government by the Indians in 1865.[1] Although these lands were occupied by squatters, Davenport evidently believed that many of them would be unable to meet the government's price, and he would be

[1] For a discussion of Indian reservations in Kansas, see Annie H. Abel, "Indian Reservations in Kansas and the Extinguishment of Their Title," *Transactions of the Kansas State Historical Society*, VIII (1903–1904), 72–109.

able to purchase large amounts of land when it was offered for sale. He entrusted $3,500 to Orlin Thurston, one of the promoters of the town of Humboldt, Kansas, and directed him to use it in purchasing Osage land. The title to the ceded lands of the Osages, however, was not settled simply, and the sales anticipated for 1869 were not carried out. Thurston did buy several parcels of land for Davenport in Wilson and Neosho Counties, but he loaned the remainder of his funds on real estate security, promising "extra rates of interest."[2] At least two of the half-dozen or more borrowers surrendered the deed of their land as security for their loans.[3] Davenport wrote to Thurston, "I had hoped to have secured land in sufficient quantity to make it an object, for the distance of the investment. . . . The loaning of money was not what I anticipated, the main object being a land investment."[4]

It was not long before the Davenports were displeased with Thurston. Despite urging and cajoling the Kansan refused to submit accounts.[5] Finally the brothers decided to place the administration of the loans, which Thurston had negotiated, in the hands of E. E. Fuller of Ottawa, Kansas.[6] Ira Davenport eventually summed up his opinion of Thurston in the phrase a "coniving [*sic*] whispering fellow,"[7] and when an extortionate medico charged the younger Davenport $10.00 for an unsuccessful vaccination against smallpox, he fulminated, "Its the worst fraud I have had in some years. I am now trying to get the same M.D. to go to Humboldt, & vaccinate Thurston."[8]

E. E. Fuller, a New Yorker who had known the Davenports before he located in Kansas, was situated in Franklin County at Ottawa. Thinking himself always on the verge of riches, Fuller was by turns merchant in Ottawa and Texas and later a miller at Ottawa. He was not a good businessman, however, and was unable to make a success of his ventures. Fuller was lending funds for John Davenport in Franklin County as early as 1870 at 12 per cent per year with a commission of 6 per cent per year. The commissions were split between Fuller and the Daven-

[2] John Davenport to Orlin Thurston, Humboldt, Kans., Apr. 25, 1871; Ira Davenport to Thurston, Aug. 31, 1871.

[3] W. S. Burns to P. P. Elder and Co., Ottawa, Kans., Mar. 27, 1871.

[4] Ira Davenport to Orlin Thurston, Nov. 17, 1869; Ira Davenport to E. E. Fuller, Ottawa, Kans., Aug. 19, 1869.

[5] Ira Davenport to E. E. Fuller, May 3, 1870, Aug. 23, 1871, Nov. 6, 1871.

[6] *Ibid.*, Aug. 23, 1871, Nov. 6, 1871, Apr. 23, 1872, Oct. 14, 1872.

[7] *Ibid.*, June 3, 1876.

[8] *Ibid.*, Apr. 8, 1872.

ports.[9] Until 1873 Fuller supervised most of the business of the Davenports in the vicinity of Ottawa. When he departed for Texas his duties were transferred to Horace Smith and P. P. Elder.

Horace Smith was cashier of the First National Bank of Ottawa. He assumed general supervision of the loans negotiated by Fuller and loaned additional funds for the Davenports during the decade. In April of 1873 John Davenport sent instructions to Smith:

> Loan out my bal on property worth three times amount of loan, at low valuation, improved farms—to good prompt men, int annually—2 years time or 3—coms 3 per cent per year—credit half coms to Ira's act & half to Edward Fullers—title to farms perfect—party getting loan pays all expense of Abstract & making out papers—recording mortgage—like small loans of $400 & $500—I have reduced the coms—Ed used to charge 6%—you can loan out my bal. . . . Any other mortgages of mine paid up? . . . In sending account of loan, state time it runs.[10]

As the 1870's passed, Smith submitted applications to Bath less frequently although his work was apparently satisfactory.

Territorial statesman, lawyer, soldier, Indian agent, banker, editor, and farmer, P. P. Elder was the most colorful figure who watched over the affairs of the Davenports in Kansas.[11] As a young man Elder came to the Territory of Kansas from Vermont. He pre-empted land south of Ottawa, and his name appears among those of the attorneys on the District Court Records of Franklin County in 1858. As a Republican he played a leading role in the political struggles of the territorial period. He served for a time in the Union Army as a captain but withdrew to become an Indian agent. Returning to Ottawa, he served several terms in the state legislature. In 1870 he was Republican lieutenant governor, but as the years passed his political thinking became progressively more radical, and he was the Populist speaker of the House of Representatives in Kansas in 1891.

In 1870 Elder organized the First National Bank of Ottawa and was its first president. After selling out his holding in this bank, he operated a private bank for a time under the style of P. P. Elder and Company.

[9] John Davenport to E. E. Fuller, Aug. 25, 1870.

[10] Although directed to Smith, these directions were included in John Davenport to P. P. Elder, May 20, 1873; see also *ibid.*, Oct. 17, 1873.

[11] William E. Connelley, *A Standard History of Kansas and Kansans* (Chicago, 1918), II, 1,137, 1,156, 1,161; III, 1,228; IV, 2,396.

Table 3. Loans made under the supervision of John and Ira Davenport in Kansas.

Year	No.	Amount	Prevailing rate—%	Foreclosed or deeded
1868	7	$ 6,500	12	1
1869	21	10,806	12	1
1870	18	12,442	12	3
1871	10	10,400	12	3
1872	37	48,167	12	7
1873	25	19,169	12	3
1874	45	17,690	12	5
1875	73	29,615	12	3
1876	62	26,280	12	2
1877	34	18,395	12	1
1878	30	15,365	12	—
1879	46	17,062	10	2
1880	65	46,147	10	1
1881	45	17,816	8	4
1882	21	14,785	10	2
1883	11	10,550	8	—
1884	1	600	7	—
1885	8	6,240	8	—
1887	2	8,500	8	—
1889	4	1,740	8	—
1890	2	2,500	7	—
1895	1	700	7	—
1896	1	700	7	—
1901	1	400	6	—
1903	1	350	5	—
Total	571	$342,919		38

Elder and his partner began to close out their private banking firm early in 1872, and in the process they decided to accept a considerable amount of real estate rather than force any of their debtors into bankruptcy. Elder borrowed $10,000 from the Davenports at 12 per cent to assist in carrying this property, and he agreed to repay the brothers from the proceeds as the real estate was sold.[12] But far from being able

[12] P. P. Elder to John and Ira Davenport, Feb. 4, 1872; Kansas Loan Ledger, pp. 97–99.

to repay the loan, Elder instead saw other creditors obtain four judgments against the partnership over the next two years.[13] The First National Bank at Ottawa acquired these judgments and in 1875 offered to accept $8,000 for them, although their face value with accumulated interest was more than twice this sum. John Davenport advanced the money on the security of additional real estate controlled by Elder.[14] In 1882 Elder discharged this obligation, but the original loan of $10,000 still stood, inflated by arrears of interest. Swollen still further by an additional amount with which Elder hoped to round out a farming unit of optimum size for his feeder operations, the debt was agreed to total $16,000 in April of 1882, although the rate of interest had been dropped to 8 per cent by this time.[15]

Elder's relations with the Davenports remained close, and occasionally they lent additional sums to him on short term with which to purchase feeder stock.[16] At the same time Elder performed various services for the brothers. He supervised the management of their real estate in Franklin County and advised them in 1879 that their agent in Paola was too untrustworthy to be allowed to collect money for them.[17]

By 1881 Elder's thinking was not of the type usually expected in an ex-banker. On learning that the Davenports were investing in Wall Street, he wrote to John Davenport, "I believe you had better keep out of Wall St Stocks by all means—I understand the whole develtree there —Banks cannot rule this government much longer—no more than Slavery did—The end is foreshadowed sure as there is a 'God in Israel.'"[18] Smith, writing in November of 1882, confided to John

[13] P. P. Elder to Ira Davenport, Dec. 15, 1873, to John Davenport, Mar. 13, 1875. The judgments were as follows: in Douglas County District Court, *National Bank of Lawrence* vs. *Elder and Walruff* in cases 2306 and 2385, in 1872, to the amount of $5,299.53 and in Franklin County District Court, *First National Bank of Kansas City, Missouri* vs. *Elder and Walruff* and *Bowen* vs. *Elder and Walruff* in cases 1321 and 1359, in 1874, to the amount of $10,411.20.

[14] P. P. Elder to John Davenport, Mar. 26, 1875; also P. P. Elder and John Davenport, Agreement, July 29, 1875; Kansas Loan Ledger, p. 180; John Davenport to P. P. Elder, Aug. 16, 1875, to H. J. Smith, July 15, 1875, and Aug. 9, 1875.

[15] John W. Deford, Ottawa, Kans., to John Davenport, Apr. 21, 1881; P. P. Elder to John Davenport, Jan. 1, 1882, Feb. 15, 1882; Kansas Loan Ledger, p. 97.

[16] H. J. Smith to John Davenport, Nov. 21, 1878; Ira Davenport to H. J. Smith, Oct. 6, 1879.

[17] P. P. Elder to John Davenport, June 6, 1879; John Davenport to P. P. Elder, Aug. 20, 1873, June 18, 1874.

[18] P. P. Elder to John Davenport, Mar. 16, 1881.

Davenport, "I am mighty sorry he is going to the Legislature this winter —He will make war on *interest.*" [19] In the next summer Smith described the trouble he was having with Elder over the way in which the latter was repaying a feeder loan to the Davenports:

Elder absolutely refuses to pay interest on any other basis than that all payments are to be applied on principal—thus: when this 2000 note was due he paid 1200 but he would not allow the interest then due to be taken out of the payment but insisted that the whole of the 1200 should be considered as a payment on the *principal* and he would pay the interest at the last end. . . . Elder wont compound worth a cent.[20]

By 1887 Elder's debt to the Davenports was still standing at $16,000. In April of that year he wrote:

The prices of beef & hogs are so low that the interest will impair my capital at the present rate of interest. It now takes 2 steer & 2 hogs to pay the same sum as one did in 1883 or 84. Life is too short for me to wait for sales under the present conditions of trade & business. I have done everything that mortal man can do—and can and have made money when all my neighbors engaged in a Similar business lost.[21]

A year later Elder was in no better condition. He argued that it was impossible to pay interest at the rate of 8 per cent per annum:

I had just as live deed that land at once to Ira as to try to meet 8 pr ct. This would perhaps be the best way—But I do not feel right in abandoning the land and you men after you have been so kind to me in the past—Every part of the farm is in the best possible condition for use or sale—I have expended large sums of money to put the land buildings & fences in good repairs & feel like keeping them so. . . . I propose to make every effort to sell trade or in any way to get out & pay that mortgage . . . as it is not a question to you men as to losses but as to how much interest you can get . . . is [it] asking too much to be permitted to pay up back interest at 6 per cent. . . . Some of my neighbors . . . have lost from 2 to 5000. . . . The devilish dressed beef men is the cause.[22]

Ira Davenport reduced the rate of interest to 6 per cent.[23]

In March 1889 Elder sold a portion of his land. He arranged to have

[19] H. J. Smith to John Davenport, Nov. 27, 1882.

[20] *Ibid.*, Aug. 10, 1883.

[21] P. P. Elder to John Davenport, Apr. 10, 1887.

[22] *Ibid.*, Apr. 21, 1888.

[23] *Ibid.*, May 30, 1888.

the purchasers write a mortgage to be held by Ira and guaranteed by himself. Elder's old mortgage was to be released and a new one written to cover the diminished security. Ira Davenport refused to accept the new mortgage because it did not include a clause waiving appraisement. Since such a clause had not been included in the original mortgage, Elder maintained: "He must not demand or expect other terms in the new mortg than he has in the old. I have always regarded that law waiving the appraisement of land in mortg sale—with no equity of redemption as the most infamous and dangerous law to mortgagor that any state has or ever had." [24] Ira acceded to Elder's request, concluding in a letter to his brother, "This ought to bring this d—d business to a head. Elder writes from his point of view—talks about 'slaving the best years to pay this debt'—one would think it was a security debt that he had had no money for. Who the deuce wanted him to make a debt? Whose money is this but his own borrowed from us?" [25] Not until the depression years of the 1890's had given way to more prosperous times, however, was Elder to free himself from his burden of debt, and even then Elder sacrificed most of the security in that process. Although Elder had been a banker and for years had helped to watch over the affairs of nonresident moneylenders, he was one of the most vocal of the agrarian radicals in Kansas and most energetic in proposing amendments to the collection laws of the state. The preceding paragraphs should make the anomaly more understandable.

During 1872 the Davenports received several letters from F. M. Shaw, the cashier of the First National Bank of Paola, in which he offered to lend their funds at remunerative rates. After checking on Shaw's business reputation with Elder and Fuller, Ira Davenport decided to test the man.[26] One of the brothers contacted him in person while west in late 1872. Shaw made his first loan for the Davenports in January 1873, and in August of that year the brothers suspended lending temporarily until his work had a chance to prove its quality.[27]

Lending was begun at a rate of something over 15 per cent in a state where the legal maximum stood at 12 per cent. The interest obtained above the legal rate of course was described as commission. By the summer of 1873 Shaw was arguing that 15 per cent was the highest rate

[24] *Ibid.*, Mar. 25, 1889.

[25] *Ibid.*, Attached memorandum.

[26] Ira Davenport to P. P. Elder, Oct. 16, 1872, to E. E. Fuller, Oct. 14, 1872.

[27] Ira Davenport to F. M. Shaw, Aug. 4, 1873.

which could possibly be obtained in his area. Ira Davenport replied that a reduction of the commission to 3 per cent a year should not be entirely at the expense of the Davenports. He suggested that he would be content with a third of the commission, which he argued was not enough to return a profit but would pay for the labor of accounting to those for whom the Davenports were lending funds.[28]

Davenport believed it to be well within the power of borrowers to pay 15 per cent, but he did not think that Kansans had a right to expect such low rates until the collection laws were remedied. Since the agrarian radicals later claimed that the collection laws of Kansas had been rewritten in the interests of the moneylenders during the late 1860's and early 1870's, this was an interesting observation. Evidently the Davenports regarded aspects of the law of Kansas as unfavorable to the mortgagee. In Kansas the deed of trust was treated as a simple mortgage collectable only through the courts, and a stay law prevented the sale of a mortgagor's land until six months had elapsed after judgment was rendered.[29]

In their early dealings with Shaw the Davenport brothers did not leave the mortgage papers at Paola but rather held them at Bath, New York. They refused to send notes or releases before Shaw reported that the mortgagor had made his payment at the bank in Paola.[30] Shaw was warned to keep his loans down to several hundred dollars in size. Applications for loans on city property were not accepted.[31] The removal of the Indian reservations from eastern Kansas left its imprint upon titles in the region. The Davenports steadfastly refused to lend on land where the first white owner had obtained his title from an Indian. In August 1875 John Davenport summed up his attitude on Indian titles when he returned mortgage papers backed by an Indian title, writing, "I must return these papers and certainly shall return any more you send in, as I do not want them and will not accept them." [32] Davenport never explained his distrust of Indian titles, but undoubtedly he believed them dangerous because of the very real possibility that they had been fraudulently obtained from the Indian grantee of the government.

By 1876 the Davenports were well satisfied with Shaw and recom-

[28] *Ibid.*, Sept. 6, 1873. [29] *Ibid.*

[30] John Davenport to C. A. Leighton, Paola, Kans., Oct. 27, 1873.

[31] John Davenport to F. M. Shaw, July 27, 1874, Jan. 14, 1875, Sept. 6, 1877.

[32] *Ibid.*, Aug. 31, 1875; also Jan. 16, 1873.

mended his services to other members of the community in Bath. One of these was a young lawyer, Reuben Robie. John Davenport cautioned Shaw:

He fears the big interest as all new and safe men do in the East—who have not been West—& seen your good farming country & the men & security—You know it is an old adage the bigger the interest the greater the risk—He is a good safe man—a young lawyer—has some little means of his own, will receive more from his Father's Estate when it is all settled—he's careful—Send him none but the best applications. He asked me if I believed you really personally went out & examined each piece of land you loaned on? I assured him you did & looked into *taxes too*—& stir the men up 30 days before due.[33]

Robie asked that the applications be submitted for his inspection before loans were finally closed. When Shaw neglected to do this in one case, he was sharply reprimanded by John Davenport.[34]

In 1876 John Davenport introduced another feature of the lending business into his relationship with Shaw, who was now operating his own bank under the title of F. M. Shaw and Company. Davenport objected to a loan which Shaw had proposed to him but offered to take it if Shaw would guarantee it.[35] Until this time there was little use of the guarantee in the lending business of the Davenports, although their agents in both Illinois and Iowa occasionally guaranteed a loan which appeared to be irregular in some respect. Eventually the guarantee became a cardinal feature of the lending business of the major western mortgage companies. The guarantee, however, never became characteristic of the Davenports' lending in Kansas.

In 1877 the Davenports instructed Shaw to merge all of their accounts.[36] One reason for this change in policy was undoubtedly a desire on the part of the Davenports to simplify their business, but it may also have marked the realization that it was no longer possible to obtain rates in Kansas which were above the legal rate. Undoubtedly the original division had been made as a safeguard against the action of the usury law. By the late 1870's competition among lenders was such in Kansas that the Davenports were forced to forego their share of the commission.

[33] John Davenport to F. M. Shaw, Jan. 8, 1876. [34] *Ibid.*, May 23, 1876.
[35] John Davenport to F. M. Shaw and Co., July 5, 1876.
[36] John and Ira Davenport to F. M. Shaw and Co., Mar. 16, 1877.

In Kansas as elsewhere the Davenports were faced with borrowers who wished to close out their loans before they came due. Like most lenders they preferred not to close out loans prematurely, since to do so meant that the funds must be reloaned to a borrower who might be less reliable than had been his predecessor. In addition, interest rates tended to drop constantly in the western states in these years. Money accepted before maturity usually had to be reloaned at a lower rate of interest than formerly if placed out in the same community. In August 1877 the Davenports explained to Shaw that they would accept loans before maturity only if the borrower paid the interest up to the original terminal date.[37] This policy did not prevent borrowers from selling their land, but it did prevent a loss to the Davenports. In exceptional cases, however, where the borrower had been prompt and the loan had been small, the Davenports did consent to release loans before they were due.

In 1877 Shaw inquired if the Davenports would care to invest in chattel mortgages. Such paper carried a higher rate of interest than did long-term mortgage paper, but the brothers were uninterested. They replied that chattel mortgages were a good investment for the local lender who could supervise them in person, but they preferred to stick to real estate security.[38]

Until late in 1877 Shaw was apparently the Davenports' favorite agent in the state of Kansas. In November 1877 Ira Davenport returned some of the securities which Shaw had offered, writing that they were unsatisfactory. He claimed also that the Kansan had delayed repeatedly when asked to remit balances from the account at Paola, and informed him that he was fully aware of a recent run on Shaw's bank.[39] Shaw managed to conciliate the brothers, and in June 1878 John Davenport complimented him upon the loans which he had been making for them.[40] But by August Shaw was again late with his remittances and in submitting mortgage papers which he had promised to the Davenports.[41]

Late in 1879 Shaw and the Davenports came to a parting of the ways. It was discovered that the agent had not reported all of the payments made to him by mortgagors. Ira Davenport wrote, "I doubt if you have

[37] *Ibid.*, Aug. 7, 1877.
[38] *Ibid.*, Sept. 3, 1877.
[39] Ira Davenport to F. M. Shaw and Co., Nov. 3, 1877.
[40] John Davenport to F. M. Shaw and Co., June 23, 1878.
[41] *Ibid.*, Aug. 14, 1878.

any better business upon hand than setting yourself right with me. . . . I shall not let these matters delay nor any circumstances or cost of sending good money after bad. . . . It is not the money it is the outraging of confidence."[42] The Davenports transferred their business in Paola to the law firm of Jones and Maxwell. In January 1882 the brothers summed up their loss. Aside from a joint investment in tax certificates with Shaw on which some $500 was owing, Shaw had not accounted for $360 which he had collected for them.[43] The Davenports did not prosecute Shaw because they needed his evidence in court cases which were pending in the early 1880's.[44] Others were less forebearing, and Shaw spent at least a portion of 1880 in jail.

In 1879 the Davenports began to do business with the firm of Young and Yates of Thayer, Kansas. Thayer lies in Neosho County, and titles were granted late in that area since it had formed a part of the Osage reservation. Before 1879 Young and Yates had been the local agents of F. M. Shaw in Thayer. One of the brothers visited their office while he was on an inspection trip in Kansas during the late 1870's. Young and Yates offered to supply good real estate loans if the additional middle man—Shaw—was cut out so that they could place them at a low commission. They promised that funds could be made to return a 2-per-cent commission for the Davenports if placed at 9 or 10 per cent.[45] The capitalists from Bath were not so firmly attached to Shaw that they rejected such overtures. They allowed Young and Yates to make a few small loans of $200 and $300 at 12-per-cent interest and asked for no share of the commission. They instructed the agents from Thayer to charge as small a commission as was consistent with careful work. They instructed them to examine the county records and to certify to the correctness of abstracts. Loans were to be made only on improved farmland and were not to exceed one-third of the appraised value of the property. All loans were to be made in the name of John Davenport. The brothers emphasized to the agents that they were to look after the loans until they were properly closed out and that they were interested in "prompt men as well as good security."[46] In reply to the question of the agents W. S. Burns

[42] Ira Davenport to F. M. Shaw and Co., Jan. 2, 1880.

[43] John and Ira Davenport to Jones and Maxwell, Paola, Kans., Jan. 7, 1882.

[44] *Ibid.*, Jan. 20, 1880.

[45] J. A. Young and W. J. Yates, Thayer, Kans., to John and Ira Davenport, Jan. 3, 1879.

[46] John and Ira Davenport to Young and Yates, Jan. 25, 1879.

wrote that the Davenports preferred interest to be taken annually since it was less trouble for both lender and borrower. Loans might run for five years, since they were not interested in obtaining the land. In contrast to the lending agencies which were then beginning to multiply rapidly, the Davenports had no mortgage forms of their own but used any adequate form which the agent could provide.[47]

For the most part Young and Yates seem to have done satisfactory work for the Davenports. In 1879 they were reprimanded for suggesting that a loan should be made on unimproved land, and in the same year the Davenports neglected a suggestion that they might wish to take over some loans and enlarge them for farmers who were unable to pay out. Young and Yates explained that these men had borrowed money in 1874 and 1875 and had been unable to pay off their loans in the ensuing years of depression. The agents believed that the next five years would be more prosperous and desired to increase the loans and carry them for another five years. To such suggestions the Davenports were unsympathetic.[48]

In March 1881 Young and Yates informed the Davenports that money was so plentiful that it was impossible to obtain more than 8 per cent with a commission, or a straight rate of 10 per cent. They confided that they were lending money for Crippen, Lawrence, and Company of Concord, New Hampshire, who gave them a commission of 2 per cent of the face of the loan when funds were loaned at 10 per cent; when contracts were made at 9 per cent Young and Yates paid Crippen and Lawrence a commission of 2 per cent out of the fee which the Kansans charged the borrower and when the lending rate was dropped to 8 per cent this commission was raised to 4 per cent of the face of the loans. Young and Yates asked permission to place money at 10-per-cent interest and to be allowed to deduct a commission of 2 per cent of the face of the loan from the interest payments.[49] To this proposal John Davenport agreed, but reiterated that the loans should be small in amount, that the title should be correct, that the agents should personally inspect the real estate, that the borrowers should keep their taxes paid up and should pay their interest promptly.

[47] Young and Yates to John and Ira Davenport, Jan. 31, 1879; John and Ira Davenport to Young and Yates, Feb. 4, 1879.

[48] Young and Yates to John and Ira Davenport, Sept. 24, 1879, June 29, 1881.

[49] *Ibid.*, Mar. 29, 1881, Apr. 11, 1881.

In November 1881 Young and Yates informed the Davenports that they were transferring their business to Kansas City. To take their place at Thayer, they recommended a local real estate agent, E. L. Barnes.[50] Barnes sought to take over the Davenport agency as it had been left by Young and Yates, and his correspondence with the New Yorkers is marked by his smooth, coherent, and plausible style.[51] Unfortunately, his style served to cover a certain business unorthodoxy. For a time he made new loans for the Davenports, although a suggestion that he could obtain 1½ to 25 per cent per month for them on chattels was disregarded.[52] In 1883 Barnes, who had organized a partnership with one Lyman of the same place, became increasingly dilatory in his correspondence with the Davenports.[53] Finally in disgust, they asked Jones and Maxwell to investigate the situation at Thayer.

Jones and Maxwell reported immediately that there had been much fraud in the real estate loan business at Thayer and promised to investigate. Soon they were able to report further information. Barnes, they found, had no business standing whatsoever. Lyman, his partner, had considerable capital which he had obtained in a previous partnership with two cattle dealers. They had rustled a herd of cattle and appropriated the proceeds. All three of the men had been arrested; one of them was sent to the penitentiary; a second escaped from the officers and was still wanted by the state; only Lyman had stood trial and been acquitted. The sheriff who had arrested the cattle dealers informed Jones and Maxwell that Lyman had actually been the worst of the lot and had obtained all of the money for the cattle. Jones and Maxwell reported, however, that some of the citizens of Thayer believed that he had since reformed.

Finding it impossible to obtain satisfaction from Lyman and Barnes through the mail, Jones and Maxwell investigated in person. They found no outright fraud, but Lyman and Barnes had been holding up the remittances destined for the Davenports and using them for a few months to finance the greater share of the stock and grain business done in Thayer. When accused, the partners freely admitted the practice and

[50] *Ibid.*, Nov. 29, 1881.

[51] E. L. Barnes, Thayer, Kans., to John Davenport, Dec. 9, 1881, Dec. 21, 1881, Jan. 24, 1882, Mar. 7, 1882.

[52] *Ibid.*, Jan. 25, 1882.

[53] *Ibid.*, Apr. 12, 1882, memo of John Davenport.

agreed to settle with the lawyers from Paola. Jones and Maxwell demanded 10 per cent on all balances which they had held. The Davenports, therefore, received interest on their money and the whole affair turned out to be more interesting than disastrous.[54]

After 1880 the Davenports tapered off their lending in the state of Kansas. Ira Davenport was withdrawing his personal funds for investment on Wall Street and in Michigan timberland. Loans drawn at 12 per cent had ceased to be the rule in 1878. The time was approaching when the trust funds at the disposal of the brothers must be surrendered. No one agent in Kansas had ever given complete satisfaction. When the time came for retrenchment, investments, therefore, were cut back earlier in Kansas than in Illinois or Nebraska, where the agents had inspired more confidence. For the remainder of the decade, however, the Davenports continued to invest money through their more trustworthy Kansan agents. The First National Bank of Ottawa, John Deford (the attorney of the Davenports in Ottawa), R. J. Waddell (a loan agent of the same town), and Jones and Maxwell of Paola all negotiated a few loans during the 1880's, and six loans were accepted from 1890 on. It is very possible that the Davenports would have withdrawn completely from Kansas had they not been the owners of a certain amount of property which had to be administered. By accepting the occasional application from these agents, they augmented the income of the westerners and made them more attentive to the interests of the Davenports.

As usual, the lending business necessitated some traffic in land. The letters of the brothers to their agents in Kansas contain the usual protestations that they loaned only for the interest and did not wish to acquire real estate.[55] Some thirty-eight loans, however, or between 6 and 7 per cent of those made in Kansas, were foreclosed. Another nine were involved in litigation. The land book of the Davenports shows only twenty-nine parcels of land obtained by foreclosure, and it is possible that the real estate behind the remaining nine loans was bid in by other parties at the sheriff's sale. In at least one instance Horace Smith of the First National Bank of Ottawa took foreclosed property from the

[54] John Davenport to Jones and Maxwell, Mar. 7, 1883; Jones and Maxwell to John and Ira Davenport, Feb. 15, 1883, Mar. 7, 1883, Mar. 29, 1883.

[55] John Davenport to F. M. Shaw, Oct. 12, 1877; John and Ira Davenport to Young and Yates, Feb. 4, 1879; Ira Davenport to Jones and Maxwell, Jan. 20, 1880.

Davenports at cost because he had negotiated the loan and argued that the foreclosed land was, therefore, his responsibility.[56] It was possible to calculate the return on investment which the Davenport brothers received from twenty-four foreclosed farms in Kansas. On the average they held these farms ten and one-half years, and they invested an average of $1,247 in each before sale. On their investment the return per loan was 2.5 per cent, and the average return on each dollar invested in foreclosed real estate was but one per cent. Of all the states in which they operated, the Davenports were least successful in selling their foreclosed land in Kansas.

The Davenports did not confine themselves solely to moneylending and real-estate speculation in Kansas. In 1876 F. M. Shaw convinced Ira Davenport that tax certificates were a profitable form of investment. Shaw agreed to attend to the detail and invested about $1,000 of Davenport's money at the tax sale in Miami County in that year. Shaw promised Davenport 10 per cent on his investment and one-half of all returns above that figure. Since tax certificates were returning 24 per cent for the first year and 36 per cent thereafter until a deed was issued, the investment appeared to be a good one. The tax certificates, however, represented small sums ranging from five dollars upward, and since they might be redeemed at any time by the owner of the property against which they stood, the bookkeeping and calculation of returns was burdensome. In 1877 Ira Davenport wrote to Shaw: "These tax certificates are going to be an endless computation & question of arithmetic between our respective accountants—However interesting such dealings are . . . do not buy any more certificates & we will work out of what we have and keep to the department of loaning." [57] Henceforth the Davenports bought tax certificates only as they needed to protect the title of property on which they held mortgages.

County bonds were another type of investment which the Davenports occasionally purchased in Kansas. In 1876 they empowered Shaw to buy Johnson County bonds to the value of $1,000.[58] County officials often issued warrants prior to the collection of taxes in order to tide their municipalities over a period of scanty funds. In 1875 Ira Davenport

[56] H. J. Smith to John and Ira Davenport, Mar. 7, 1879.
[57] Ira Davenport to F. M. Shaw, Jan. 18, 1877.
[58] John and Ira Davenport to F. M. Shaw, May 9, 1876.

invested in a quantity of warrants issued by Labette County.[59] In the 1880's John Davenport purchased stock in a sorghum sugar mill which was being built in Ottawa.[60] Occasionally the Davenports speculated in corn. E. E. Fuller bought corn for John Davenport in the early 1870's, and both brothers held quantities of the grain during the decade.[61]

[59] Ira Davenport to F. M. Shaw, May 10, 1876.
[60] John W. Deford to John Davenport, Oct. 30, 1884.
[61] John Davenport to P. P. Elder, May 15, 1877.

IV

NEBRASKA

IN NEBRASKA the lending operations of the Davenport brothers were linked more closely to speculation in land than in any other state. Between 1870 and 1904 John and Ira Davenport held title to some 63,000 acres of land in twenty-two counties of Nebraska. Some 57,000 acres were acquired by purchase from three railroads, the state of Nebraska, and the federal government. Most of the remaining acreage was a result of moneylending. The real estate was scattered from Sarpy County on the eastern boundary of the state to Cherry County in northwestern Nebraska, although the greatest acreage lay in Dodge, Pierce, Wayne, Madison, and Lancaster Counties.

The brothers made their first purchase of land in Nebraska in 1870, when John Davenport purchased 18,000 acres of land in Dodge and Cuming Counties from the Union Pacific Railroad. As in Kansas, the brothers entered the state with the intention of purchasing land and then combined the supervision of their real estate with moneylending. In contrast to the 571 loans totaling $342,919 loaned in Kansas between 1870 and 1900, John and Ira Davenport loaned $1,128,892 in Nebraska, divided among 1,610 loans (see Table 4).

Table 4. Loans made under the supervision of John and Ira Davenport in Nebraska.

Year	No.	Amount	Prevailing rate—%	Prevailing rate to the Davenports—%	Foreclosed or deeded
1871	39	$29,010	12	12+	7
1872	27	18,805	12	12+	7
1873	10	4,073	12	12+	—
1874	63	19,871	12	12	4
1875	31	7,103	12	12	1
1876	3	5,900	12	12	1
1877	32	12,383	12	12,10?	—
1878	190	58,806	12	12,10?	2
1879	59	26,126	10	10,8.5?	—
1880	172	68,121	10	8.5	1
1881	108	44,735	10	8.5	—
1882	91	54,780	10	8.5	—
1883	183	111,050	9	8.5	1
1884	74	49,075	9	7.5,8	—
1885	73	46,596	10	8.5	—
1886	80	68,740	9	7.5	1
1887	56	44,570	9	7.5	2
1888	27	14,772	10	8	13
1889	47	50,700	10	8	5
1890	83	78,400	8	7	1
1891	36	52,735	8	7	2
1892	36	49,270	8	7	—
1893	13	47,200	7	6	—
1894	16	25,221	7	6	—
1895	17	26,900	6	6	—
1896	9	11,300	6	6	—
1897	8	17,850	6.5	6.5	—
1898	3	15,500	6	6	—
1899	6	15,100	5	5	—
1900	18	54,200	5	5	—
Total	1,610	$1,128,892			48

The spring of 1871 found Ira Davenport in Lincoln, Nebraska, where he established contact with Amasa Cobb and Major J. F. Sudduth of the First National Bank of Lincoln and made some loans on real estate.[1] For about two years Sudduth supervised the lending of funds furnished by Ira Davenport in addition to administering the payment of taxes on land owned by the Davenports south of the Platte River.[2] These early loans were drawn at 12 per cent, and evidently Ira Davenport derived a commission of 3 per cent for himself on extensions as well as on new loans.[3] If these terms appear difficult by present-day standards, Davenport was evidently in a position where he could pick and choose. He wrote in 1872, "The application of Judge Hilton I will not be able to fill first for present want of funds and also I dont want to loan only to those satisfied with my rates. The distance of the field of operations, the care necessary, and the time and expenses of trips are sufficient offsets without having dissatisfied borrowers." [4] Farm property was preferred and lending was to be done on a conservative basis. "I don't want to go over one third cash valuation upon improved or partially improved farms by which I mean enough tillage to show a good proportion to the untilled," wrote Davenport. He concluded, "I have enough demand for money to take only the best." [5]

In 1872 Ira Davenport followed the usual practice of the Davenports by halting lending in the Lincoln area until the loans could prove their quality.[6] The capital of Nebraska had been established at Lincoln in 1867. Until the depression of 1873 the city enjoyed a period of real estate speculation, as merchants and capitalists endeavored to stake out their claims in a city which they believed would be a great western metropolis. The price of farmland in the surrounding area was also affected. Apparently some of the loans of 1871 and 1872 in the Lincoln area were made to overoptimistic businessmen and farmers who were gambling on a continued rise in land values. In June 1873 Ira Davenport foreclosed his first mortgage in Nebraska.[7] Other loans were in a doubtful condition. In July 1874, after the real estate bubble was broken, Ira Davenport summed up his opinion of the loans made at Lincoln: "The result of my loaning in Lincoln is not going to be gratifying. I want the money back not the land. . . . There being such

[1] Ira Davenport to J. F. Sudduth, Lincoln, Neb., July 7, 1871.
[2] *Ibid.*, June 17, 1872. [3] *Ibid.*, July 7, 1871. [4] *Ibid.*, Sept. 1, 1872.
[5] *Ibid.*, Apr. 2, 1872. [6] *Ibid.*, Oct. 2, 1872. [7] *Ibid.*, June 21, 1873.

amount of taxes on these lands is not encouraging. I now suppose I will have to hand the entire list over to the General [Cobb] for settlement." [8] Again he wrote, "Enclosed is a list of loans in arrears & back taxes from which I think you will see, with what I have already in suit that I have sufficient grounds for feeling that Lincoln has not proven an attractive or successful field for loaning." [9] In all, the Davenports assumed title to the security backing fourteen of the fifty-odd loans which they made in the Lincoln area, either by foreclosure or by informal settlement, and two others were taken to court but settled short of foreclosure. Some 1,000 acres of land were placed on their land book as a result. After 1874 the brothers ceased lending in Lancaster County. Foreclosures there, however, dragged into the 1880's, and in 1882 B. F. Cobb, the real estate agent in charge of their affairs in Lincoln, collected the principal on one loan which had been extended and forged the release. In sequel Cobb went to the penitentiary, and the loan was foreclosed when the borrower claimed that his responsibility for the loan ended when he paid the principal to Cobb.[10]

While in Nebraska during 1871, Ira Davenport arranged that E. O. Crosby, a real estate agent of Fremont, Nebraska, should supervise the payment of taxes on the land of the Davenports which lay north of the Platte River. Apparently Ira Davenport made a few loans in the vicinity of Fremont in 1871, and Crosby was allowed to lend Davenport funds occasionally in the early part of 1872.[11] The Fremont *Tribune* reported in July that Captain W. S. Burns was in Fremont assessing the possibility of lending money.[12] In October, Crosby was advertising the fact that he had money to lend. In that same month Ira Davenport replied to a request from Crosby for more funds, "I have not thought of increasing the amt now out in Dodge until I saw how the loans now made were met. It is something of an experiment and wants to be worked slowly at first." [13]

In 1873 or early in 1874 the decision was made to channel all lending in Nebraska through Crosby, and the ninety-four loans made in the state during 1874 and 1875 were negotiated by him. Crosby submitted the applications and abstracts to the Davenports and they chose the

[8] *Ibid.*, July 7, 1874.

[9] *Ibid.*, July 27, 1874.

[10] Ira Davenport to W. H. Munger, Fremont, Neb., Sept. 18, 1885.

[11] Ira Davenport to E. O. Crosby, Mar. 11, 1872, Mar. 17, 1872.

[12] Fremont *Tribune*, July 26, 1872.

[13] Ira Davenport to E. O. Crosby, Oct. 26, 1872.

loans which appeared satisfactory to them. There is some question whether the notes and mortgages were drawn up in Fremont or at Bath, but in all probability they were drafted by Crosby. Ira Davenport made it clear that Crosby was not to represent himself as the agent of the Davenports:

> There is one point . . . which we must have understood—that is—that you are in no respect our agent but the Agent of the Borrowers—make this known. . . . Do not assume any forms or signatures of agency except as for the parties you apply for loans for—and there can be no tracing you as what you are not. We have been through this trouble once in Illinois & as the result *we now have no agents.* Assurances of friendly persons or City Councilmen are nothing to keeping your own bars up.[14]

Later Crosby was instructed to concentrate his business in Dodge County, and the Davenports reminded the agent of the type of information which they needed before they could decide on loans:

> Prefer to loan in Dodge Co & to farmers near our land—Please be a little more particular in sending in applications as to value of their land—State what land is worth with improvements & without—We dont want any land to take on mortgage—want to loan at ⅓ cash value—State how far from market land lies—that is the station they sell wheat or grain at. . . . You can get some idea of worth of land by what land sells for—We want to know value of our security—you can get opinion of farmers who know the land—So when you send in applications state value of land with improvements & in raw state—Inquire also what kind of a farmer the applicant is.[15]

To keep themselves informed of conditions in Nebraska, the brothers were subscribing to both the Fremont *Tribune* and the Fremont *Herald* for a time in 1873, but asked Crosby to renew their subscription to the "best one for local & State items" only.[16]

By 1876 business relations with Crosby were becoming strained. He was not forwarding his accounts promptly and discrepancies appeared frequently in his reports. During the mid 1870's Crosby built the Fremont Opera House and evidently drew on the funds of the Davenports to help him finance the project. Pressed by Ira Davenport, he tendered the brothers a mortgage on his house in Fremont and on eighty acres of land nearby. Other creditors were also pressing, and in January 1877

[14] *Ibid.*, July 7, 1874. [15] *Ibid.*, Oct. 26, 1874.
[16] John and Ira Davenport to Crosby and Newton, Dec. 22, 1873.

Crosby decided that a trip to California was the best solution to his difficulties. In June 1877 Ira Davenport estimated that Crosby was some $2,900 in debt to the brothers. The record is not clear, but evidently the Davenports escaped with a minor loss.[17]

When Crosby departed for California, the brothers prepared a list of the loans under his supervision, which they sent to A. P. Hopkins, a private banker of Fremont. Hopkins took over the administration of the loans and then carried on the lending business as well. The transfer was not completely free of risk. Ira Davenport warned Hopkins:

> The laws of Nebraska are so curius [*sic*] upon agents & usury—that it seems that even if you recd all the Coms. & we only the legal interest, yet if you can be made to appear you rec coms as our agent that taints our loans with usury. This places us in an awkward position as regards sending any of our borrowers or applicants to you, but we will try to do so as best we can. . . . What I say about applicants & present debtors who write us, refers to the fact that they came to us instead of them going to you & our difficulty is to have them go to you without sending them—We can probably manage it.[18]

Although the agreements which they had with their representatives in Nebraska are less clear than in other states, the brothers unquestionably procured a portion of the commission for themselves when they began to lend funds there. Beginning in 1874 the supreme court of Nebraska interpreted the usury law most stringently in a series of decisions.[19] If it could be proven that the western agent acted in any way under the direction of the eastern lender, the western agent's commission was calculated as part of the interest rate. The loans negotiated by Crosby bore a uniform rate of 12 per cent. Presumably he obtained a commission from the borrower. In all probability the Davenports relinquished any share of the commission after the unfavorable decisions were handed down.

It is impossible to discover the exact terms of the agreement which Hopkins made with the Davenports in 1877. Possibly it was agreed that

[17] Ira Davenport to E. O. Crosby, Jan. 1, 1876, Apr. 6, 1876, May 13, 1876, Feb. 10, 1877, June 23, 1877, to G. L. Loomis, Fremont, Neb., Feb. 2, 1877, to Hopkins and Wilson, Fremont, Neb., Feb. 9, 1877; Hopkins and Millard to John and Ira Davenport, Jan. 15, 1880, Feb. 24, 1880.

[18] Ira Davenport to Wilson and Hopkins, Aug. 31, 1877.

[19] *Philo* vs. *Butterfield, Nebraska Reports,* III, 256, *Cheney* vs. *White, ibid.,* V, 261, and *Cheney* vs. *Woodruff, ibid.,* VI, 151.

he should subtract a commission of 2 per cent per year from the interest payments on the loans which he had negotiated. Such an agreement would have banished all fear of prosecution under the usury law. If this was the case, however, the loan ledgers of the Davenports do not show it. In 1879 the legislature of Nebraska lowered the legal maximum rate of interest from 12 per cent annually to 10 per cent, necessitating a new agreement between Hopkins and the Davenports. The banker suggested that 2 per cent per annum on the principal would be a fair commission. Loans would be made at 10 per cent and the commission deducted from the interest payments. Hopkins admitted that the 8 per cent which would be left for the Davenports "looks pretty small." [20] After considerable correspondence and a trip west by Ira, the new commission rate was settled at 1½ per cent per annum, leaving the Davenports 8½ per cent return on their funds.[21]

Hopkins, with his partner, Millard, acted as the agent of the Davenports for some five years. During this time he gave excellent service and encountered few of the difficulties which invariably marked the work of less efficient agents. Apparently he was allowed to accept applications immediately when he believed the loan to be an unquestionably good one. Where the Davenports had themselves used the county newspapers to draw up lists of mortgagors who had not paid their taxes in the early years of Crosby's agency, Hopkins evidently prepared his own lists. Then he paid the taxes of the delinquents to keep the lien of the Davenports incontestable.[22] Lending over a somewhat larger field than Crosby, Hopkins made at least 529 loans.

Hopkins had no qualms about foreclosure, when he believed it necessary. In April 1880 he asked for the mortgage papers of one Sinkula who had borrowed $250 on the security of eighty acres of land in Dodge County. The land, he wrote, "is good but man is poor stick, drinks & pays nothing, better foreclose." [23] On the other hand, in January 1881 he suggested that borrowers in Butler County should be given special consideration. These men owed both interest and principal after a year in which dry weather had prevented them from raising any crops. Hopkins suggested that the Davenports must decide whether they would enlarge

[20] A. P. Hopkins to John and Ira Davenport, June 6, 1879, July 17, 1879.

[21] Ira Davenport to A. P. Hopkins, Aug. 15, 1879; Hopkins and Millard to John and Ira Davenport, Apr. 12, 1880.

[22] Hopkins and Millard to John and Ira Davenport, Mar. 14, 1881.

[23] *Ibid.*, May 22, 1880.

the loans to those who had been prompt with their interest payments or whether they expected to have all of their loans paid when due. He suggested that borrowers who had been prompt in the past should be helped out, but that payment should be asked of those who had been slow in their payments even before the drought. The latter could obtain enlarged loans from another agency. The Davenports consented to enlarge their loans to the men who were regarded as responsible and had ample security. Otherwise the men would be expected to obtain loans elsewhere with which to pay off their obligations to the Davenports. Where loans were to be enlarged, the mortgagors were to give a second mortgage for the additional amount.[24]

The case of David C. Reynolds illustrates another aspect of the lending operations of the Davenports in Nebraska. When the legal interest rate was lowered from 12 per cent to 10 per cent a year, Reynolds found himself paying interest on a loan at 12 per cent which in May 1880 still had three and one-half years to run. Reynolds allowed his interest payments to lapse and suggested that he would either allow his loan to go to foreclosure or would settle before proceedings were invoked, as the Davenports might wish. Hopkins suggested that Reynolds was trying to force the Davenports to close out his loan in order that he might obtain funds elsewhere at 10 per cent. Hopkins, after reporting the situation, offered to accept payment of the loan if Reynolds would pay up his back interest, complete with interest on the delinquent interest and 3½ per cent for the unexpired term of the mortgage. Reynolds eventually accepted this proposition, although its terms obviously vitiated any profit which he had hoped to obtain from refinancing at a lower rate of interest.[25] The decline in interest rates in the west after the early 1870's presented a constant problem to lenders. As mortgagors saw their neighbors obtaining loans at interest rates below those which they were paying, they endeavored to refinance. The mortgagee, on the other hand, was anxious that they should not refinance, since the proceeds of the loan must be reloaned at the current rate.

Late in 1882 A. P. Hopkins merged his private banking business with that of Lucius D. Richards and M. L. Keene to form the Fremont National Bank, of which he became president.[26] Richards and Keene with-

[24] *Ibid.*, Jan. 12, 1881; Davenport memorandum on margin.

[25] *Ibid.*, May 29, 1880, Dec. 24, 1880.

[26] Fremont *Weekly Tribune*, Jan. 19, 1883.

drew from active banking, sitting merely on the board of directors of the new bank while they devoted their time to selling real estate and lending money for nonresidents. In organizing the new bank it was agreed that Hopkins' agency for the Davenports be transferred to Richards and Keene if the New Yorkers agreed.[27] Henceforth Richards supervised all of the lending done by the Davenports in the state of Nebraska.

Richards was born in Vermont in 1847. In 1862 he enlisted in the Union Army at the age of fifteen and re-enlisted in 1863 when his term of enlistment expired. In 1870 and 1871 he was working as a civil engineer for the Sioux City and Pacific Railroad Company, and for this corporation he built the first fifty miles of track. In 1872 he gave up engineering and homesteaded eighty acres of land in Pebble Township, Dodge County, to the north of Fremont. Commuting his homestead to a cash purchase in the mid 1870's, he moved to Fremont, where he entered the real estate business. With the departure of Crosby he was given the supervision of the real estate belonging to the Davenports north of the Platte. In 1880 Richards went into partnership with M. L. Keene, who had been county clerk for several terms and who held considerable real estate near Fremont. Real estate was the main interest of the partners, but in 1882 they took a brief fling at banking.[28]

In January 1883 Richards sought permission to loan funds in Antelope County, up the Elkhorn Valley from Fremont. Richards, Keene, and several of their associates had speculated heavily in the town plat of Neligh, the county seat, some years previously, and Richards claimed to know the county well.[29] When Richards suggested expanding the lending field, the Davenports exchanged their opinions of Richards' ability. John Davenport believed Richards to be capable, but was somewhat reluctant to expand operations because the loans made by Hopkins had been, in a sense, backed by a banking institution, while Richards and Keene had no such resources behind them. He suggested that since Hopkins was English he was more cautious than Richards; unquestionably, however, the latter knew the topography of Nebraska better than Hopkins did. The brothers decided to experiment with a few loans in

27 Richards and Keene to John and Ira Davenport, Dec. 11, 1882.

28 Fremont *Weekly Tribune*, May 6, 1880, Feb. 9, 1882; "Biographical Notes," *ibid.*, July 10, 1890, Aug. 7, 1890. Richards was the Republican candidate for governor in 1890.

29 *Ibid.*, May 6, 1880.

Antelope County.[30] The decision acted as an opening wedge and Richards eventually carried the lending activities of the Davenports well into northern and western Nebraska.

Mortgage companies were springing up rapidly throughout the west at the time, and in July 1883 Richards suggested to John and Ira Davenport that they take part in organizing such a company in Fremont. The promoters of a corporation being formed in Omaha had offered stock to Richards and Keene; they hoped to lend the funds of investors at rates which would return 8 per cent on the investment capital and a commission to the company. While refusing their offer, Richards believed that such an institution might well be organized in Fremont. Richards claimed that he had been able to procure a better rate of interest than any of the other lending agencies in the region because the Davenports were allowing him to accept applications immediately if he regarded them as unquestionably first class. Borrowers were willing to pay for the promptness with which he filled their applications. He believed that a sound incorporated company could keep this advantage and at the same time vastly expand operations. Other directors of the Fremont National Bank approved of the plan. Richards believed that a 20-percent levy on a capitalization of $250,000 would provide adequate capital with which to begin. He asked for the advice of the Davenports and inquired if they would take stock in the new company.[31]

In his reply to Richards, Ira Davenport approved of the suggested company with reservations. If Richards were to be the "*unquestioned manager*," the Davenports would lend through the company. Hitherto they had refused to deal with such companies, and Ira added that they would still prefer to have Richards act as their agent alone but realized that it might be necessary to form a company to stave off competition. They would not take stock in the company, but offered to recommend its services to other eastern businessmen if it was made up of men like Hopkins and if Richards was the active manager.[32] The Western Trust and Security Company was organized and began business in 1885 with L. D. Richards as president, J. L. Baker, vice-president, and J. W. Goff,

[30] Richards and Keene to John and Ira Davenport, Jan. 26, 1883; draft of John Davenport to Ira Davenport on reverse of letter; Ira Davenport to John Davenport, Feb. 3, 1883.

[31] L. D. Richards to John and Ira Davenport, July 31, 1888.

[32] Ira Davenport to L. D. Richards, Aug. 7, 1883.

secretary treasurer. The paid-up capital was $60,000. The loans negotiated for the Davenports formed the core of the company's business.

As in Illinois, Iowa, and Kansas, the volume of funds placed out annually varied in relation to other demands on the brothers for money. The 183 loans, totaling $111,050, which Richards negotiated in 1883 represented the largest amount of funds that was loaned in Nebraska during any one year. However, $68,740 was loaned in 1886 and $78,400 in 1890, while $15,000 loaned in 1888 was the smallest sum placed in the state after 1876 and before 1896. Thus there was no uniform flow of funds through Richards' hands. After 1891 the amount invested in Nebraska mortgages annually by the Davenports tapered off.

Lending operations under Richards and Keene and the Western Trust and Security Company followed the pattern evolved under Crosby and Hopkins. Farm loans were preferred on a reasonable valuation. For the most part, loans were drawn for periods up to five years. In 1883 at Richards' urging some experimenting was done with loans drawn for ten years, but these do not appear to have been numerous—few mortgagors who were aware of the decline in rates could have been interested in committing themselves for such a period of time.

Rates of interest and commissions during the years of Richards' control are worth some attention. Until 1890 a majority of the mortgage contracts bore a rate of 9 per cent in all but three years, 1885, 1888, and 1889. In those years 10-per-cent loans predominated. In 1890, 8 per cent became the dominant rate, and in 1893 loans at 7 per cent were in the majority. A 6-per-cent rate held until 1898, but the majority of the twenty-four loans negotiated in 1899 and 1900 were written at 5 per cent. Until 1893 these rates included the commission of Richards or of the Western Trust and Security Company. For the most part, this commission amounted to 1½ per cent of the loan per year. From the 10 per cent shown on a majority of the loans made during 1888 and 1889 a commission of 2 per cent of the loan per year was deducted. The increased commission probably did not mean additional returns to the Western Trust and Security Company. The 10-per-cent rate was obtained by entering the frontier counties of Cherry, Brown, Holt, and Rock, and the 2 per cent was undoubtedly split with local agents.

After 1894 the prevailing rate shown on the mortgage papers was the actual rate obtained by the Davenports. For a time in the early 1890's lending was suspended completely, and when it was begun again, Ira

Davenport desired that all of the commission on the new loans should not be deducted from the first interest payment, but instead, be taken out each year as interest payments were made. Davenport had always considered that Richards' practice had involved taking payment for services that might not be completed until at least five years later. He argued in addition, "It is not so much the amt that is taken out in advance as it is the change of position that has taken place of late years between the lender and the borrower. We pay the Coms now that he paid & it seems common sense that we should not pay all in advance."[33] Since Davenport did not suggest the change in procedure until loaning had been under way for some months, Richards did not accept the suggestion with pleasure, writing:

I do not particularly object to your decision that our commission shall be taken out annually on loans made during the past year except as a matter of bookkeeping & that it is retroactive. We have made loans for you all these years at a total rate & you have paid the Commission out of the first interest recd & when we resumed loaning nothing was said of a change in the plan & the business was continued as of old. You assume that the gradual lowering of the rate has changed the conditions. Should the fact of a lower rate necessarily change the plan under which we have been working & especially without notice? Would it not be better to let the method under which we have worked stand to date & change it as you suggest on further loans? or we might pursue the plan of the Ins Companies, make the papers net to you & get our pay from the borrower, when possible at the time the loan is made. We can not always do this & in such cases the annual commission would apply.[34]

This last arrangement was apparently satisfactory to Davenport, for a majority of the mortgage papers drawn in the succeeding years bore a rate net to Ira Davenport.

Under the company, Richards and his colleagues expanded their lending field rapidly. From Antelope County they moved north and west. By 1888 they were using local agents in Cherry, Holt, Brown, and Rock Counties. By 1890 it was apparent that the loans in these areas were not turning out satisfactorily. Western Nebraska had been in the grip of a "real estate boom" between 1885 and 1887. Relatively unim-

[33] Ira Davenport to the Western Trust and Security Co., Nov. 21, 1894; see also *ibid.*, Oct. 24, 1894.

[34] L. D. Richards to John and Ira Davenport, Nov. 26, 1894.

proved farms stood as security for the loans in this region. In the summer of 1887 drought returned to the plains states and settlers began to flow out of the sand hills area of northwestern Nebraska. In February 1890 Richards explained to the Davenports that some of the mortgagors of the company in Holt, Antelope, and Brown Counties were far in arrears after three years of poor crops and low prices. Where possible, the company was buying the deeds to the land from these borrowers. Richards assured the Davenports that the loans did not represent more than 40 per cent of the value of the land at the time they were made and that they had been inspected from the office at Fremont. He offered to sell such farms to the Davenports for between $600 and $1,000 and suggested that they would make a profitable investment. Were it not that the company had ample use for all of its funds he believed that the farms would have made a profitable investment for it.[35] From this date on, the correspondence from the Western Trust and Security Company contains numerous references to the foreclosures in northwestern Nebraska. In most cases the treasurer of the company hastened to point out that the borrowers were able and hard-working but that the cumulative force of hard times had finally forced them to the wall. It was necessary to take possession of the security backing loans made for the Davenports in the same area.[36]

In March 1891 Richards wrote apologetically to John Davenport:

> I am very sorry these loans have turned out this way but have no fear but they will pay out in a little time. The Oregon Short Line Ry is surveyed through the Southern part of Brown & Cherry Cos & is built to O'Neill but the close money markets stopped them. We paid com on these loans & if they do pay out we should be permitted to retain the amount from the proceeds when sold—We have made no loans in the section for nearly two years & are trying to get out of it as fast as we can. Taking deeds when title can be got at a less expense than cost of foreclosure. Will look after your lands so acquired & try & rent them.[37]

Twenty-seven of the 249 loans made between 1887 and 1891 were eventually closed out by foreclosure or deeding.

Well understanding the boom and bust psychology of western real estate men and town promoters, the Davenports became uneasy as the

[35] *Ibid.*, Feb. 2, 1890.
[36] J. W. Goff to John and Ira Davenport, Apr. 24, 1890, Nov. 11, 1891.
[37] L. D. Richards to John Davenport, Mar. 15, 1891.

western mortgage companies began to slide into receivership after 1888. In December 1891 Ira Davenport asked Richards to explain a clipping from the Fremont paper which referred to the financial collapse of a mortgage company in Fremont. Richards explained that the mortgage company was that of George Dorsey, Richards' greatest rival in Fremont, where the two contended not only for leadership in the business community but also for control of the Republican Party. Richards wrote piously, "If the truth was known, it was conceived in fraud and it has been kept up ever since." [38] The Western Trust and Security Company, however, was not completely sound either. Having ventured into the mortgage debenture business, it was hard put to meet its commitments during the 1890's. Finally, Richards and Keene took over the real estate which the company had foreclosed.[39] These events had no direct effect upon the Davenports, whose loans were not guaranteed by the company, but their confidence was shaken. Ira Davenport noted of an irregular loan which his brother had taken in June 1893 as a favor to Richards, "I wouldn't do more of this—first because I went away from Fremont with an impression that R & K wanted *holding in* some on loaning as you will see by the foreclosures lately made far north in the new counties." [40] For some time prior to 1893 Richards had been reloaning one half of the collections, but during a large part of that year lending was halted completely. Fear of obtaining unsatisfactory loans was not the only factor dictating such a measure; the western mortgage loan was not the remunerative investment it had once been. "The rates offer small coms for those who attend to it & interest for those who loan," wrote Ira in the same year.[41]

Between 1871 and 1900 the Davenports took over title to the security advanced by forty-eight of their borrowers in Nebraska. This was 3 per cent of the total number of loans made in the state, although another eight loans were contested in the courts. Of the fifty loans which Cobb and Sudduth negotiated in the Lincoln area during 1871 and 1872, almost 30 per cent ended in foreclosure or by the borrower deeding his security. Although Crosby's agency terminated unhappily, the loans which he negotiated for the Davenport brothers turned out reasonably

[38] L. D. Richards to John and Ira Davenport, Dec. 21, 1891.

[39] Interview with Fred Richards, Sr., Fremont, Neb., July 26, 1949.

[40] Richards and Keene to John and Ira Davenport, June 21, 1893, undated memorandum on letter, Ira to John Davenport.

[41] Richards and Keene to John and Ira Davenport, Feb. 17, 1893.

well. The security was taken on six out of ninety-seven loans. Hopkins had the best record of all the agents in Nebraska. Only four loans were foreclosed out of a total of 652. Although the loans of 1888 and 1889 damaged the average of Richards and the Western Trust and Security Company, the over-all result was good; twenty-four loans, or some 3 per cent of the 785 loans made under the direction of Richards, ended with the Davenports in possession of the security.

In four of the cases of foreclosure in Lancaster County the defendants alleged usury. In one of these cases the Davenports judged it the better part of valor to settle the case informally rather than to ask for a full judgment from the courts. The loan was one which had been made in Lincoln in the year 1873 through Major Sudduth. C. M. Parker of Lincoln, Nebraska, allowed his loan to become delinquent during 1878. When he did not pay the taxes on his property in 1879, B. F. Cobb, the agent of the Davenports in Lincoln, took a judgment on the property by default. Parker maintained that the claim of the Davenports was outlawed by the statute of limitations and in May of 1880 changed his plea to usury. Cobb then transferred the case to the Circuit Court of the United States, where he thought that there was a better chance of obtaining a fair trial. "Our Dist Judge," wrote Cobb, "is, we think, a little weak in the *back* outside of the certain 'clique' of attorneys whom he seems to favor especially." [42]

The case, according to Cobb, hinged on whether or not Sudduth had charged a commission for his services. Ira Davenport argued that even so, Parker had no grounds for pleading usury. "Sudduth," wrote Davenport, "was not my agent—Parker applied I presume to him, he made the loan and of course charged for his trouble.[43] Parker claimed that Sudduth had charged a commission of $120 on a loan of $1,000 drawn at 12 per cent per annum. Early in 1881 Ira Davenport estimated that he had $1,900 invested in the case. Parker's attorneys inquired if a compromise could be effected and Ira Davenport offered to accept a judgment of $1,500. The attorneys refused to consider anything above $1,000. B. F. Cobb outlined the alternatives:

> We have worked the matter up thoroughly and from what we have learned, I dont see how we can possibly hope to win the case,—as they will unquestionably be able to make Sudduth out an agent, at the time this loan was

[42] B. F. Cobb to John and Ira Davenport, May 19, 1880.

[43] Ira Davenport to B. F. Cobb, July 2, 1880.

made, and if they do succeed in that, usury is established and you only get a judgment for the difference between 1,000.00 & the amt of Int that has been paid—and the 120.00 Commission will also be taken from the 1000—So if we go trial and get beaten, instead of getting $1,000.00 you will get less then $700.00 In their offer of judgment for $1,000 they were to pay costs and attorneys fees.[44]

It was on these terms that the case went to final trial. Ira Davenport pled for a judgment of $1,000 and it was granted by the court. Execution of the judgment was stayed for nine months on the petition of the defendant.

The transfer of this case to the federal court illustrates a procedure which was attacked by the agrarian radicals. Richards informed the Davenports that he transferred all cases to the federal court if $500 or more were involved.[45] Federal judges were allowed to include an allowance for attorneys' fees in the judgment—a practice which was forbidden in the district courts of Nebraska.

By no means had all of the foreclosed property in Nebraska been sold at the date of Ira's death, but accounts had been closed on twenty-nine farms. On the average, the Davenports held them for eight and one-half years and had invested $778 in each by the time that they were sold. The average return per loan was 10 per cent, with a return on each dollar invested of 9 per cent—the best showing in any of the five states in which the Davenports loaned money.

[44] B. F. Cobb to John and Ira Davenport, Nov. 25, 1881.
[45] L. D. Richards to John and Ira Davenport, June 12, 1886.

PART 2

THE MIDDLEMAN

The J. B. Watkins Land Mortgage Company

FED by the rapid rush of settlement into the plains states and by the accumulation of capital in the hands of eager investors throughout northeastern America and in Britain, the western mortgage business reached a peak of activity in the 1870's and the 1880's when land mortgage companies were organized. To estimate the number of these companies exactly is an unrewarding if not impossible task. More than 150 of them came under the surveillance of the fiscal officials of Connecticut, Massachusetts, New York, and Vermont during the years between 1888 and 1895.[1] Most of the companies were organized in the states lying west of the Mississippi River, but some were incorporated in the central and northern states of the eastern seaboard and a few found their genesis abroad. When drought and low prices combined to spread acute depres-

[1] The *Annual Reports* of the Connecticut Bank Commissioners, 1888–1895, of the Massachusetts Commissioner of Foreign Mortgage Companies, 1890–1895, of the New York Superintendent of Banking relative to Foreign Mortgage, Loan, Investment and Trust Companies, 1891–1896, and of the Vermont Inspector of Finance, 1889–1893, provide the most satisfactory data on which to base an estimate.

sion over the plains states after 1887, the mortgage companies fared badly.

At the University of Kansas there are preserved today many of the business records of the J. B. Watkins Land Mortgage Company. Although not entirely complete, the collection allows the student to reconstruct the history of one land mortgage company.

V

SEEKING INVESTORS

JABEZ BUNTING WATKINS was born in Pennsylvania in 1845. After teaching school in Virginia, Pennsylvania, Illinois, and Wisconsin, he graduated from the Law Department of the University of Michigan in 1869. In the following year he began the practice of law at Champaign, Illinois.[1] His first letterpress book shows him making collections, taking pension cases, and acting as agent for at least one insurance company. At the same time he was working up another side line which was ultimately to make him a fortune. This was the farm mortgage business.

Early in 1871 Watkins was acting as the local agent in Champaign for Corydon Weed of Bloomington, Illinois, a veteran loanbroker who obtained funds from the eastern states for investment.[2] Already, how-

[1] William E. Connelley, *A Standard History of Kansas and Kansans* (Chicago, 1918), V, 2407; Standard Publishing Company, *Kansas* (Chicago, 1912), III, 1200–1202; *National Cyclopedia of American Biography* (New York, 1926), XIX, 105; Lawrence *Daily Journal World,* Feb. 5, 1921.

[2] J. B. Watkins to Corydon Weed, May 7, 1871; Henry Dickinson, New York, N.Y., to C. M. Gaylord, Savona, N.Y., Nov. 28, 1877. Unless otherwise noted all correspondence cited is in the J. B. Watkins Papers, held in the Library of the University of Kansas, Lawrence, Kans.

ever, Watkins was endeavoring to place himself directly in contact with investors in order to obtain more investment capital and the larger share of the commissions which brokers like Weed obtained. In January 1871 he traveled east and interviewed the officials of the National Capital Life Insurance Company of Washington, D.C. He was told that he might lend the funds of the company on mortgages bearing 10-per-cent interest if he insured every person to whom such a loan was made. Watkins refused to agree to this proviso. Instead he offered to allow the company 2½ per cent in advance on all the loans which he made while at the same time making every possible effort to sell insurance.[3] The offer was evidently rejected.

Letters written in March and April 1871 illustrate the kind of business which Watkins was endeavoring to build up. To George W. Elder of Lewiston, Pennsylvania, he promised 2½-per-cent commission paid in advance on all the money which the Pennsylvanian could obtain for him.[4] To F. F. Wendell, a New Yorker, he sketched his method of loaning in some detail:

> You ascertain that A has $1000 to loan for five years, communicate that fact to me. B comes into my office, wants to borrow $1000 for five years. Says he has one hundred acres of land worth thirty dollars per acre. I fill out a blank application with his statement under oath, as to the *value* and *condition* of said farm. Also get the certified statement of three freeholders who are acquainted with the land to the same facts. B must furnish an Abstract of title, showing that his land is free of *all* incumbrances, then he executes a note for $1000 payable in five years at your office or where the lender desires. Also ten interest notes of $50.00 each payable at regular intervals of six months each, at the same place. Also a Trust Deed of said farm as security for the payment of these several notes which Deed contains a power of sale in twenty days, which is duly recorded in this county where the land is situated. These papers thus executed I send to you. You will present them to A and get the draft for $1000, less your $25 comm, payable to B which you will send to me. One of the great arguments in your favor in getting money on the above terms and conditions is that the several installments are compelled to be paid *promptly,* otherwise the property will be sold in *twenty* days. Something I presume unknown in your country. And then the lenders business is all done at home—he don't realize the fact that his money is away from home. And he has no trouble with it at all, but gets his interest

[3] J. B. Watkins to John B. Patterson, Washington, D.C., Feb. 24, 1871.
[4] J. B. Watkins to G. W. Elder, Lewistown, Pa., Mar. 7, 1871.

regularly every six months. I think if you present this system in the true light you cant fail to get some money at once. If you can do so enlist others in the cause.[5]

Plan and practice, however, did not always coincide. Two weeks later Watkins agreed, under some protest, to negotiate loans for the Covenant Mutual Life Insurance Company of Chicago for a commission of one-half per cent of the principal.[6]

By 1873 Watkins had made considerable effort to expand his mortgage business. In 1872 he reversed the usual procedure of loan agents and went west to Wisconsin to raise funds.[7] In Illinois he was building up a network of local agents whom he contracted to pay $10.00 per loan out of a commission paid by the borrowers which varied from 7 to 10 per cent of the loan.[8] At the same time Watkins made arrangements with Wilson and Toms, mortgage brokers of Bloomington, to act as their local agent at Champaign. He was by this time advertising in the local newspapers and by handbill.[9] In May 1872 he sent an advertisement to the *Independent*.[10] Although he accumulated property worth several thousand dollars, it is difficult to estimate the degree of success which Watkins achieved in his efforts to establish himself as a mortgage broker at Champaign in the years before 1873.[11] Without doubt the greatest asset acquired in these early years was a thorough understanding of the loaning business rather than a large working capital or an extensive clientele.

In August 1873 Watkins transferred his business to Kansas in order to obtain "a wider field of operations, more choice of securities & better rates." [12] He located at Lawrence, a city with a population of between 6,000 and 7,000 people.[13] Although, in his correspondence, Watkins never explained his reasons for choosing the little city above the junction of the Kaw and the Wakarusa, it is possible to suggest a few of them. The banking resources of Kansas City were convenient, as was

[5] J. B. Watkins to F. F. Wendell, Fort Plain [*sic*], N.Y., Apr. 12, 1871.

[6] J. B. Watkins to C. B. Holmes, Chicago, Ill., Apr. 24, 1871.

[7] J. B. Watkins to W. E. Brewer, Raymond Center, Wis., Mar. 25, 1872.

[8] J. B. Watkins to Robert M. Jameson, Paxton, Ill., Mar. 23, 1872, to S. B. Whitham, Hillsboro, Ill., Apr. 18, 1872.

[9] J. B. Watkins to Wilson and Toms, Bloomington, Ill., Apr. 6, 1872.

[10] J. B. Watkins to *Independent*, New York, N.Y., May 17, 1872.

[11] J. B. Watkins to Wilson and Toms, Bloomington, Ill., Apr. 6, 1872.

[12] J. B. Watkins to Charles Demand, Boston, Mass., July 29, 1874.

[13] Kansas, census roll, 1875, held at the Kansas State Historical Society in Topeka, gives the population of Lawrence as slightly over 7,000.

the seat of the federal court at Topeka, but a loan agency at Lawrence would be spared the competition for business and possibly for labor that would be encountered in the more populous centers. In 1870 a north-south line marking the center of population on the map of Kansas would have fallen along the eastern boundary of Douglas County, in which Lawrence was the county seat.[14] Finally, railroad connections were available both to the south and to the west. At Lawrence, then, Watkins set up office, with his brother-in-law for clerk, on the second floor of a store building which faced Massachusetts or "main" street.[15]

Watkins began his labors in Kansas at a favorable time. The depression of 1873 and its aftermath brought disillusion to many eastern investors. Holders of railroad securities suffered severe losses,[16] while the insurance companies underwent a weeding out process which eliminated many of the weaker organizations and aroused distrust among investors.[17] In some eastern states the savings banks which had been rising rapidly in public favor found themselves in financial difficulties.[18] At the same time, the last forty years of the nineteenth century was a period when capital was being accumulated rapidly in the northeastern states. Not only were large fortunes amassed but clerical and professional workers were often able to lay by modest competences. Finally the long-term interest rate was declining, stimulating those who possessed capital or savings to look for new avenues of investment. Conditions were favorable in the mid 1870's, therefore, for the western mortgage broker with his promise of high interest and a security as substantial as the soil itself.[19]

Once established at Lawrence, Watkins set about enlarging his clientele of investors. For the next ten years under the style of J. B. Watkins and Company he endeavored to publicize the western farm mortgage as a form of investment. Almost from the beginning of his efforts Watkins placed most of his newspaper advertising in the religious press.

[14] J. B. Watkins to D. W. Clapp, Iowa City, Ia., Feb. 8, 1879.

[15] Lawrence *Daily Journal World*, Feb. 5, 1921; J. B. Watkins Land Mortgage Company, *Perkins* vs. *Watkins in Magistrates Court; The President of the Western Farm Mortgage Co. F. M. PERKINS* vs. *J. B. WATKINS, Libel Suit for $10,000 Damages* (Lawrence, Kans., 1887).

[16] Henry Dickinson, New York, N.Y., to Charles Thompson, Manchester, Eng., Nov. 28, 1877, to J. B. Watkins and Co., Feb. 9, 1878.

[17] Henry Dickinson to A. N. Bentley, Greenville, N.Y., Dec. 27, 1877.

[18] Henry Dickinson to J. B. Watkins and Co., Jan. 18, 1878.

[19] J. B. Watkins to Rev. S. T. Thompson, Muncey, Pa., July 17, 1874.

These religious newspapers were read in the substantial homes of the east—whose occupants, if not rich, were at least saving—and they proved a more successful medium for Watkins' evangelical work than did the secular press. It is impossible to compile a complete record of the papers which he utilized, but the list in the notes to this chapter seems to be a representative one.[20]

In addition to spreading abroad the virtues of the farm loan business Watkins attempted to scotch any slurs which appeared. Thus he took violent exception to an item in the New York *Times* [21] describing the disastrous bankruptcy of Corydon Weed, his one-time superior in Illinois. He pointed out to the editor of that paper that the business laxity of one man should not be used to condemn the farm loan as an investment and the mortgage broker as a type.[22] In a circular prepared about this time he advanced the same argument and cited his own exemplary if rather brief record.[23]

Eastern investors suspected of having large amounts of money for investment were invited to visit Lawrence at Watkins' expense.[24] Here they found the young man to be a thoughtful host, eager to explain the details of the mortgage business to them. On long drives through the Kansas countryside they inspected the farms of Kansans who desired

[20] *The Watchman,* Boston, Mass.
The Evangelist, New York, N.Y.
Illustrated Christian Weekly, New York, N.Y.
Springfield *Republican,* Mass.
Christian Secretary, Hartford, Conn.
The Public, New York, N.Y.
The Presbyterian, Pittsburgh, Pa.
The Standard, Chicago, Ill.
Christian Advocate, Pittsburgh, Pa.
The Christian Intelligencer, New York, N.Y.
The Christian Union, New York, N.Y.
The Independent, New York, N.Y.
The Christian at Work, New York, N.Y.
The Churchman, New York, N.Y.
The Methodist, New York, N.Y.
The Examiner and Chronicle, New York, N.Y.
The Weekly Witness, New York, N.Y.
The Church Union, New York, N.Y.
The Baptist Weekly, New York, N.Y.
The Christian Advocate and Sunday School Journal, New York, N.Y.
New York *Weekly Tribune,* New York, N.Y.
The New York Financier, New York, N.Y.
Zion's Herald, Boston, Mass.
Philadelphia Sunday School Times, Philadelphia, Pa.

[21] "Collapse of Western Mortgages," editorial, New York *Times,* Nov. 11, 1877.

[22] J. B. Watkins to Editor, New York *Times,* Dec. 19, 1877.

[23] Henry Dickinson to J. B. Watkins and Co., Dec. 24, 1877.

[24] J. B. Watkins to Nathaniel Gordon, Exeter, N.H., June 2, 1877; Henry Dickinson to Charles Thompson, Manchester, Eng., Nov. 28, 1877.

to tap the coffers of the east. If inspection palled, Watkins' shot gun and the omnipresent prairie chicken provided a pleasant change. When such investors expressed pleasure at what they saw, their testimony was incorporated into advertising circulars for use in the east and abroad.[25]

The task of persuading eastern investors to buy mortgage securities was really a twofold one. Not only had Watkins to prove that the farm mortgage was a superior type of investment but also that "Bloody Kansas" and the "Great American Desert" were myths—that Kansas was actually a rich and productive state, peopled by healthy, honest, and peaceful husbandmen.

The inquiring investor learned that as a mortgagee he would hold a mortgage duly executed according to law and recorded in the appropriate county records, a principal note or bond with semiannual interest notes attached, an abstract showing the chain of title on the mortgaged property from the United States down to and including his mortgage, the original application of the mortgagor describing the property, an examiner's report written by Watkins or by one of his employees, and a map of the premises.[26]

Watkins pointed out by letter and by circular that the investment which these papers represented returned a rate of interest difficult to duplicate in the east. When he first moved to Kansas, he loaned at 12 per cent and sometimes proffered the eastern investor a portion of his commission in addition.[27] At times also he guaranteed the prompt payment of interest by the borrower. If it became necessary to hold the investor's money for a time before allocation to a borrower, Watkins promised to pay interest on it during the delay.[28]

The young broker emphasized that high rates did not mean a high risk. The loans were small, falling generally between $300 and $1,000 in size, while the majority of them did not exceed $500. Loans did not exceed a third of the value of the property. In addition, since the areas were but recently settled, the rapid rise in land values further acted to keep the loan down to a small proportion of the property's value. Loans were made only to resident farmers for productive purposes; speculators must seek elsewhere for financing. Watkins regarded the

[25] J. B. Watkins and Co. to J. Y. Heald, Wilmington, Del., Dec. 14, 1877.
[26] J. B. Watkins to Rev. S. T. Thompson, Muncey, Pa., Apr. 18, 1874.
[27] Henry Dickinson to Prof. Debolson Wood, Hoboken, N.J., Oct. 26, 1882.
[28] J. B. Watkins to J. B. Clark, Albion, N.Y., June 30, 1877.

value of western village or city property as too uncertain for security in this age of town booming and paper cities. No loans were made in townships where enthusiastic taxpayers had bonded themselves so heavily that property values were affected. As a climax Watkins could argue that the position of his headquarters in the midst of the lending field allowed him to make these rules more than pious wishes. He was in a position to pick out the very best of securities.[29]

Watkins promised that he would keep mortgagors under supervision and watch to see that they paid their taxes and did not damage the security. Although customarily interest was collected by the Lawrence office and remitted to the mortgagee, lenders possessed all of the documents necessary if they decided to assume complete control of their loans. If a borrower allowed his payments of interest to lapse, the lender still had little to fear, claimed Watkins. The indenture which he held was a first mortgage and contained a clause empowering him to institute foreclosure proceedings within thirty days. Other clauses in the mortgage provided that past due interest and principal should bear 12-per-cent interest, that the attorney fees should be paid by the mortgagor, and that damages to the amount of 6 per cent of the loan should be assessed as a penalty for breaking the contract.[30] Finally, although he did not make the assurance an absolute guarantee, Watkins informed investors that they would not have to assume the ownership of any real estate. When necessary he himself would assume payment of loans and take over the title to the land of delinquent mortgagors.[31] As his business expanded Watkins found it necessary to drop some of these allurements and to modify others, but they are a fair sample of the arguments with which he bombarded investors in the mid 1870's.

In the minds of many eastern investors the State of Kansas was inseparably connected with drought, famine, and grasshoppers. In 1875, the year following a major visitation of locusts, Watkins was able to quote a satisfied customer who said that interest coupons on loans ar-

[29] J. B. Watkins and Co. to G. M. Parks, Washington, Kans., Aug. 12, 1876, to Q. A. Annen, Las Vegas, N.M., June 9, 1877, to B. S. Stone, Mexico, N.Y., June 12, 1877, to Henry G. Bronson, Hartford, Conn., Aug. 14, 1877; J. B. Watkins to H. C. Dodge, Amherst, N.H., June 23, 1877, to R. L. Cochran, Franklin, Pa., Mar. 12, 1879.

[30] J. B. Watkins to Sidney W. Jackson, Jericho, Queens Co., Long Island, Jan. 6, 1874.

[31] J. B. Watkins to H. L. Ward, Norwich, N.Y., June 12, 1877.

ranged by Watkins "are paid promptly at maturity, grasshoppers or no grasshoppers." [32] To an investor inquiring about drought he wrote:

We establish a limit west of which it would not be safe to loan on account of want of moisture & rainfall by observation and statistics. . . . The eastern line of the rainless belt has been moving westward ever since the settlement of this state began. We remember when the whole region of this state was 'The Great American Desert'. . . . Just in the same proportion as the country has been opened up to cultivation the rainless limit has receded. We are not yet prepared to believe that it will during this generation recede beyond the western limits of the state. But we believe that the entire state will some time be settled. We are satisfied that the rainless belt has retreated before the march of civilization and that wherever civilization has pressed hardest there the limit is farthest west.[33]

Aiding Watkins and other loanbrokers interested in creating a favorable opinion of Kansas throughout the east were the advertising activities of the land-grant railroads and of the state itself. Interested as they were in selling their lands and building up population in the plains states, the railroads flooded the eastern states and Europe with literature which painted a glowing picture of agricultural opportunities beyond the Missouri.[34] During the 1870's the Kansas government entered the field. A commissioner of immigration was appointed and the state board of agriculture began to publish yearly reports. Handsomely bound and printed, these reports contained schedules showing the agricultural production of the organized counties in addition to county maps and other information of general interest. Here was statistical ammunition which the loan agent could use to good advantage in proving the productivity of Kansas farms.[35]

To businessmen who would act as his agents in obtaining eastern funds Watkins paid a small commission. In 1874 he was offering them 4 per cent of the value of the loan on mortgages returning 10 per cent to the investor.[36] In some cases these men were also investors and received the commission on the personal funds which they invested. By 1877 agencies at Buffalo, Albion, Batavia, Rochester, Syracuse, Rome,

[32] J. B. Watkins to Lyman Kimball, North Ferrisburg, Vt., Aug. 13, 1875.

[33] J. B. Watkins to Edward Lewis, Philadelphia, Pa., Jan. 3, 1878.

[34] See Glenn D. Bradley, *The Story of the Santa Fe* (Boston, 1920), ch. 5, for an account of the colonizing activities of one railroad in Kansas.

[35] Henry Dickinson to J. B. Watkins and Co., Dec. 24, 1877.

[36] J. B. Watkins to W. E. C. Lyons, Nashville, Ill., July 15, 1874.

and Johnstown in New York, at Wilmington, Delaware, Boston, Massachusetts, Warner, New Hampshire, and at Ferrisburg, Vermont, were handling western farm mortgages negotiated by J. B. Watkins and Company of Lawrence.[37] By this time Watkins had been able to reduce the commission paid to such agencies to 1½ per cent.[38]

In 1876 Watkins decided to go one step further in his efforts to establish eastern contacts and to open a branch office in New York. To manage this branch he hired a retired importer, Henry Dickinson. For thirty years Dickinson had served as the American resident partner of a British hardware firm. Not only had he numerous business contacts, but his appointment solidified Watkins' connection with the Society of Friends, which was to prove of great value. Although not a member of the Society himself, Watkins as a Pennsylvanian had great sympathy with their religious tenets. Silas Deane of Ferrisburg, Vermont, who handled Watkins' securities as early as 1874, was a member of the Society, and Miles J. Dart, whom Watkins hired as his first real estate inspector, had been raised in the faith in Vermont. Henry Dickinson was also a Friend and had not only an extensive acquaintanceship with members of the faith in the eastern United States, but as an expatriate Englishman he also had acquaintances among the British Quakers. Substantial, saving members of the middle class for the most part, the Friends in the northeastern states, in increasing numbers, henceforth channeled their savings into farm mortgage securities. Dickinson made a point of attending the yearly meetings, where he could mollify dissatisfied investors and speak a good word for his western investments to those who as yet had not sampled them.

Under the agreement which he had made with Watkins, Henry Dickinson was to receive, in addition to a salary of $2,000 annually, a commission on all investment funds which he procured from his friends in England.[39] Early in 1877 he placed advertisements in a group of British papers which included the London *Friend*, the Glasgow *British Friend*, and the Sheffield *Independent*.[40] By the fall of that year he had investors in London, Glasgow, and Ireland.[41] The immediate result of

[37] J. B. Watkins and Co. to Henry C. Bronson, Hartford, Conn., Aug. 14, 1877.

[38] *Ibid.;* also J. B. Watkins and Co. to Donald McIntyre, Johnstown, N.Y., June 25, 1877.

[39] Henry Dickinson to J. B. Watkins and Co., Dec. 26, 1877.

[40] *Ibid.*, Dec. 19, 1877, Dec. 24, 1877.

[41] Henry Dickinson to Charles Thompson, Manchester, Eng., Nov. 28, 1877.

his advertising, however, was not striking. He placed more reliance in building up an organization of agencies. A Friend and justice of the peace in Manchester expressed interest, and a firm of financial agents in London replied to his inquiries with a proposal to form a joint stock company to deal in American mortgages, but the work of finding agents went slowly.[42] The novelty of the securities, bearing a rate of interest almost double the current British rate, and the previous unhappy experience of British investors in America, along with the agitation of the silver question at the time, caused Dickinson's overtures to receive a cautious reception.[43]

With an eye on the British field Dickinson and Watkins set to work to improve their lures. Since Dickinson reported that "anything tending to repudiation more or less has a strong effect upon the sensitive nerves of Englishmen," [44] Watkins decided to specify in his mortgage form that debts would be collected in gold coin.[45] Dickinson also suggested "that the antiquated line of thought prevalent in old countries should have as much consideration as is proper" and advised the use of red wafer seals on the bonds, rather than a printed seal, and a very complete mortgage form, including as many safeguards for the investor as possible.[46] Finally it was decided that Watkins himself should go to England in order to organize the business in the British Isles.

In the spring of 1878 Watkins landed in England bearing a letter of reference from George Opdyke and Company, his bankers in New York. In addition Dickinson had written ahead to his friends in order to pave the way. In one letter he described Watkins' financial standing as strong and Watkins himself as "industrious in his personal habits, not self indulgent but very economical and of good judgement." [47] Apparently Watkins' personal qualities were of sufficient caliber and his securities tempting enough to impress the British. When he left England after a stay of some months he had made considerable progress toward working up a profitable business. In London he had organized a branch office presided over by H. G. Chalkley, a Quaker financial agent of Bishopsgate Street.

[42] Henry Dickinson to J. B. Watkins and Co., Jan. 18, 1878.

[43] Henry Dickinson to J. B. Watkins, Feb. 21, 1878. [44] *Ibid.*, Feb. 16, 1878.

[45] *Ibid.*, Feb. 16, 1878; Henry Dickinson to Charles Thompson, Manchester, Eng., Feb. 26, 1878.

[46] Henry Dickinson to J. B. Watkins and Co., Dec. 24, 1877.

[47] Henry Dickinson to Charles Thompson, Manchester, Eng., May 6, 1878.

By setting up a London office, Watkins was able to solve a problem which had arisen over the payment of interest. The English bankers, Barclay and Company, had objected to honoring the interest coupons of Watkins' securities because they would have to deduct income tax from each coupon. The added labor which this involved, would, the bankers argued, nullify any profit which they might derive from the Kansan's account. In addition British security holders who were not liable for the payment of income tax would be put to the trouble of demanding a rebate from the government. But with the local office in operation investors had merely to send their interest coupons to Chalkley, who would honor them with drafts drawn upon a local account at Barclays.[48] In addition, the establishment of a London office meant that Watkins now had someone in England who could energetically promote the business and mollify unhappy investors at all times.

While his superior was in England, Dickinson was preparing a circular for use in Great Britain, directed to "my friends in Great Britain and Ireland and Investors generally" and advertising "First Mortgage Bonds, Eight per cent interest in gold, guaranteed payable at the National Bank of Commerce, New York, U.S. and Barclays." A paragraph of this circular demonstrates Dickinson's ingratiating approach:

> During nearly thirty years residence in the United States . . . I have observed large losses made by my countrymen through injudicious investments whilst at the same time the wealth of the United States has been largely and steadily on the increase but not so much by special enterprises which have been very fluctuating, as from the cultivation of the soil. The old maxim "there is nothing so safe as land" is still true, though the returns may be less fascinating, they are much more reliable.[49]

When the circulars were completed Watkins advised Chalkley that he could not use them too freely.[50]

While he was in England, Watkins arranged to pay six minor agents one per cent on all investment funds which they could supply. Chalkley, he hoped, would add to the number of these subagents rapidly.[51]

The attempt to operate abroad brought Watkins face to face with the problem of exchange. After much inquiry he settled on the plan

[48] J. B. Watkins to Charles Thompson, Manchester, Eng., Dec. 21, 1878.
[49] Letter Press Book No. 2 (New York ser.), pp. 393–396.
[50] J. B. Watkins to H. G. Chalkley, Dec. 21, 1878.
[51] *Ibid.*, Nov. 23, Dec. 21, 1878.

which he described in answer to an English inquiry during 1879. The lender was to furnish the amount of sterling that would make a specified number of dollars in New York. This would be loaned for five years paying 8-per-cent interest in gold in New York. J. B. Watkins and Company agreed during the five years of the loan to redeem interest coupons in London at four shillings to the dollar. No rate was fixed for the return of the principal at the end of the term of the loan; at that time the dollars would be waiting for the British investor in New York to be reinvested or called home as he saw fit. If the investor chose to recall the money it would be sent at the rate of exchange then current.[52]

The eastern and foreign citadels were not stormed without some difficulties. Especially irksome was the problem of the guarantee. During the first three years in which he was at Lawrence, Watkins guaranteed neither the interest payments nor the principal of the mortgages which he sold. Actually, however, he saw to it that all interest was paid promptly and stood ready to take the land if necessary and to assume payment of the loan. Watkins decided to capitalize on custom and advertise the fact that he guaranteed both the prompt payment of interest and the principal at maturity. Investors immediately began to question the financial strength behind the guarantee, and Watkins in disgust retrenched to a mere guarantee of the interest. By 1879 he had decided to discard the guarantee entirely.[53] Once he was committed to it, however, the importunities of the investing public forced him to retain the guarantee in his business practice.[54] In itself, guaranteeing the interest was only a minor concession, but it pointed the way to a guarantee of the principal. Given a period of stiff competition this might well be the next concession. When this became the case—as eventually it did—the risk of the business was largely concentrated in the hands of the loanbroker.

Both in England and in America, Watkins found it necessary to fight the pervading fear among investors that the currency of the United States might be depreciated in concessions to the silver and fiat money forces. To soothe such forebodings, Watkins for a time wrote some of

[52] J. B. Watkins to William Nield, Reading, Eng., Jan. 23, 1879.

[53] J. B. Watkins to Reverend C. H. Richmond, Saranac, N.Y., Sept. 19, 1879, to Henry Dickinson, Nov. 23, 1878.

[54] J. B. Watkins and Co. to Henry Dickinson, July 7, 1880; M. J. Dart to J. B. Watkins, July 26, 1880; Henry Dickinson to J. B. Watkins, May 28, 1880.

his mortgage contracts in terms of "gold coin" rather than "lawful money" when investors desired it.[55] In a sense this proved to be robbing Peter to pay Paul. Watkins confessed that "due to the agitation by politicians" he was having much trouble in getting such papers signed. In several cases he had redrawn papers three and four times only to have the mortgagors refuse to execute contracts containing the gold clause.[56]

In other cases Watkins found investors deeply impressed by the frailty of human flesh. If Watkins were to die, they asked, who would see to it that borrowers paid their taxes and interest promptly or took the land if such became necessary? No doubt the business title of J. B. Watkins and Company was adopted to give the impression of permanence and to forestall such questioning. In the early 1880's, however, Watkins perfected his answer to the queries by organizing a trusteeship pledged to wind up the business after his death. He named as his trustees, Miles J. Dart, his lieutenant since 1874; D. M. Sprankle, Watkins' cousin who was also employed at the Lawrence office; and Alexander Thomson, a brother-in-law of Watkins and professor at Iowa State College.[57]

It was customary among some western businessmen who carried on a part-time brokerage business to send the applications of borrowers to the east.[58] The investor then could make his own choice. Watkins found it necessary to convince his clients during the late 1870's that this practice was no longer necessary. In a period when competition for mortgage securities had been less keen, when the broker served only a few investors, and when he had taken none of the risks of the business, such practice was quite feasible. But by this time Watkins' business was sufficiently large that he found it impossible to send each potential investor a separate list. Orders for the same mortgage followed each other to Lawrence, and investors were dissatisfied when told that it had been necessary to substitute other securities for the ones which they had selected. Henceforth Watkins generally pointed out that he stood the risk on the mortgage securities which he sold.

[55] J. B. Watkins and Co. to Hopkins and Taber, Holton, Kans., Mar. 13, 1879, to William H. Dodge, Great Bend, Kans., Mar. 24, 1879.

[56] J. B. Watkins to Edward Lewis, Philadelphia, Pa., Dec. 28, 1878.

[57] J. B. Watkins to Heald and Company, Wilmington, Del., Oct. 24, 1881.

[58] Davenport Collection, Collection of Regional History, Cornell University, Ithaca, N.Y., *passim;* Hawkes Papers, Kansas State Historical Society, Topeka, Kans.

Surely his judgment could be trusted, therefore. Competition among agencies, he argued, was too keen to permit the added delay which came from sending applications east.[59]

The experience with George Opdyke and Company was disconcerting. When he first established his business in New York, Watkins had opened an account with this firm of bankers. Investors could obtain their installments of interest merely by presenting interest coupons from their mortgage bonds to Opdyke and Company. While Watkins was abroad in the late 1870's, he learned through Dickinson that Opdyke and Company were attempting to sell western mortgages to his customers. The bank had become the eastern agent of another western loanbroker and was trying to fatten off the Lawrence clientele. The New York account of J. B. Watkins and Company was promptly removed to the National Bank of Commerce.[60]

To work in the east, Watkins found, a company required a favorable rating from the commercial agencies. In 1878 he was unhappy to find himself rated by Bradstreet and Company as worth only some $10,000.[61] Some of his more alert investors immediately inquired how a man of so little capital could guarantee the payment of interest on his securities.[62] Watkins demanded an examination by the Bradstreet agency and assured his investors that his rating should have been some six times that published. Although he blamed rivals in Lawrence for submitting the unfavorable report, he was never able to prove the charge.[63] Within a few years the reports of his financial strength in the commercial guides were sufficient to satisfy most investors.

[59] J. B. Watkins and Co. to A. W. Gilbert, Ross, O., July 9, 1879.
[60] Henry Dickinson to J. B. Watkins and Co., Apr. 18, 1878.
[61] Henry Dickinson to J. B. Watkins, Feb. 16, 1878.
[62] J. B. Watkins to Edward Lewis, Philadelphia, Pa., Feb. 19, 1878.
[63] J. B. Watkins to Henry Dickinson, Dec. 30, 1880.

VI

SEEKING BORROWERS

IN THE west Watkins set about the task of finding borrowers with an energy equal to that which he displayed in contacting eastern investors. By the summer of 1875 he claimed to be advertising funds to loan in one hundred newspapers in Kansas.[1] A year later he had begun the practice of sending advertising circulars to all farmers in eastern Kansas whom the assessment rolls showed to have property which would provide adequate security for a loan.[2]

In the first few years at Lawrence the method of making loans underwent a process of development. Farmers who wrote letters of inquiry received application blanks and the terms on which Watkins loaned money. If they remained eager to make the loan, Watkins or his inspector visited them, made sure that the farms were ample security for the money requested, and closed the loans.[3] Sometimes one of the newspapers at a county seat carried an advertisement informing the

[1] J. B. Watkins and Co. to M. D. Wright (address not given), Aug. 28, 1875.

[2] J. B. Watkins and Co. to D. M. Sprankle, Wichita, Kans., Mar. 16, 1876.

[3] J. B. Watkins and Co. to Samuel H. Early, Clay Centre, Kans., Aug. 4, Aug. 6, 1874.

farmers of the county that a representative of J. B. Watkins and Company would be present on a given date to take applications and to inspect loan securities.[4] Much more usual, however, was the practice of making arrangements with the register of deeds or with some lawyer, banker, or real estate agent located at a county seat.[5] At first these men merely collected applications which were submitted to Lawrence. When a sufficient number of applications had been accumulated at Watkins' office to justify the expense of a trip to that particular county, he or his inspector made the journey and inspected the security offered by the applicants.

As soon as Watkins believed that the resident understood his method of loaning and the type of security desired, he transferred the business of inspection to him as well. The agent was still subject to periodic visits from members of the Lawrence office, but they made no attempt to inspect every farm on which he proposed a loan. Before the law he was still the agent of the borrower,[6] although his fee was usually a percentage of the commission paid by the borrower to J. B. Watkins and Company.[7]

For several years after 1875 agents who were considered especially worthy of trust were given several counties in which they made all of the inspections. In the county seats local men gathered applications and received a flat fee for their services, while the inspecting agent received a percentage of the commission.[8] But this system was soon abandoned, and the local representatives made their own inspections subject to periodic examinations by an inspector from the office at Lawrence. To avoid friction between agents it was usual to appoint only one in a county.[9] Agents received the benefits of Watkins' advertising and generally placed ads of their own in the local papers. At times Watkins offered to bear part of the local agents' advertising expenses.[10]

4 J. B. Watkins and Co. to Ellsworth *Reporter*, June 7, 1876.

5 J. B. Watkins and Co. to M. Reasoner, Concordia, Kans., July 17, 1876.

6 J. B. Watkins and Co. to Henry P. Churchill, Cawker City, Kans., Mar. 15, 1882.

7 J. B. Watkins and Co. to M. Noyes, Parsons, Kans., July 16, 1875, to D. M. Sprankle, Wichita, Kans., Apr. 6, 1876.

8 J. B. Watkins and Co. to D. M. Sprankle, Wichita, Kans., June 9, 1876.

9 J. B. Watkins and Co. to Adams and Altdoerffer, Larned, Kans., Nov. 21, 1879, to D. M. Sprankle, May 22, 1882.

10 M. J. Dart to E. S. Bertram, Council Grove, Kans., May 29, 1876.

By the late 1870's local agents were usually appointed in the following manner. When it was decided to push into a new county, an inspector from the Lawrence office visited the county seat to choose one of the more reputable members of the business community as agent. In many cases overtures had already been received from several would-be agents of the town, and the inspector was given all the information which the Lawrence office had been able to gather on their abilities and habits before he arrived. The newly chosen agent received a full explanation of the business from the inspector; then he immediately entered upon the full duties of an agent, taking applications, inspecting securities, and closing the loans. The trial period in which a local representative was allowed only to gather applications was discarded. However, under the new plan, the new agent was not allowed to operate long without a return visit from the inspector, and his applications received extremely careful examination at the Lawrence office.

From the Lawrence office the local agent received blank applications, statements, and abstracts.[11] When a farmer applied for a loan, the agent filled out an application on the basis of his statements. Such an application listed the size of the loan desired, the applicant's marital status, his indebtedness, the acreage of his farm, the acreage in crops, the improvements on the farm, the amount of stock owned, and the owner's valuation of his farm. The farmer made his affidavit pledging that the statements in his application were true. Three other parties who were acquainted with the land also made affidavits on the application as to the value of the land.

Next the agent made a personal inspection of the property and filled out the statement. This document contained much of the material included in the application but was intended for the private use of the Lawrence office. As such, it included the agent's candid evaluation of both the applicant and his property. Sometimes it contained material thought better kept off the application, which might eventually come into the hands of an eastern investor. If a farmer had lost his crop by drought the previous year, no reference was made to the fact on the application, but it was faithfully recorded on the statement.[12] The office staff at Lawrence therefore could weigh the possibility of further

[11] The over-all description of lending in the late 1870's is based on J. B. Watkins and Co. to W. A. Madans, Lyndon, Kans., July 21, 1877.

[12] J. B. Watkins and Co. to John Dawson, Alma, Neb., Mar. 18, 1881.

drought before making a decision on the loan. A map of the property completed the statement.

Once the statement was prepared, the agent, the register of deeds, or an abstracter made up a memorandum abstract showing all conveyances of the land and any judgment or taxes which stood against it. These latter entries were made in pencil.[13] The completed application, statement, and memorandum abstract were forwarded to Lawrence. If approved there, the office staff drew a bond and mortgage on the property and sent it out to the agent along with the abstract. After the agent had the note and mortgage signed by the borrower and executed he returned the bond to Lawrence and filed the mortgage for record with the register of deeds. A check was sent to the borrower as soon as the bond, or note, returned to the office and it was learned that the mortgage had been filed for record.[14] The commission owing to J. B. Watkins and Company was deducted before the check was sent out, as was the money necessary to pay off any taxes or judgments already on the land. Such liens were paid off by the local agent or by draft sent directly to the county officers and the pencil notation erased from the abstract.[15] As soon as the mortgage was filed, it was entered on the abstract. The abstracter certified to the correctness of the abstract while the county treasurer and the clerk of the county court certified that no taxes or judgment liens stood against the land. The local agent then forwarded the abstract and mortgage to Lawrence. The papers representing the loan stood ready for transfer to the east.

The arguments which Watkins used to obtain local agents were short but potent. He pointed out that his wide advertising,[16] his determination to keep lending rates lower than those of any competitor,[17] and the promptness with which he could fill loans [18] guaranteed that his representative would obtain the lion's share of local business. The lawyers, real estate men, and bankers who formed the financial fraternity in

[13] J. B. Watkins and Co. to J. H. Drewing, Troy, Kans., Feb. 4, 1876.

[14] By 1880 borrowers in some cases were allowed to draw drafts on J. B. Watkins and Co. on the day when the executed paper was returned. J. B. Watkins and Co. to Sholer and Leigh, Mankato, Kans., Dec. 18, 1880.

[15] J. B. Watkins and Co. to E. Mills, Burlingame, Kans., Oct. 20, 1874, to J. D. Vasoter, Waveland, Kans., Apr. 13, 1876.

[16] J. B. Watkins and Co. to M. D. Wright (address not given), Aug. 28, 1875.

[17] J. B. Watkins and Co. to J. H. Crossman, Humboldt, Kans., June 1, 1876.

[18] J. B. Watkins and Co. to Scott and Ross, Erie, Kans., Feb. 18, 1876.

the frontier towns of Kansas were a notoriously lean and hungry group. It was not difficult to recruit agents.

One of the problems which perplexed Watkins in the early years was that of preventing the local agents from charging extortionate rates. He realized that if he was to build up a business with a future he must try to keep the good will of the farming community. To a prospective agent at Republican City, Kansas, he wrote, "Nor will we fill loans for anyone who proves to be extortionate upon the borrower. We charge reasonable rates. And expect local parties, without responsibility to charge living compensation only. We speak of this in the start because of past experience."[19] A year later he wrote to an agent whom he had empowered to make his own examinations:

We want you to build up a permanent business & on a sound basis. One great trouble we have is in the matter of charges. . . . Here is the basis we have fixed upon with our locals who have full charge of their field. They shall on loans of $1000 & upward charge a commission of 10%. On less than $1000 charge $5 extra. This is to include *all* charges and expense except for abstract & recording mortgage. And in no case will an over charge be sanctioned by us. From the above charges we will give you a discount to be your compensation in full for all services rendered in connection with this office. And we shall expect you to do promptly and in good order anything required to be done, in and about loans or applications coming through you. And in your best efforts to build up a large and safe business in your section also to protect the interests of your applicants that they may not be overcharged or defrauded by others in connection with the loan.[20]

At times Watkins and his employees found it necessary to tutor their agents. One young man at Humboldt, Kansas, was the particular target of letters of advice from Miles J. Dart, who was acting as inspector in 1876. Dart wrote to the agent:

you will need to be very careful and conservative in all cases & don't make too strong promises. Study your field carefully in all its bearings. Study how to get the most & best work with least expense. Study the character of the country, its soil & value in different localities. When travelling through the country take notes of everything you see and hear that can in any way be of value to you in the Future. Talk freely to farmers & get their experi-

[19] J. B. Watkins and Co. to W. H. Fletcher, Republican City, Kans., Aug. 7, 1874.
[20] J. B. Watkins and Co. to M. Noyes, Parsons, Kans., July 16, 1875.

ences for the district relative to crops, values, etc. & then draw your own conclusions.[21]

Again, Dart gave a most enlightening sketch of the factors to be considered in evaluating securities in southeastern Kansas:

We consider the best class of upland to be limestone slope. This class of land we regard as being nearly and in some cases quite as good as bottom. A good limestone upland 80 a[cres] within 8 miles of railroad with a man and his family living on it, in a house worth $400, with good well and outbuildings worth $300, all fenced, with 60 a[cres] in cultivation, the balance timber, or number one pasture, with an orchard of 200 peach trees—bearing & as many apples with plenty of small fruit for home use, 10 head of cattle with as many hogs and team enough for the place, would be security for $500. This is about as good an 80 a[cres] as you would find & consequently this is as much as we would care to put on any 80 a[cres] unless, say, it would lay adjoining Humboldt, *all* in cultivation & *good deal* better improvements than in above mentioned case, when we might put $600 on it but never above this and very *rarely* above *$500.* If a bachelor lived on such a farm as the one first named we would not allow him over $400, unless we were personally acquainted with him & knew him to be all right. Same if a woman lived on the place—widow. An ordinary 80 a[cres] of upland that can all be cultivated with 50 a[cres] in cultivation and nearly as good improvements as named in first, with a good family on it, would be good security for $400. If bachelor or woman lived on it we wd [*sic*] not give them over $300. And the last named is as poor a piece of land as we would care to do *anything* with. We can not do anything *at all* on mills or on city property. Can only work on *improved farming lands.*[22]

Finally, Dart warned that it was not always wise to show borrowers the form of the mortgage until they had signed the application because "sometimes parties become discouraged on seeing these."[23]

In some respects the relations of J. B. Watkins and Company with its agents remained constant throughout the first ten years of operation in Kansas. The firm never bought mortgages;[24] the securities which Watkins sold in the east and abroad had been supervised at every stage by his own organization. Nor did Watkins ever waver from the axiom that he wanted only the best class of loans obtainable. Agents were told that it mattered little what they did with second-rate work as long

[21] M. J. Dart to J. H. Crossman, Humboldt, Kans., July 24, 1876.
[22] *Ibid.*, July 31, 1876.
[23] *Ibid.*, Aug. 21, 1876.
[24] J. B. Watkins and Co. to James H. Crossman, Humboldt, Kans., Apr. 1, 1876.

as it was not submitted to Lawrence.[25] All documents submitted by local agents had to be in a fine legible hand. Loans were always made in even hundreds.[26] Mortgage papers always had to be dated the first of a month. Agents were advised not to touch a loan until they knew that title to the land was flawless or could be made so at once.[27] Agents were discouraged from lending to borrowers who wished to pay off debts to other loan companies. If the other company regarded the security as good they would renew the loan, argued the Lawrence office staff.[28]

Subject to change was Watkins' attitude toward loaning on final certificates and loaning to settlers who wished to use the money for proving up by commuting their homesteads to cash purchase or by using the pre-emption act. Title was nominally vested in the settler when he received a certificate and receipt from the officers of his district land office showing that he had presented his final proofs and paid his final fees. Once the settler had obtained his certificate he had still to receive his patent from the General Land Office. If he had made fraudulent proof, there was no guarantee that his claim might not be canceled before he received the patent. Some lenders were willing to accept the risk involved and to lend to settlers who had not yet received this patent. Even more dangerous was the financing of settlers who had yet to obtain their final certificate. In this case the money had to be paid to the settler and by him to the local land office before—in the eyes of the law—he had the land to mortgage. Any arrangement made to solve the difficulty was at best risky. Mortgage papers bearing a date prior to that on the receiver's receipt could be repudiated without difficulty.

When prospective borrowers were plentiful, Watkins refused all applications based on final certificates or submitted in the hope of obtaining funds with which to make proof. However, when eastern funds backed up on the books at Lawrence and the applications of borrowers were scarce, Watkins sometimes relented and handled such loans.[29]

25 J. B. Watkins and Co. to E. G. Bertram, Council Grove, Kans., July 17, 1876.

26 M. J. Dart to J. H. Crossman, Humboldt, Kans., June 9, 1876.

27 J. B. Watkins and Co. to Scott and Ross, Erie, Kans., Feb. 18, 1876.

28 J. B. Watkins and Co. to Theodore Hurtz, Scandia, Kans., Apr. 22, 1880.

29 J. B. Watkins and Co. to Samuel H. Early, Clay Centre, Kans., Aug. 4, 1874, to W. H. Knight (address not given), Feb. 11, 1876, to S. H. Hustoedt, Caledonia,

Watkins regarded a county as fit territory for business as soon as its records were set up so that title could be traced and the farms boasted sufficient breaking and improvements to guarantee that the owners would not abandon them at the first provocation. Although once J. B. Watkins and Company became established in a county they continued to make loans on applications which they considered suitable, Watkins claimed that the loans made in the period of settlement were the most satisfactory.[30] If possible he preferred to precede other loan agencies into the field. Priority allowed his agents to pick out the very cream of the applications and guaranteed that the loans could be made at a high rate of interest and commission. In addition, since the value of land in the frontier counties rose rapidly in the first few years of settlement, it was easy to turn the land of any defaulter over at a price sufficient to cover the inconvenience of taking the property.

In his search for mortgage securities Watkins rapidly extended his operations over a large portion of the western plains states. On his arrival at Lawrence, Watkins began to lend money in the portion of eastern Kansas which stretched to within thirty miles of the sixth principal meridian in the north and stopped some ninety miles short of the same line in the south.[31]

In the spring of 1876 Watkins was endeavoring to establish agencies in all counties east of the sixth principal meridian in Kansas.[32] At the same time he so needed applications that he extended his lending field eastward into the western counties of Iowa and Missouri.[33] By late 1877 he had extended his western limit ninety miles past the sixth principal meridian in the north and twenty-four miles in the south.[34] Two years later applications were being received from counties as far west as Osborne in the north and Edwards in the south.[35] One of the Lawrence staff estimated the number of agencies at over one hundred.[36]

D.T., Mar. 13, 1880, to W. R. Hoole, Zion Valley, Kans., May 10, 1880, to T. G. Flaland, Grand Forks, D.T., Dec. 9, 1880; M. J. Dart to A. Hubbard, Spencer, Ia., Aug. 7, 1876, to L. J. Best, Aug. 30, 1876.

30 J. B. Watkins to Edward Lewis, Philadelphia, Pa., Dec. 18, 1877.

31 *Ibid.*

32 J. B. Watkins and Co. to Register of Deeds, Seneca, Kans., Mar. 4, 1876.

33 M. J. Dart to D. M. Sprankle, Wichita, Kans., Sept. 23, 1876.

34 J. B. Watkins to Edward Lewis, Philadelphia, Pa., Dec. 18, 1877.

35 J. B. Watkins to D. W. C. Clapp, Iowa City, Ia., Feb. 8, 1879.

36 J. B. Watkins and Co. to Welch and Drew (address not given), Feb. 13, 1879.

As the drought of 1879 and 1880 temporarily checked any further extension to the west, J. B. Watkins and Company looked northward for new applications. By early May of 1881 agencies had been established in some twenty counties of south-central Nebraska.[37] On a trip shortly afterward one of the field inspectors organized "a good many" more.[38] At the same time some sixteen agencies were set up in Dakota Territory by correspondence.[39] Meanwhile business had been suspended in Iowa, where rates had slumped downward in advance of those in the states to the west.[40]

In the spring Watkins visited Dakota in order to investigate disturbing reports which he had received from the territory, to inspect the agencies which had been set up by correspondence, and to organize others. He found that numerous companies and agencies were bringing in investment funds rapidly. Lending rates consequently were falling. In addition, loans were being made on land values which Watkins believed were grossly inflated. Much of the work was centered on the tricky task of supplying settlers with the money necessary to prove up.[41] Finally there was considerable difficulty in finding reliable agents. After surveying the situation, Watkins decided to withdraw from the territory entirely. For some years, however, his attorney reaped the reward of the Dakota venture in foreclosures and snarled titles.[42]

In the fall of 1881, after his decision to withdraw from Dakota, Watkins was eager to find an area into which he could profitably expand his lending activities. Dart was dispatched south to investigate the possibilities in Texas. The disorders attendant on reconstruction in Texas had given Texas a reputation of which eastern capitalists were frightened. Investment funds therefore had been slow to flow into the state. Dart, however, decided that satisfactory loans could be made in Texas at good rates of interest and commission. Dallas was selected as the proper site for a branch office supervised by Dart. Preparations to move into Texas were cloaked in secrecy. On Dart's return Watkins broached the subject to Henry Dickinson, writing:

[37] M. J. Dart to H. C. Reynolds, Blue Rapids, Kans., May 5, 1881.
[38] M. J. Dart to J. B. Watkins, Sioux City, Ia., June 15, 1881.
[39] M. J. Dart to J. B. Watkins, Spencer, Ia., June 4, 1881.
[40] Henry Dickinson to Jerome H. Wheeler, Worcester, Mass., Nov. 1, 1882.
[41] M. J. Dart to W. D. Russell, Yankton, D.T., April 30, 1881.
[42] W. J. Patterson to J. B. Watkins, Aug. 14, 1882, to Coughran and McMartin, Sioux Falls, D.T., May 9, 1882; T. H. Rudiger to J. B. Watkins, July 29, 1882.

We . . . shall turn a considerable portion of European capital there, and will place some American capital where it will be sat[isfactory] to the parties furnishing it, but *we do not want it to become known in this country that we are doing business in Texas.* It is therefore important in soliciting that you do not let the matter be known except to parties who keep their business strictly to themselves. We are confident that as soon as it becomes known we are there other cos will be looking in that direction also and we shall have to compete with them as we have been doing here.[43]

When the decision was made to enter Texas, the agencies in Nebraska were abandoned.

Having convinced investors that loans on Kansas farms were unequaled as investments, Dickinson was now faced with the problem of persuading them that loans made in Texas were no less safe without alerting the loaning fraternity to Watkins' new venture. Dart did his best to provide ammunition. A letter written by him in the spring of 1882 to Dickinson pointed out the high fertility of the soil, the rapid expansion of railroad mileage in the state, the speedy growth of manufacturing and business, and the great variety of crops and mineral resources. Unlike farmers in the winterbound states to the north, Texans were able to graze their cattle all year round with perfect safety. Although titles had been somewhat complicated in an earlier period they now presented little more difficulty than did titles in the north. As a clincher Dart wrote:

After an extensive campaign of several months in the state I conclude that, while now and then a man is shot, there is less secret mischief; less getting into the confidence of men to betray it than in the north and east. . . . The shot gun and bowie knife question I believe to be greatly overstated. . . . I wish to impress the fact that there is less perfidy and trickery among men who pretend to be decent than in many other localities which have a higher name for morality than Texas.[44]

The subsequent development of the loan business in Texas will be discussed in Chapter XI.

[43] J. B. Watkins to Henry Dickinson, New York, N.Y., Dec. 5, 1881.
[44] M. J. Dart to Henry Dickinson, New York, N.Y., Apr. 15, 1882.

VII

EARLY PROBLEMS

BY 1879 J. B. Watkins and Company were lending funds beyond the ninety-eighth meridian in Kansas. Loans were being negotiated in the tier of counties east of Dodge City in the Arkansas Valley. In this year partial drought struck western Kansas, and the following year was even more unfavorable for the growth of crops. At the same time the rapid expansion of business and the growing distance between Lawrence and the lending field made the task of overseeing local agents increasingly difficult. These circumstances helped to bring Watkins his first serious difficulties.

Trouble struck first in Kingman County. In the spring of 1880 Miles Dart, who was in charge of obtaining mortgage securities at the Lawrence office, appointed R. G. McClain to the post of local agent at Kingman. Some of the county officers and other responsible residents of Kingman County had recommended him highly. At the time D. M. Sprankle, the field inspector, was suffering from an injured hand and was unable to visit McClain immediately on his appointment. Before Sprankle made his inspection, McClain submitted a few applications which appeared satisfactory and were approved at Lawrence. The completed papers were in time also forwarded to Lawrence and a number of drafts drawn on behalf of the supposed mortgagors by McClain.

At this point a minor confederate of McClain's became dissatisfied and confessed to Sprankle that the papers being submitted from Kingman were forgeries. Miles Dart was immediately summoned to Wichita, where he met Sprankle. After a conference the two set out by team for Kingman, turning aside twice to view tracts of land on which McClain had submitted applications. In both cases they found that the land was still a part of the public domain and that the supposed mortgagor was unknown in the district.

There followed a week of high drama. When he arrived at Kingman, Dart found it necessary to drive to Hutchinson for additional legal aid. Leaving Kingman at six in the evening, Dart was back the next morning after a seventy-mile drive during the night. The county attorney was also involved, and suspicion pointed to other county officers as well, including the register of deeds. As deputy sheriff the preceding year McClain had once shot a man through the neck at seventy-five yards with his revolver and to arrest a man so skilled in self-defense seemed highly dangerous. Dart and Sprankle, however, managed to have McClain, the county attorney, and another confederate arrested on charges of forgery and misuse of the county seals. Once caught, the confederates tried with little success to buy off their accusers. Two of them obtained their freedom on bond, but McClain was unable to obtain bondsmen. Legal proceedings dragged on at Kingman for several days, keeping Dart constantly on tenterhooks. He found himself in a town without a jail attempting to guard a prisoner whose friends seemed legion.

At the end of three days Sprankle was forced to return to Wichita. Rumor spread that an attempt would be made to release McClain by force. Twice during the following night his confederates managed to hand the prisoner a revolver, but on each occasion the sheriff's pistol was at McClain's head before he could use it. The following night the sheriff, weakening under the strain, imbibed so freely that Dart could see little help in prospect if efforts were again made to release McClain. The loan agent thereupon had himself sworn in as deputy sheriff and acted in that capacity for two days until the prisoner was safely lodged in the Hutchinson jail.

Returning to Lawrence Dart wrote to his superior in England:

> Owing to the gravity of the offences, I decided to put sufficient force on the prosecution so that there will be no failure in getting the full extent of the law. I know of no instance where the honor of the state has been prostituted to a greater extent, and feel that if all of them get the full extent of the law that justice will then be but poorly satisfied and the honor of the state insufficiently vindicated.[1]

Despite his intentions, Dart's plans for the culprits were eventually foiled. McClain broke jail, was rearrested after a reward had been posted by the governor, and eventually escaped again. Although he was found in the late 1880's, Watkins decided not to renew the case. McClain's confederates jumped bond, and the ex-county attorney eventually died in a gun fight. Five drafts drawn by McClain on the Lawrence agency totaled some $2,300. Of these, two had been honored before the plot was discovered. Payment was stopped on the remaining three.[2]

Far less spectacular than the McClain affair but potentially more dangerous to the business was the optimism of local agents in the counties along the ninety-eighth meridian. Operating in counties which were for the most part organized in the 1870's and were still being settled, the agents were often overgenerous in the size of loans which they recommended. In part this tendency was due to the perennial optimism with which most of the western businessmen regarded the area where they had cast their lot. No doubt, however, the fact that their fee was a percentage of the loan also had something to do with their actions.

In the fall of 1879 Dart was cutting the size of loans recommended by agents in the newly settled counties of the Arkansas Valley by one-fourth.[3] Of twenty-eight applications sent in by the agency at Larned

[1] M. J. Dart to J. B. Watkins, London, Eng., May 17, 1880.

[2] This account is based on the following: M. J. Dart to J. B. Watkins, London, Eng., May 17, 1880, to T. L. Nixon, Wichita, Kans., May 8, 1880, to J. M. Dean, North Ferrisburg, Vt., May 19, 1880; Henry Dickinson to J. B. Watkins, London, Eng., May 28, 1880; A. L. Selig to M. J. Dart, Dallas, Tex., Feb. 23, 1882; T. H. Rudiger to Sheriff H. R. Watts, Wichita, Kans., July 6, 1882; J. B. Watkins and Co. to F. E. Gillett, Kingman, Kans., July 12, 1882, to Kohn Bros. and Co., Wichita Bank, Wichita, Kans., May 15, 1880, to Governor John P. St. John, Topeka, Kans., July 12, 1882, to Merchants Detective Association, Kansas City, Mo., Aug. 19, 1882; *Kingman County Citizen,* May 7, June 18, June 25, July 23, 1880.

[3] J. B. Watkins and Co. to D. M. Sprankle, Wichita, Kans., Sept. 22, 1879.

in Pawnee County, Dart declined twelve completely, approved seven fully, and accepted the remainder on condition that they be scaled down or that the perishable improvements be insured. The loans ranged in size from $200 to $500.[4]

In some cases the reckless manner in which agents recommended loans indicated outright dishonesty. Such was the case in Mitchell County. Here agents were located at both the county seat and an outlying town. Dart had done his best to dampen their enthusiasm. "If you continue to water valuations in north-western Kansas, the country will all run away one of these days," [5] he wrote in the spring of 1881 to one of them. Finally, in rapid succession, two of the Lawrence staff, and then J. B. Watkins himself, inspected the loans which they had been making. Watkins showed his displeasure by jailing the agents on a charge of obtaining money under false pretenses.[6]

In part the guilt in this case lay with the inspector who had been examining loans in northwestern Kansas. Although well meaning, he had approved loans on property for greater sums than it would have brought in the market. Watkins discharged him, writing, "I would not be true to my patrons, to do business in the future upon your judgment, in view of the discoveries I have made in the localities mentioned." [7]

The position of agent in the western counties was by no means without difficulty. In drought years the real estate business on which most of the western lawyers and real estate men depended for part of their income was seriously curtailed. They were under pressure to turn a dollar wherever they could. With their crops destroyed, many of the better element among the settlers desired a loan to tide them over. Another large group among the settlers—those who were easily discouraged or had been merely holding their land as a speculation—also desired loans. These settlers, however, wished merely to get as large a loan as possible and to leave. In effect, in the absence of other buyers, they wished to sell their land to a mortgagee. They were quite prepared to swear to an extreme valuation on their land and had little difficulty in finding others of their ilk to add their supporting affidavits on the

[4] J. B. Watkins and Co. to Adams and Altdoerffer, Larned, Kans., Oct. 25, 1879.

[5] J. B. Watkins and Co. to U. B. Mumford, Beloit, Kans., Apr. 15, 1881.

[6] J. B. Watkins to T. B. Sweet, Topeka, Kans., Oct. 12, 1881, to M. J. Dart, Dallas, Tex., Apr. 28, 1882; J. B. Watkins and Co. to H. G. Reynolds, Blue Rapids, Kans., June 3, 1882; Beloit *Gazette,* Aug. 20, Sept. 3, Oct. 29, 1881.

[7] J. B. Watkins to H. G. Reynolds, Blue Rapids, Kans., Aug. 27, 1881.

application. Thus the local loan agent already in a receptive mood found himself besieged with applicants eager to raise as much money on their security as possible.

Dart's letters to the west in the fall of 1881 illustrate the situation as it appeared from Lawrence. To one of his inspectors he wrote: "Noth ing but the strictest caution will insure safety in a loaning business in western Kansas. Men that had previously built up good characters and reputations have gone to utter demoralization in western Kansas." [8] A local agent at Greenvale was told;

> If property can not be fairly valued in Western Kan[sas], we will withdraw our business from there altogether. . . . If Western Kansas does not want to utterly ruin herself she had better go out of the business of trying to sell out to loan agents. They are all getting their eyes peeled & will soon refuse to work them at all unless they receive different treatment.[9]

Another local representative learned that "such work as is going on in western Kansas is simply devilish. Unless it stops soon loan companies will be compelled to abandon the field." [10]

J. B. Watkins and Company did withdraw from some of the western counties, including Pratt and Stafford. Loaning was continued in Edwards County because the local agent there was believed to be an exceptionally conservative judge of land values.[11]

Although good crops came again to the counties of the ninety-eighth meridian in 1881, J. B. Watkins and Company still suffered the effects of the drought and the careless work of agents during the previous two years. By June of 1882 there were over 700 loans in default.[12] In July the local agent at Kingman learned, "From recent personal investigation made in your field we find that the leaving mania is not dead yet; that people are only waiting for some loaning company to make them loans to enable them to get out of the country." [13] A few months later Watkins and his lieutenants decided to withdraw from even those western counties where the agents had proven themselves to be of

[8] M. J. Dart to Earl Joslin, Lyons, Kans., Sept. 5, 1881.

[9] M. J. Dart to Aaron Ford, Greenvale, Kans., Sept. 8, 1881.

[10] M. J. Dart to W. H. Dodge, Great Bend, Kans., Sept. 8, 1881.

[11] J. B. Watkins and Co. to L. W. Higgins, Kinsley, Kans., Sept. 1, 1881. Higgins was later a full-time employee.

[12] T. H. Rudiger to J. B. Watkins, June 21, 1882.

[13] J. B. Watkins and Co. to F. E. Gillett, Kingman, Kans., July 19, 1882.

exceptional ability.[14] By the fall of 1883 some 40,000 acres of real estate had fallen to Watkins by foreclosure or had been merely deeded over by the mortgagor.[15] Since he had promised the mortgagees that he would not allow them to take any land, he assumed payment of the loans and took the land in his own name. This action tied up considerable operating capital and created considerable anxiety in the minds of Watkins' staff.[16]

Watkins directed that letters be sent to mortgagors in Mitchell County pointing out that the agents had been jailed and that every one who had sworn to false valuations was a party to their activities. So long, however, as mortgagors stayed on their land and paid their interest, they had nothing to fear from J. B. Watkins and Company. But defaulters and those who abandoned their land would find themselves pursued by a deficiency judgment.[17] It is impossible to discover the effect which this argument had in keeping the settlers on their land. Certainly there was strong feeling in the section against Watkins, who had transferred his suits from the county to avoid a miscarriage similar to that which had allowed the Kingman ring to escape.

While Watkins was meeting his first major problems in the lending field, trouble struck in the Lawrence office.[18] Since 1875 Watkins had employed as his cashier F. M. Perkins, whom he had previously known in Wisconsin. Until 1879 Watkins had permitted his staff to draw advances against their salaries. During 1878 Perkins allowed his books to slip behind. Finally, when Watkins hired an additional bookkeeper and the books were brought up to date, he found Perkins to be some $2,500 in his debt. After considerable urging Perkins converted a farm which he owned into cash, borrowed $500 from the Merchants' Bank of Lawrence, and gave Watkins a note for the residue. Immediately after the affair was thus settled in the spring of 1880, Watkins left for England.

Shortly after his return from running McClain to ground in Kingman

[14] J. B. Watkins and Co. to L. W. Higgins, Kinsley, Kans., Nov. 7, 1882.

[15] This figure was arrived at by subtracting real estate of Jan. 1, 1881, from that put into J. B. Watkins Land Mortgage Company in 1883.

[16] T. H. Rudiger to M. J. Dart, June 27, 1882, to J. B. Watkins, July 18, 1882.

[17] J. B. Watkins and Co. to Arthur Brown, Blue Hill, Kans., Jan. 10, 1882.

[18] In general this account is based on the stenographic record of *Kansas* vs. *Perkins* given in Lawrence *Daily Tribune* Dec. 20, 1880, to Jan. 3, 1881, inclusive, and *Perkins* vs. *Watkins in Magistrates Court; The President of the Western Farm Mortgage Co. F. M. PERKINS* vs. *J. B. WATKINS, Libel Suit for $10,000 Damages* (Lawrence, Kans., 1887).

County in May of 1880, Dart learned from local agents at Washington and Scandia, Kansas, that Perkins was soliciting the locals to work for a new farm mortgage company of which he was president. To agents who would gather applicants for the new company Perkins promised swifter attention to applications and loans than that given by J. B. Watkins and Company. Because of his previous difficulty with Perkins, Watkins had left Dart in charge of the Lawrence office. Dart used his authority to discharge Perkins. With Perkins' discharge began a struggle which over the next eleven years was to embitter the business life of Lawrence and at times drive Watkins to the verge of mental exhaustion.

A few days after Dart had removed the cashier, Dickinson reported from New York that the eastern investors of J. B. Watkins and Company were receiving circulars from Perkins. During the years at Lawrence, Watkins had published all of his advertisements in the eastern press under the heading "Western Farm Mortgages." Perkins and his colleagues had named their new company the Western Farm Mortgage Company. In their first circular to the east they advertised a record of nine years' business. The number of mortgages, the acreage of security, and other details of their past history were identical with the record which Watkins had been advertising. The circular, however, advertised mortgages bearing 9 per cent, an increase of 2 per cent over the rate returned on the securities handled by Watkins.

Dart found in addition that Perkins had used his position as cashier to leave the finances in a precarious state. It had been Perkins' task upon receiving orders from the east to select applications already approved by the security department and order the mortgage papers drawn in the name of the investor. After the bond and mortgage were returned from the local agent with the signature of the mortgagee, Perkins drew a draft in favor of the borrower. Without waiting for the local agents to fulfill all their duties, Perkins had drawn some $40,000 of such drafts in excess of the available bank accounts in Lawrence and New York.

With Dickinson's help and advice Dart set about meeting the challenge. Circulars and letters were prepared which explained the situation to the eastern investors.[19] Other circulars were sent to the local agents in the loan field assuring them that J. B. Watkins and Company was

[19] J. B. Watkins and Co. to H. J. Ludlow, Troy, N.Y., June 2, 1880; M. J. Dart to Lucius Atwood, Rome, N.Y., June 4, 1880.

still very much alive and prepared to handle applications with even less delay than formerly.[20] To Dickinson the western manager dispatched orders to convert a fund of mortgages which he had on hand at New York into cash and to advertise for more investment funds. Arrangements were made with the Merchants' Bank at Lawrence and the National Bank of Commerce in New York to honor any overdraft that might occur in the accounts kept there. Dart wrote to Watkins urging him to strengthen the accounts as soon as possible.[21] In a later letter he gave his evaluation of Perkins:

> Frank now stands peer of Judas Iscariot, Benedict Arnold, and Jefferson Davis. . . . That he proposed to destroy this business completely and build his own upon the ruins thereof there is no doubt. He proposed to accomplish it before your return. He has been defeated and I desire that you give the balance of the force that stood by me in this emergency much credit.[22]

When Watkins returned to Lawrence in the fall of 1880, he threw himself vigorously into the fight against the Western Farm Mortgage Company. Chagrined at the narrow escape of his business from catastrophe and infuriated by the calculated planning with which Perkins and his colleagues had endeavored to steal his agencies and clientele, he was determined to break the new company. In early December he published in the Lawrence *Tribune* and certain Kansas City papers an article entitled "Fraud and Embezzlement" which described the birth of the Western Farm Mortgage Company.[23] Its president, F. M. Perkins, promptly entered civil and criminal suits on the charge of libel and sued for damages. Watkins countered by charging Perkins with embezzlement. During the next year and a half the four cases arising from the controversy went through the courts. First came Watkins' suit against Perkins before Magistrate L. S. Steele, followed by Perkins' three actions against Watkins. In no case was the plaintiff successful.

At this range Watkins' case against Perkins does not appear a particularly strong one. Although it was shown that Perkins had opened the books of J. B. Watkins and Company to members of the new company, that he had solicited Watkins' clients for patronage, and that he had attempted to have Dart on vacation at the time when the new company was being organized, the case of necessity centered on the concrete fact that he had overdrawn his accounts. This aberration had already been settled amicably, and to resurrect it was to flog a dead

[20] M. J. Dart to J. B. Watkins, June 22, 1880. [21] *Ibid.*, June 5, 1880.
[22] *Ibid.*, June 12, 1880. [23] Lawrence *Daily Tribune*, Dec. 3, 1880.

horse. Nor was Watkins able to prove completely at the trial that other members of the staff had not at times also overdrawn their accounts.

The Perkins' version of the whole affair appeared in the Lawrence *Daily Journal* at the conclusion of the case argued before Magistrate Steele.[24] The idea of a company had originated with the defendant's brother L. H. Perkins and a few other businessmen of Lawrence. They had requested F. M. Perkins to take over active management of the company but from a sense of duty he had refused to do so until Watkins should return. When Dart had decided to take over he had been only too happy to go. Watkins had been frightened by the competition of the new company when he returned and had decided to ruin the company's reputation in general and that of F. M. Perkins in particular. Excerpts from Steele's decision were quoted with approval:

> It is fair to presume that he [Watkins] knew of and permitted the defendant to overdraw his account. . . . From such a state of facts I cannot believe that J. B. Watkins believed the defendant guilty of a fraudulent or wrongful act in relation to his funds, and this prosecution seems to me to savor less of a desire to vindicate the law than the gratification of vindictive motives. The evidence shows an intense feeling on the part of the prosecuting witness against the defendant and shows that he has spared no efforts or means to injure and ruin him.[25]

There were, however, some cynical enough to suggest that Steele might have held the scales of justice more evenly had not both he and Perkins been officers in the same Masonic Lodge.[26]

But if Watkins was unsuccessful in the attempt to prosecute his former cashier, the latter was equally unsuccessful in proving libel. In the cases brought against him Watkins was able to show that the statements made in his newspaper article and in subsequent articles and letters were essentially correct.[27] Technically Perkins might not be guilty of embezzlement but the ethics of his actions were certainly open to question. Beyond attempting to prove that Perkins had been overworked and underpaid and questioning Watkins' methods of business, the counsel for the prosecution could do little against the evidence which the defendant introduced. Only the criminal action for libel

[24] Lawrence *Daily Journal*, Jan. 4, 1881.

[25] Lawrence *Daily Journal*, Jan. 4, 1881. See Topeka *State Journal*, Jan. 6, 1881, for a sarcastic rejoinder.

[26] M. J. Dart to Edward Burbeck, Racine, Wis., Feb. 15, 1881.

[27] Civil Actions 5003 and 5045 and Criminal Action 709 filed in Douglas County District Court, 1880.

was allowed to go to a decision. The verdict was "not guilty." In the courts the battle had ended in a bloodless victory for Watkins.

While the legal warfare raged the case was also being argued in the court of public opinion. Perkins and his colleagues had immediately begun to advertise in the papers utilized by Watkins. To the editors of these papers Watkins wrote accounts of the Western Farm Mortgage Company's attempt to steal his business and urged that the advertising of such a villainous group be dropped.[28] In some cases he promised further advertising only on condition that the advertisement of the Perkins company be canceled.[29] In other papers he inserted counter-advertising just above the Western Farm Mortgage Company ad.[30]

Watkins endeavored to insert favorable descriptions of his struggle in influential eastern papers.[31] When he was successful, he ordered large numbers of the issue and sent them to his investors and to other papers. A stenographic report of one civil case which Perkins brought against Watkins was prepared in pamphlet form [32] and sent to investors and to the eastern press.[33] Included were the affidavits of the jurors swearing that they would have acquitted Watkins if the case had been allowed to go to a decision. Another pamphlet used in the struggle bore the euphonious title: *What Our Patrons Say of Us and How They Regard the Attempt by the So-called Western Farm Mortgage Company to Steal Our Business.*[34]

In the original circular of the Western Farm Mortgage Company, Perkins had included a list of references of whom investors might inquire the standing of the new company. Watkins and Dart now bombarded these gentlemen with their version of the Perkins affair.[35] In some cases at least Perkins had obtained permission to use their names by claiming that J. B. Watkins and Company had been a partnership which was being dissolved amicably.[36] When the true state of

[28] J. B. Watkins to *Observer*, New York, N.Y., Feb. 19, 1881.

[29] J. B. Watkins to the *Examiner and Chronicle*, New York, N.Y., Feb. 19, 1881, to Springfield *Republican*, Springfield, Mass., July 1, 1881.

[30] J. B. Watkins to B. C. Everinchen, *Illustrated Christian Weekly*, New York, N.Y., Mar. 16, 1881.

[31] J. B. Watkins to Henry Dickinson, Jan. 19, 1881.

[32] Published in 1881 and again in 1887.

[33] J. B. Watkins and Co. to Springfield *Republican*, July 1, 1881.

[34] Published by J. B. Watkins and Co. at Lawrence (1881?).

[35] M. J. Dart to J. B. Watkins, May 28, 1881.

[36] J. B. Watkins and Co. to Amasa Proctor, Cavendish, N.Y., June 1, 1880.

affairs was explained to them they withdrew their support from the Western Farm Mortgage Company.[37]

Perkins and his cohorts did manage to obtain enough business to stay in operation, but the new company did little damage to the volume of Watkins' business. The advertising which Watkins and his competitors had done over the last few years was bringing larger and larger amounts of funds from the east. The main problem of the business in 1881 lay in the difficulty of obtaining enough good applications to fill the orders received from investors. In another respect, however, the incorporation of the Western Farm Mortgage Company had serious consequences. Watkins had become one of three partners operating the Merchants' Bank and president of that institution. As his lending business continued to expand rapidly, he had grown to be one of the most important figures in the business life of Lawrence. This rapid rise was not accomplished without exciting jealousy in the business community. With the formation of the Western Farm Mortgage Company, Watkins' enemies had a vehicle for their opposition.

Although neither Perkins nor any of the other officers of the new company had any surplus capital of their own [38] they were able to borrow at the National Bank of Lawrence.[39] The Lawrence *Journal* openly espoused their cause while the Lawrence *Tribune* rallied to the aid of Watkins.[40] The business community of the little city split into rival camps. There followed fifteen years of struggle, in the course of which Watkins took his difficulties with the National Bank of Lawrence to the courts [41] and established his own national bank and newspaper. Politics embittered the situation as well, for Watkins was a Democrat and many of his opponents stalwart Republicans. One of the latter described an election as a "question of *supremacy*" to decide "whether he and his friends should *run things* or *Watkins*." [42] Henceforth Watkins was never free from an active opposition at home ever ready to circulate rumors of his impending insolvency or to submit unfavorable reports to the commercial agencies.

[37] J. B. Watkins to T. C. Evans, Boston, Mass., July 12, 1881.

[38] J. B. Watkins to Bradstreet Co., Kansas City, Mo., May 4, 1881.

[39] J. B. Watkins to W. H. Mott, New York, N.Y., Mar. 4, 1881; also *J. B. Watkins* vs. *National Bank of Lawrence*, Case 6100, filed in District Court, Douglas County, 1887.

[40] See Lawrence *Daily Tribune*, Dec. 10, 1880.

[41] See *J. B. Watkins* vs. *the National Bank of Lawrence, op. cit.*

[42] Paul Brooks to J. B. Watkins, July 14, 1892.

VIII

EARLY RATES AND RECORD

THE moneylender found that the rapid turnover of the settlers, the scanty improvements on the farms, and the often haphazard administration of law and order combined to make the risk of lending in newly settled counties greater than in older areas. In general the older the county, the lower were the rates of interest. There were, however, factors which affected the speed with which the rates dropped. Money was loaned at lower rates in counties where railroads had been built than in those which were still without such facilities.[1] Borrowers in areas where the title to land was unusual or in doubt had to pay high rates for their money if they were lucky enough to obtain funds at all. Within specific counties differences of soil played a very important part in determining the rate charged. For instance, the sandhills along the Arkansas were forbidden territory to the agents of J. B. Watkins and Company.[2] The lender who would risk his money there could demand higher rates than those current in more fertile adjacent areas. At

[1] M. J. Dart to G. M. Parks, Washington, Kans., Nov. 12, 1878.

[2] J. B. Watkins and Co. to S. M. Nolder, Stafford, Kans., Dec. 22, 1879; M. J. Dart to Earl Joslin, Lyons, Kans., Sept. 5, 1881.

times Watkins gave his agents permission to cut commissions in order to obtain the choicer loans or to increase the flow of applications.[3] Rates were calculated so that the borrower might choose between a high rate of interest and a small commission or a low rate of interest and a large commission. It was customary as well to reduce the percentage of commission charged on loans as they grew larger in size.[4]

The rate of interest which was specified in the mortgage and on the mortgage bond was but a part of the price which the borrower paid for his loan. There were in addition other charges—the commission paid to the mortgage agency, the commission paid to the local agent, an examination fee, clerk's fees for drawing up the mortgage papers, the cost of the abstract, and the fees charged for recording the mortgage in the county records. If the local agent was an abstracter, he sometimes received the fee for preparing the abstract. Recording fees were always paid to the county register of deeds. Custom varied in handling the other charges. At times they might be listed separately for the mortgagor, or they might be lumped into a single total but, however it was done, the mortgagor usually paid them.

Abstracting and recording charges were relatively stable, but the other charges varied. This fact makes it impossible to learn exactly what the individual borrower paid for his money, if no source of information but the county records is used. In addition, it is impossible to tell which of two borrowers paid the highest charge for his loan. A low rate of interest was sometimes accompanied by a large commission. The loan which on the record appears to have been made at a high rate of interest may have had all of the service charges except the cost of recording and abstracting included in the rate.

During his first ten years in Kansas, Watkins had no set system of paying his local agents. His only hard and fast rule held that a local agent was entitled to payment for his services.

When he was establishing his business Watkins paid local representatives who merely gathered applications for him at the rate of $7.50 for each application on which a loan was eventually made.[5] When the agent assumed the task of inspecting the applicant's farm, he usually

[3] J. B. Watkins and Co. to Scott and Ross, Chanute, Kans., July 27, 1875, to Z. Jackson, Ellsworth, Kans., Mar. 4, 1879.

[4] J. B. Watkins and Co. to D. M. Sprankle, Wichita, Kans., Nov. 27, 1878.

[5] J. B. Watkins and Co. to S. A. Atwood, Hutchinson, Kans., May 31, 1876.

received a percentage of the commission; usually this percentage amounted to 2 per cent of the loan. Some agents, however, obtained a flat fee of $12.00 per loan.[6] To other agents Watkins gave the privilege of collecting their own payments from the borrower. But when some of the agents took advantage of the borrowers, he began to deduct the commissions of local agents from the loans at the Lawrence office. At the end of each month the local agent received payment on all loans completed in his county during that month.

By 1879 Watkins was changing back to the practice of allowing local agents to obtain their commission from the borrower.[7] In doing so, Watkins urged that the agents should not be greedy. Two per cent of the face of the loan was an ample fee, he believed. Watkins' action was evidently designed to relieve the Lawrence office staff of a duty which took much time and sometimes led to recriminations with the local agents. It did, however, increase the power of the local agents over the borrower. But the changeover was by no means complete. Some of the agreements made with agents during 1880 provided that the fees were to be deducted in Lawrence.[8]

In 1874 Watkins was drawing his mortgages on Kansas farms at 12-per-cent interest. In that year he offered to loan $500 at a commission of 8½% with clerk's fees of $5.00 and inspection fees of $25.00 to a farmer living at Blue Rapids. This post office, in Marshall County, was somewhat beyond the western limit of his lending field.[9] When reduced to percentages the total cost of such a loan amounted to 12-per-cent interest annually plus service charges totaling 14½ per cent of the loan. Watkins suggested that if several of the neighbors also desired money he would apportion the examination fees among them thereby reducing the cost to $10.00 or less apiece. This would have reduced the cost of the loan to 12-per-cent interest and some 12½ per cent in service charges. Since his mortgages usually ran for periods of three to five years, Watkins calculated that 1 per cent of interest

[6] See letters written July 3, 1876 to July 6, 1876 to agents in Missouri, Iowa, and eastern Kansas.

[7] J. B. Watkins and Co. to Green and Marr, Fort Scott, Kans., Nov. 28, 1879; Theodore Hertz, Scandia, Kans., in *Perkins* vs. *Watkins* (Lawrence, Kans., 1887), p. 84.

[8] J. B. Watkins and Co. to S. M. Grigsby, Milan, Mo., Apr. 13, 1880; but see J. B. Watkins and Co. to Stephen Husvedt, Caledonia, D.T., Feb. 9, 1880.

[9] J. B. Watkins and Co. to Samuel Hill, Blue Rapids, Kans., Aug. 4, 1874.

was equivalent to a cash commission of 3 per cent. On this basis of reckoning the farmer at Blue Rapids would have obtained his loan at 17 per cent, or, if two of his friends had joined him, at 16 per cent. To a farmer located at Louisville, Kansas—a location somewhat more accessible than Blue Rapids—Watkins offered money at a total cost of 15 per cent per year.[10]

Watkins was by no means unique in his efforts to channel eastern funds into the west. In 1880 he calculated that there were some forty major agencies or companies lending funds in Kansas.[11] As investors paid heed to their advertising, the competition among the agencies to find suitable securities became increasingly stiff. Both interest rates and the commissions fell rapidly. Where, in 1874, Watkins was drawing mortgage papers returning 12-per-cent interest, he had, in three years' time, reduced the rate to 10 per cent.[12] In 1880 his investors were receiving 8 per cent on their mortgage investments.[13] A few months later some securities were being drawn at 7 per cent.[14] Watkins followed a policy of dropping the rate first on securities intended for England,[15] where the long-term interest rate was lower than the long-term rate in eastern America.

Watkins' borrowers, of course, benefited by the decline in rates. During 1880 Watkins was lending money at the eastern edge of his lending field at a straight 10-per-cent annual interest.[16] All service charges but abstracting and recording were included in the 10 per cent. Local agents received 2 per cent from J. B. Watkins and Company for their services. Since the mortgages returned 7 per cent to the investors, such loans were actually made at 7 per cent with a commission of 7 per cent going to Watkins and 2 per cent to the local agent. Early in 1882 Watkins was offering funds to agents in Missouri at 7-per-cent interest plus a commission of 4 per cent, provided that they would submit applications to the value of $10,000 and look to the borrowers for their own commissions.[17] Rates were higher on the western edge

[10] J. B. Watkins and Co. to W. A. Limbacher, Louisville, Kans., Aug. 6, 1874.
[11] J. B. Watkins to Chas. Stoddard (no address given), Mar. 9, 1881.
[12] J. B. Watkins and Co. to Rev. J. J. Pomeroy, Rahway, N.J., July 23, 1877.
[13] J. B. Watkins to Geo. A. Dockstader, New York, N.Y., Feb. 18, 1880.
[14] J. B. Watkins to H. P. Hall, Saratoga, N.Y., Sept. 12, 1881.
[15] J. B. Watkins to H. G. Chalkley, Dec. 31, 1880.
[16] J. B. Watkins and Co. to S. M. Grigsby, Milan, Mo., Apr. 13, 1880.
[17] J. B. Watkins and Co. to E. M. Randolph, Edina, Mo., Feb. 21, 1882.

of the lending field, but here too they were dropping rapidly. Late in 1881 money was being offered at Kingman for 8-per-cent interest and a total commission of 10 per cent.[18] At Lincoln the interest rate was down to 7 per cent and a total commission of 10 per cent, while some firms were lending funds at 7-per-cent interest and a commission of 9 per cent of the loan.[19]

So rapid a fall in the price of money caused consternation among the loan agents in Kansas—and someone among them suggested a combination should be formed to maintain rates.[20] Both T. B. Sweet, the president of the Kansas Loan and Trust Company of Topeka, and J. B. Watkins were very energetic in popularizing the scheme and either one of them may have been the originator.

During the last nine months of 1880 J. B. Watkins or his staff sought co-operation from out-of-state agencies doing business in Kansas. Most important of these was the Corbin Banking Company of New York and New Hampshire—an agency with a field of operations equaled by few of its competitors.[21] Correspondence was also directed to T. J. Chew of St. Joseph, Missouri, who loaned large sums of money for the Phoenix Mutual Life Insurance Company of Hartford. The Travelers' Insurance Company of Hartford were informed that

> the present modus operandi of one cutting under another appears to be leading logically to such a decline in rates as that no one can afford to do business. It is our judgment that the plan of rate cutting does not necessarily secure the best class of work, and that all loaning companies of character should take a stand in relation to uniform rates.[22]

Corbin alone professed pleasure at learning the views of his friends in the business, but even he gave no encouragement.[23]

In the fall of 1880 the agencies in Kansas came to an informal agreement under which all of their agents at local points were urged to combine and charge a uniform rate.[24] A spokesman of J. B. Watkins and Company soon informed Sweet that the rates of their local agent

[18] J. B. Watkins to W. E. Gillett, Kingman, Kans., Oct. 11, 1881.

[19] J. B. Watkins and Co. to J. D. Miller, Lincoln, Kans., Dec. 19, Dec. 30, 1881.

[20] J. B. Watkins to T. B. Sweet, Mar. 31, 1880.

[21] J. B. Watkins and Co. to Corbin Banking Company, New York, N.Y., May 26, 1880; to T. B. Sweet, May 22, 1880.

[22] J. B. Watkins and Co. to the Travelers' Insurance Company, Hartford, Conn., Nov. 29, 1880.

[23] J. B. Watkins and Co. to T. B. Sweet, Nov. 30, 1880.

[24] *Ibid.*

at Lyons had been undercut by all competitors despite an agreement of only a few days' standing. He concluded, "It is evident that the plan for a combination of local agents does not start out brilliantly if we have correct information from Rice County."[25] A few days later the agency at Lawrence was maintaining that the loan companies should receive 8-per-cent interest and 5-per-cent commission (or a commission of 7 per cent if the fee of the local agent was included) in all the counties lying east of the sixth principal meridian and in Jewell, Smith, Republic, Osborne, Mitchell, Cloud, Russell, Lincoln, Ottawa, Barton, Ellsworth, Saline, McPherson, Rice, and Reno to the west of the same line. To the west of this field rates should be higher again.[26]

In January 1881 representatives of the Kansas loan agencies drew up articles of agreement at a meeting held in the office of T. B. Sweet at Topeka.[27] Watkins sent a copy of the agreement to T. J. Chew and asked him to secure the signatures of all the loanbrokers of St. Joseph. Once the scheme was in operation, he explained, any lender who dropped his rate below those of the association would immediately find himself underpriced by the other members of the association until he co-operated. Since the legislature in Kansas was hostile to the interests of the loanbrokers, the new organization was to have a lobbying function as well.[28]

During the early months of 1881 the executive committee of the Loan Agents' Association endeavored to draw up a schedule of rates. Watkins sent his suggestions to Sweet.[29] He fixed a western boundary for the combination's field by running a line roughly along the ninety-eighth meridian. To the east of this boundary he divided the counties into two groups. Where local conditions demanded a rate which was lower than usual the counties were placed in an excepted list. The remaining counties made up what Watkins called a general list (see Table 5 below). Unfortunately he did not list the counties to be placed in the two schedules. Except when money was loaned at 10 per cent or a higher rate of interest, local agents were to obtain their commission

[25] *Ibid.*

[26] J. B. Watkins and Co. to Western Loan and Trust Co., Topeka, Kans., Dec. 8, 1880.

[27] J. B. Watkins and Co. to Central Loan and Trust Co., Topeka, Kans., Jan. 14, 1881.

[28] J. B. Watkins to T. J. Chew, St. Joseph, Mo., Jan. 26, 1881.

[29] J. B. Watkins to T. B. Sweet, Feb. 17, 1881.

from the borrowers.[30] Watkins also recommended that a large loan should never be made for a smaller commission than that charged for a small loan. This rule would, he believed, remove at least one of the incentives which caused borrowers to ask for needlessly large loans. Competition was still to operate in the newly opened counties lying beyond the western boundary line.

Table 5. Percentage rates suggested by Watkins in 1881.

	EXCEPTED LIST					
Loans	$500 or less		$500 to $1,500 *		$1,500 and over	
	Int.	Com.	Int.	Com.	Int.	Com.
	7	7	7	6	7	5
	8	4	8	3	8	2½
	9	1	9	½	9	0
	10	2 out †	10	2 out	10	1½ out
	12	2 out	12	2 out	12	1½ out
	GENERAL LIST					
Loans	$500 or less		$500 to $2,000		$2,000 and over	
	Int.	Com.	Int.	Com.	Int.	Com.
	7	9	7	8	7	7
	8	6	8	5	8	4
	9	3	9	2	9	1
	10	0	10	1 out	10	1½ out
	12	2 out	12	2 out ‡	12	1½ out

* Changed in the official table of rates to $2,000. J. B. Watkins to G. T. Wood, Doniphan, Kans., Feb. 10, 1881.

† The portion of the local agent's commission paid by the mortgage agency from the contract rate.

‡ Two per cent out on less than $1,500, 1½ per cent out on $1,500 and over.

While attempts were being made to draft a schedule of rates, Watkins continued his efforts to bring Chew and Corbin into the combination. The former claimed that he had contracted with local agents to supply them with funds at lower rates than those proposed by the new

[30] As later approved by the association locals were to charge 2 per cent for loans under $2,000, 1½ per cent for loans above that figure. J. B. Watkins to G. T. Wood, Doniphan, Kans., Feb. 10, 1881.

association.[31] The latter refused to divulge the agreements which he had with his local agents and suggested that all business be pooled on the basis of the previous year's work.[32] Despite their recalcitrance Watkins suggested to Sweet that the rates of the Loan Agents' Association of Kansas [33] be put into effect on May 1, 1881.[34]

At the end of July, Watkins admitted to Sweet that the association's efforts to control rates had ended in failure. He charged that Sweet's own Kansas Loan and Trust Company had consistently undercut the combination rate as had other members.[35] Watkins still believed, however, that benefit might come from the efforts to unite the local agents into boards. Although the idea had not occurred to the founding fathers of the association, he pointed out that it could be of great use in purifying the loan business. Just at this time Watkins was attempting to prosecute his local agents in Mitchell County for lending on outrageous valuations. Such agents could be barred from the lending business permanently by setting up a blacklist. Watkins wrote:

> I should report to the association every man who would systematically recommend a greater loan than the land is security for. I would also report every man that made a business of stealing from borrowers, and of course report every one that entered into conspiracy with others to rob either the loaning agency or the borrowers. Let the fact be understood among locals that they will be dealt with in this way, and we shall have fewer attempts at robbery.[36]

Although for a time Watkins' staff and the officials of the Kansas Loan and Trust Company continued to chide each other for cutting rates, the Loan Agents' Association of Kansas slipped quietly into limbo. No references to it can be found in Watkins' correspondence after 1882. Although the loan agencies might unite in the future for a little discreet lobbying, the effort to fix rates was never revived. There was always at least one agency willing to cut below its competitors in order to fill a sudden surplus of orders. In addition, the major agencies

[31] J. B. Watkins to C. N. Beal, Topeka, Kans., Mar. 1, 1881.

[32] J. B. Watkins to T. B. Sweet, Mar. 3, Mar. 24, Apr. 5, 1881.

[33] J. B. Watkins to T. J. Chew, St. Joseph, Mo., Mar. 18, 1881.

[34] J. B. Watkins to T. B. Sweet, Apr. 5, 1881.

[35] *Ibid.*, July 30, 1881; J. B. Watkins and Co. to J. B. Watkins, May 25, June 15, 1881.

[36] J. B. Watkins and Co. to T. B. Sweet, Topeka, Kans., July 30, 1881.

did by no means all of the business. The state and private banks often dealt directly with a few eastern investors. Minor brokers both east and west also floated a large number of loans in the aggregate. Communities were not long established before local men had funds to loan.

In the spring of 1874 Watkins first ventured east from Lawrence in an effort to find additional customers for his securities. On his return he wrote jubilantly to Dart that he had been successful beyond his expectations and had decided to enlarge his little force by adding a real estate inspector.[37] Dart, an old acquaintance and investor, accepted the post.[38] Careful but energetic administration and a willing market brought rapid expansion in Watkins' business.

Through the 1870's the volume of his business doubled yearly.[39] In 1877 the office staff had turned out between thirty and fifty sets of papers in a month; it was turning out as many as 200 in 1880.[40] In February 1879 Watkins reviewed a record of 1,775 loans made on 272,486 acres of land over the previous eight years.[41] By September of the same year the total of loans negotiated was over 2,200.[42] In 1880 a veritable flood of investment funds struck the Lawrence office. By the following spring over $300,000 stood on Watkins' books awaiting allocation to western borrowers.[43] By 1883 Watkins had supervised the investment of some $5,000,000 in western farm mortgages.

Within six years from the date on which he added Miles Dart to his staff Watkins was employing an office force of eight at Lawrence in addition to his representatives in New York and London and a wide-flung net of local agents supervised by one or two traveling inspectors.[44] To make the most efficient use of his staff he divided it into departments. A security department supervised the work of obtaining applications and selected the ones on which loans could be made with safety. An interest department sent notices of pending interest installments to western farmers and forwarded their payments to eastern investors. In the 1870's, when foreclosures had been relatively few,

[37] J. B. Watkins to M. J. Dart, Hiawatha, Kans., July 15, 1874.

[38] J. B. Watkins to M. J. Dart, Caledonia Centre, Wis., Mar. 15, 1873.

[39] Statement of Frank Perkins in *Perkins* vs. *Watkins*, p. 117.

[40] J. B. Watkins and Co. to B. S. Stone, Mexico, N.Y., June 12, 1877; J. B. Watkins to Henry Dickinson, Mar. 15, 1880.

[41] J. B. Watkins to R. L. Cochrane, Franklin, Pa., Mar. 12, 1879.

[42] J. B. Watkins to Rev. C. H. Richmond, Saranac, N.Y., Sept. 19, 1879.

[43] J. B. Watkins to H. G. Chalkley, Oct. 14, 1881.

[44] *Perkins* vs. *Watkins*, p. 17.

Watkins contracted with various attorneys to handle his legal work.[45] In 1881, after drought in western Kansas had greatly increased litigation, Watkins hired a young attorney on a permanent basis and established a legal department. Since the activity of the legal department added a considerable landed estate to Watkins' assets he set up a land department to administer and sell the real estate. Thus, along with the bookkeeping or cashier's department, the security, interest, legal, and land departments formed the main divisions under which the business of the Lawrence office was organized.

As the volume of his business increased so did Watkins' income. In 1880 his net income was $34,000. On January 1, 1881, he listed his assets at $422,786 and his surplus above liabilities at $153,525.[46] Among his assets he listed 8,500 acres of land of which some 8,000 lay in Kansas.

Despite his rapidly increasing wealth Watkins at times found himself hampered by lack of operating funds. One of his most annoying problems as a mortgage broker was that of making the supply of investment funds match the demand for loans from western farmers. Although the intensity with which he was advertising modified the rule somewhat, funds for the most part came from the east in a fairly steady stream. The farmers of Kansas, however, did most of their long-term borrowing from September to December, when crops had been harvested and they could calculate their need for money.[47]

Watkins reasoned that if he could obtain a large supply of funds every fall with which to take up the surplus of applications he would be able to solve his problem. Mortgage papers could be drawn in his own name or that of Henry Dickinson and assigned as needed.[48] In 1878 he attempted to persuade the Farmers' Loan and Trust Company of New York to furnish the necessary capital with which to carry a large fund of mortgages. Promising that he was well able to pay a high rate of interest, Watkins wrote that he could use up to $80,000. For security he offered to give his note and assign the mortgages to the

[45] J. B. Watkins to O'Connel and Springer, Fort Dodge, Ia., Feb. 18, 1879; J. B. Watkins to E. S. Bertram, Council Grove, Kans., Mar. 23, 1882.

[46] Assets and Liabilities of J. B. Watkins, Jan. 1, 1881, in Letter Press Book No. 20 (Lawrence ser.), p. 388.

[47] J. B. Watkins to L. Atwood, Rome, N.Y., Aug. 7, 1877, to J. Y. Heald, Wilmington, Del., Oct. 11, 1879.

[48] J. B. Watkins to Henry Dickinson, Nov. 25, 1878, Feb. 22, 1879.

Trust Company as collateral, or, if the company so preferred, they might hold a mortgage on the farms which Watkins owned.[49] The officers of the trust company, however, were not interested in Watkins' proposal. In 1880 the Travelers' Insurance Company of Hartford agreed to such an arrangement, but at the last moment this corporation also decided that it had better uses for its funds.[50]

Such a shortage of operating capital had indirect effects on Watkins' business. Loan agencies that could carry a fund of mortgages on hand were able to give the investor his securities immediately. There was no need of the delay which ensued while the agency allocated the funds to a mortgagor and the documents were sent to a county seat for execution. Even when the flow of funds and the flow of applications were in harmony, this delay was unavoidable under Watkins' manner of doing business.[51] Despite the fact that he, at times, offered to pay interest on the funds while they were lying idle Watkins found that the delay prejudiced some investors against him.

Linked also to the shortage of operating capital was a problem in the management of real estate. The rapid rise in land values in the nineteenth century west assured Watkins that real estate could be a profitable investment. In his early years in Kansas he bought farms when he saw a bargain. These were added to the real estate taken to protect his investors. But such holdings did freeze his liquid funds. Large accessions by foreclosure and deeding in the early 1880's proved that this could happen to a serious degree. To aid him in carrying these lands he began the practice of writing and selling mortgages on his own property when in need of funds.[52] In theory the practice aided him to carry real estate until he could get a good price for it, but at a later period the policy proved to be a highly dangerous one.

[49] J. B. Watkins to Farmers' Loan and Trust Company, New York, N.Y., Dec. 23, 1878.

[50] J. B. Watkins to J. Y. Heald, Wilmington, Del., Oct. 11, 1879, to Henry Dickinson, New York, N.Y., Jan. 9, 1880.

[51] M. J. Dart to Henry Dickinson, July 26, 1880.

[52] J. B. Watkins to Henry Dickinson, Oct. 3, 1881.

IX

INCORPORATION AND DEBENTURES

DURING the early 1880's many of the mortgage agencies were transformed into corporations.[1] The motives underlying incorporation stemmed from the violent competition for securities in the west and for investors in the east. The agency with ample operating capital could tender the borrower his funds almost immediately and hand the investor his securities when he ordered them. As soon as a few agencies had swung over to the incorporated class with capital sufficient to enlarge their business, the other brokers were also under pressure to do likewise in order to hold their clientele in the east and their field of operations in the west. As settlers poured into the unsettled portions of the plains states in the great boom of the mid 1880's, company after company was organized until several hundred were hopefully attempting to do business.

[1] The *Annual Reports* of the Connecticut Bank Commissioners, 1888–1895, of the Massachusetts Commissioner of Foreign Mortgage Companies, 1890–1895, of the New York Superintendent of Banking relative to Foreign Mortgage, Loan, Investment, and Trust Companies, 1891–1896, and of the Vermont Inspector of Finance, 1889–1893, provide the most satisfactory statistical data on the mortgage companies as well as an analysis of their business methods.

As we have seen, the shortage of operating capital had long hampered Watkins in his efforts to expand the mortgage business at Lawrence. During the early 1880's the letters from Dickinson became increasingly plaintive as he described old customers lost and new ones unwon because he had no mortgages on hand which he could give to them immediately on order.[2] In answer to this problem in part Watkins incorporated his business in 1883 as the J. B. Watkins Land Mortgage Company.

During the first six months of 1883, however, the business of J. B. Watkins and Company had shown a profit of $42,000. A small operating capital can hardly be given as the sole reason for incorporating so prosperous a business. Additional explanation lies in another venture which Watkins initiated in 1882. In that year he began the purchase of 1,500,000 acres of land in Louisiana from the state and federal governments. Although a joint stock company which he had organized among his British investors provided part of the purchase money, the original outlay and subsequent development of the real estate drained off much of Watkins' surplus funds.

Incorporation was linked as well to the problem of the guarantee. Why back completely the mortgage securities which he sold, asked Watkins, if he could not benefit by the fact in advertising? A previous attempt to advertise a full guarantee of both interest and principal had brought embarrassing query into his financial strength. A company with a large paid-up capital could bear scrutiny on this score without fear.[3] Incorporation also allowed Watkins to separate his enterprises. Now that he had acquired title to considerable property aside from his mortgage business, a full personal guarantee could conceivably place it in jeopardy. With an incorporated company organized under the laws of a state like Colorado, which did not demand double liability of stockholders, Watkins would be responsible only to the extent of the shares that he himself held in the company.[4]

Since his entry into the mortgage business Watkins had found some investors loath to entrust their funds to a mere individual. He had endeavored to meet the difficulty by setting up a trusteeship pledged to

[2] Henry Dickinson to J. B. Watkins, Feb. 21, 1883, to J. B. Watkins and Company, July 25, 1883.

[3] Henry Dickinson to J. B. Watkins, July 23, 1883.

[4] J. B. Watkins to Rev. Dr. J. W. B. Clark, Haverhill, Mass., Oct. 11, 1883.

carry out all commitments to investors in case of his death. Now the formation of a company met the problem in a much simpler and more convenient way. Watkins might die but the company would live on.[5] When Watkins had possessed no real record to advertise, he had sought to give an impression of strength by operating under the style of J. B. Watkins and Company. Sometimes it was suggested that the use of such a title was misleading. An incorporated company removed this point of criticism.

Watkins incorporated the J. B. Watkins Land Mortgage Company under the laws of Colorado with a capitalization of $750,000. For the stock representing this sum he exchanged the 52,000 acres of land, which he then held in the northern states by foreclosure, deeding, and purchase, along with complete control of the business and office assets at Lawrence, Dallas, New York, and London. The business, Watkins claimed, represented a net income of over $77,000 annually. He quoted the statements of Jay Gould and James Gordon Bennett to prove that the value of a business with such an income should be not less than $777,000.[6] The new company *per se* still had no liquid working capital, but Watkins placed $100,000 at its disposal.

If Watkins had immediately unloaded large blocks of stock on the eastern market, the student could with justice suspect that the capitalization contained considerable water. Some of the other mortgage companies which were organized in this era were patently designed to bring the profits of promotion to their promoters. But while organizing his company, Watkins maintained that he would never sell more than a third of the stock.[7] He sent out a prospectus to selected groups of his investors but made no attempt to sell large amounts of stock to them.

To one eastern investor Watkins wrote that he wished to have as many of his patrons as possible take a few shares.[8] In this way he would interest them directly in the success of his company and hold them as investors. But no effort was made to launch a full-scale sales campaign. When Dickinson informed investors that the new company would doubtless return dividends of 15 per cent, Watkins' cashier rebuked him.[9] With only some 5 per cent of the stock sold to others, Wat-

[5] J. B. Watkins to Rev. Dr. J. L. Withrow, Boston, Mass., Oct. 11, 1883.

[6] J. B. Watkins to Rev. David Moore, Geneva, N.Y., Sept. 27, 1883.

[7] J. B. Watkins to Henry Dickinson, Oct. 11, 1883.

[8] J. B. Watkins to Rev. Dr. J. W. B. Clark, Haverhill, Mass., Oct. 11, 1883.

[9] T. H. Rudiger to Henry Dickinson, Oct. 16, 1883.

kins called off further sales and informed Dickinson in the summer of 1884 that the business of the company over the previous six months had been too successful to justify the sale of any more stock at par.[10] Profits from the business had been somewhat more than the $75,000 necessary to pay a yearly dividend of 10 per cent, and the sale of farms had brought in an additional $20,000.[11] It is possible that Watkins' need for funds became less pressing or perhaps the business recession of 1884 may have served to dampen the enthusiasm of his patrons for mortgage company stock. Certainly, however, he stopped selling stock far short of the amount which he might conceivably have sold and still retained control of the company. Eventually a few shares were sold to British investors, at their own request and at considerably above par. When Watkins completed his last sale of stock to a small group of British investors in May 1889, he had distributed but 493 shares, or less than 7 per cent of the total. Stockholders resided in ten states, the District of Columbia, and England. Although a few shares were held in Ohio, Indiana, and Michigan, the bulk of the stock, aside from Watkins' holdings, rested in the central seaboard and New England states. The largest amount was held in New York, where twenty-three stockholders owned 204 shares, and in Massachusetts, where ten individuals held eighty-four shares.

The new company formally replaced J. B. Watkins and Company on October 1, 1883.[12] Under the new arrangement, however, the business was no less under Watkins' control than formerly. The board of directors was made up almost entirely of his employees; [13] some of the directors did not even own stock for a time at least. As president Watkins received no salary.

Although he had listed a shortage of operating capital among the reasons which induced him to incorporate his business, Watkins effected the transformation in a way which brought him no more than an additional $75,000. Possibly this addition to his capital would have been ample had the business carried on as successfully through 1884 as in the preceding year. In 1884, however, business recession checked the flow of funds from the east, while his projects in Louisiana made

[10] J. B. Watkins to Henry Dickinson, July 18, 1884.
[11] J. B. Watkins to Rev. Dr. J. W. B. Clark, Haverhill, Mass., July 21, 1884.
[12] A. L. Stanton to J. W. Ellis, Iuka, Kans., Nov. 26, 1883.
[13] T. H. Rudiger to Henry Dickinson, Dec. 10, 1883.

constant demands on his capital.[14] Early in 1885 he found it necessary to borrow $25,000 to meet his obligations until investors should be more openhanded.[15] Watkins' reliance on bank credit was to be almost continuous hereafter.

During 1885 both Henry Dickinson and T. H. Rudiger, the secretary of the company, were deploring the fact that it was impossible to carry on a business in completed mortgages to a greater extent.[16] Watkins agreed that this change in technique was most desirable. With his approval Dickinson arranged to secure funds from a Connecticut banker who offered to advance money against a fund of completed mortgages. The plan, however, miscarried.[17] Watkins, himself, proposed to float an issue of bonds to the amount of $200,000 against his lands in Louisiana and to use the revenue in the mortgage business.[18] Difficulties arose, however, and the project was temporarily abandoned.

Despite the setbacks, Watkins decided in 1886 to switch over to a policy of doing business in completed mortgages. As he had suggested while planning incorporation, he did not intend merely to have mortgages on hand for sale to investors.[19] Rather, he planned to group mortgages to the extent of $100,000 together, deposit them with a reputable trust company and issue debenture bonds against them. Watkins' plan was hardly novel. A writer analyzing the mortgage security business at a slightly later date credited the Iowa Loan and Trust Company of Des Moines with issuing such debenture bonds in 1881.[20] But several years previous to that date Dickinson had noted that a couple of New York trust companies were selling securities of this kind.[21] When Watkins was establishing his business in England, a firm of British financial agents had suggested the establishment of a company to handle debenture bonds backed by western farm mortgages. By 1886 the mortgage debenture bond was used by a goodly number of the western agencies and companies.

[14] D. M. Sprankle to J. B. Watkins, Mar. 28, 1884. It was in 1884 that Watkins established the Watkins Banking Co., at Lake Charles, La.

[15] T. H. Rudiger to J. B. Watkins, Mar. 26, 1885.

[16] *Ibid.*, Feb. 24, 1885.

[17] Henry Dickinson to Lawrence office, Mar. 13, 1885.

[18] J. B. Watkins to Henry Dickinson, Aug. 18, 1885.

[19] J. B. Watkins to S. N. Rowell, Malta, N.Y., Sept. 27, 1883.

[20] D. M. Frederiksen, "Mortgage Banking in America," *Journal of Political Economy*, II (Mar. 1894), 203–234, 210.

[21] Henry Dickinson to J. B. Watkins, Jan. 5, 1878.

There were advantages to be gained from using the debenture bond aside from the greater promptness which its use would allow. In the lending field it was customary to give the borrower a range of interest rates and commission charges. There was no problem if the borrower chose to make his loan at the rate returned at the time to eastern investors. But if he elected to pay but a small commission and have his mortgage bear a higher rate of interest, the interest payments to investors had to be adjusted, with some risk of misunderstanding, or a note and second mortgage drawn to cover the additional interest. Since the original mortgage did not reach the investor under the debenture plan, the need for adjustment of interest or for a second mortgage was removed.

Most potent of all the arguments in favor of the debenture bond was the fact that irregular paper could be included among the mortgages backing the debenture series. There can be no doubt that Watkins' employees strove to see that loans were made on the best risks available. But in the face of ever-increasing competition for the best loans it was difficult to obtain enough gilt-edged paper to satisfy the demands from investors. At the same time there were forms of mortgage paper available in the west which did not fit the specifications necessary for sale to investors. Few lenders wished to loan their funds for shorter periods of time than five years, although there were farmers willing to mortgage excellent property to secure loans for shorter periods of time. In Texas the vendor's lien note was in common use. This type of paper rose out of sales in which the vendor retained a lien on the property which he sold. Such notes could be purchased in quantities in Texas and were often backed by excellent security. Usually, however, they were drawn for irregular periods of time. In addition, the attempt to sell even those running for five years in the east would have involved tedious explanation of real estate law in Texas. That such short-term paper and vendor's lien notes often returned higher rates of interest than ordinary mortgage loans because of their unusual features was obviously no argument against their use as backing for debenture bonds.

Finally the debenture plan allowed Watkins to place his own land under mortgage more easily and thereby gave him more capital for use in his varied ventures. Although the trust company would inspect the securities which were submitted as collateral for the debenture bonds, few investors would take the trouble to examine them. Watkins had long placed mortgages on his property in the northern states as he believed it necessary. Without exception such mortgages had been on improved farms. Moreover, a certain care was exercised to see that such securities were sold only to investors who would not object. The debenture form made the chances of complaint even smaller still. But now Watkins could also raise funds on his unimproved lands in Louisiana in the same way if he so desired.

To serve as trustee for his debenture bonds Watkins procured the Farmers' Loan and Trust Company of New York. Few organizations of its type had a better reputation than did this company. Under the terms of an agreement of January 1887 the trust company pledged itself to hold the securities backing the debenture bonds of the J. B. Watkins Land Mortgage Company.

As provided in the agreement, mortgage papers were submitted to the trust company in lots of convenient size. They were drawn in the name of Henry Dickinson and assigned to the Farmers' Loan and Trust Company.[22] Accompanying each mortgage and its note or bond was an attorney's certificate and the certificate of company loaning boards established at Lawrence and Dallas. The certificates described the mortgage and note and certified that they were free from irregularities in title or lending practice. Each mortgage was accompanied by the owner's description of the real estate on which it was drawn. An appraisal of the property's value by at least two disinterested parties completed the papers.[23] Once the documents had been examined and approved by the trust company, fully guaranteed five-year debenture bonds were issued against them. When the amount of securities behind a debenture series reached $100,000, the series was closed out and a new one begun. The $100,000 was to represent no more than 40 per cent of the value of the real estate on which the mortgages were drawn.[24] Under the agreement between the mortgage company and the trust company the latter was empowered to take possession of the securities behind any debenture series which remained unpaid for sixty days after maturity. In such a case the trust company would realize upon the securities and pay the debenture holders.

Once the debenture bond had been adopted, Watkins found that a

[22] J. B. Watkins to Dallas office, June 11, 1888. [23] *Ibid.*, Feb. 4, 1887.

[24] J. B. Watkins to M. J. Dart, Apr. 1, 1892.

working capital of between $300,000 and $400,000 was required to keep both Henry Dickinson and H. G. Chalkley supplied with the various denominations of bonds.[25] He urged both of them to work out arrangements with banking houses that would accept the debenture bonds in bulk, advance a large percentage of their face value, and hold them in exchange for the interest which they returned.[26] Almost immediately Chalkley succeeded in obtaining such an arrangement at Barclay and Company.[27] Somewhat later Dickinson made a similar bargain with Brown Brothers in New York.[28] Both banks set $100,000 as the upper limit for such advances.[29] Barclays' advanced £1 for each $6.00 of bonds and Brown Brothers 90 cents on the dollar.[30]

Since the early 1880's Watkins had been selling mortgages bearing 6-per-cent interest in England. In 1886 he dropped the rate of interest on American mortgage securities from 7 per cent to 6 per cent, with both principal and interest guaranteed.[31] Debenture bonds for the American market returned the same rate, but an effort was made to work the British clientele into 5-per-cent debenture bonds immediately after adopting the new form of paper. Orders, however, were accepted for 6-per-cent mortgages in both Great Britain and America until 1890. In that year Watkins decided to accept no further orders for mortgages and to deal only in debenture bonds.[32] Hardly had the decision been made when the stringency in the money market forced him to continue a policy of accepting orders for mortgages.[33] Although they found more favor in England, the debenture bonds sold readily in America as well.

It was still possible during the late 1880's to buy mortgages in the eastern market which returned 7-per-cent interest, but Watkins warned investors that the companies handling such securities were not reliable. Some twelve or fifteen years previously, he pointed out, there had been a great weeding out among the insurance companies. It would not be long before the mortgage companies underwent a similar period of stress. He wrote that the mortgage business was "the most rotten

[25] J. B. Watkins to H. G. Chalkley, Aug. 22, 1887.
[26] J. B. Watkins to Henry Dickinson, June 26, 1888.
[27] J. B. Watkins to H. G. Chalkley, Dec. 24, 1887.
[28] J. B. Watkins to Henry Dickinson, Oct. 13, 1888.
[29] J. B. Watkins to M. J. Dart, Feb. 17, 1890.
[30] J. B. Watkins to D. M. Sprankle, Oct. 10, 1888.
[31] J. B. Watkins to Edward Payne, Middletown, Conn., Oct. 9, 1886.
[32] J. B. Watkins to Lawrence office, July 8, 1890.
[33] W. F. Presby to Lawrence office, Oct. 11, 1890.

branch of business that I have any knowledge of in this country."[34]

For the benefit of investors, Watkins claimed that his decision to issue debenture bonds had been made in an effort to put his business on a conservative basis ready for the breakers ahead. He argued that the debenture bond was a sounder investment than had been the plain first mortgage bond. Where the latter had been backed by a single holding of real estate, the debenture bonds were supported by a large number of first mortgage securities. Any risk, therefore, was divided among all of the securities.

When he changed over to debentures, Watkins also evolved what he called a savings certificate. These were issued in denominations of $5.00 to $25.00. With no other backing than the promise of the J. B. Watkins Land Mortgage Company to honor them, the certificates returned approximately 4½-per-cent interest annually. They were intended to provide a stepping stone to the debenture bonds, whose smallest denomination was $300. The workingman who could only save a few dollars a week was able to put them into savings certificates which bore a higher rate than did an account at a savings bank. When his stock of savings certificates grew sufficiently large, the worker could exchange them dollar for dollar for debenture bonds.

The greater part of the securities used in the debenture business was obtained in Texas.[35] Despite permission to buy vendor's lien notes Dart soon found himself hard put to obtain sufficient paper to satisfy the demands of the business. In Texas it was the general custom to let vendor's lien notes run beyond maturity. Such notes were not outlawed for four years and the homestead law prevented renewals. In 1889 Dart suggested that he be allowed to take past-due notes for use in the debenture business. Despite the opinion of an eminent Texas jurist, who argued that such notes were entirely safe, the Farmers' Loan and Trust Company refused to accept them.[36]

As he changed his offerings to the investing public, Watkins also changed his advertising and sales methods. Before incorporation Watkins had advertised widely in the press of the eastern United States and of Great Britain, although he had occasionally suspended advertising while his staff worked off a surplus of orders. He emphasized his

[34] J. B. Watkins to H. G. Chalkley, Feb. 20, 1888.

[35] J. B. Watkins to M. J. Dart, June 28, 1888.

[36] M. J. Dart to W. F. Presby, June 12, 1889; Presby to Dart, June 27, 1889.

venture into the debenture trade by a $10,000 advertising contract which was designed to place his name before investors in the eastern United States and the British Empire. By 1888 Watkins was convinced that few additional patrons could be attracted through use of the press. If anything, the western mortgage had been advertised too well. The greatest problem in the mortgage business was no longer that of raising funds but rather of obtaining safe loans in the west. He believed that henceforth a steady flow of investment capital could be raised most cheaply by working through local agents and brokers in the east. It is doubtful, however, if Watkins ever had a great number of local representatives in the eastern states. Letters to no more than ten such men appear regularly in his correspondence for any length of time. It is perhaps exaggeration to estimate that fifty agents served him actively at various times in the east.

By September 20, 1893, the J. B. Watkins Land Mortgage Company was advertising that it had sold securities totaling $18,986,106 to 4,796 investors. The correspondence of the company suggests that steady customers made up little more than half of the 4,796 investors which it claimed. The value of securities sold, of course, included the sales made by J. B. Watkins and Co. and evidently also embraced some $5,500,000 of mortgage debenture bonds, as well as $1,500,000 of the notes of the Kansas City, Watkins and Gulf Railroad.[37] Scattered milestones along the corporation's path are shown in Table 6.

Analysis of 1,800 investors taken in alphabetical order from a register which was in use during the late 1880's showed that less than half of 1 per cent were institutional investors, 53 per cent were men, and the remainder women. Three eastern savings banks, a college in central New York, a missionary society, a denominational educational group, and one church congregation made up the institutional investor group. Watkins profited from his Quaker connections and undoubtedly a significant proportion of the individual investors were Friends. Prefixes revealed that at least 15 per cent of the men in the sample were ministers, teachers, or doctors. Many of the female investors, of course, were the wives or relatives of male investors. Some 28 per cent of the

[37] In a biographical sketch prepared by J. B. or Mrs. Watkins and published in William E. Connelley, *A Standard History of Kansas and Kansans* (Chicago, 1918), V, 2407, it was claimed that Watkins had supervised the investment of $12,000,000 in farm mortgages during his career. This figure falls far short of the total investment shown in Table 6 and evidently does not include debentures or railroad paper.

Table 6. Statistics in the history of the J. B. Watkins Land Mortgage Company.*

Date	Farms (acres) at date	Farms (value) at date	Loans negotiated to date	Value of loans to date	Investors to date	Securities outstanding at date	Surplus at date
Oct. 1883	52,000	$ 456,200	8,778 (May 1)	$5,592,150 (May 1)	—	—	—
May 21, 1886	83,867	—	—	—	—	—	$137,926
Jan. 1, 1889	—	—	17,790 (10,281 in Kansas)	12,674,616	3,204	—	423,917
Jan. 1, 1891	—	1,597,059	—	15,549,922	—	3,709,359	567,110
Jan. 1, 1892	—	1,721,039	21,411	17,254,522	4,600	4,336,961	587,974
Jan. 1, 1893	—	2,082,619	—	18,482,826	—	4,396,134	596,065
Sept. 20, 1893	—	—	22,607	18,986,106	4,796	—	597,916
Apr. 4, 1894	249,904						

* T. H. Rudiger to J. B. Watkins, May 7, 1884; J. B. Watkins to Henry Dickinson, May 21, 1886; Hutt to J. B. Watkins, Jan. 12, 1889; J. B. Watkins to Henry Dickinson, Feb. 16, 1889; J. B. Watkins to Percy Thompson, Feb. 18, 1892; J. B. Watkins to Miller and Houghton, Sept. 20, 1893; Land List given in Case 7083 (see Chapter XIV); New York, *Annual Report of the Superintendent of Banking relative to Foreign Mortgage, Loan, Investment, and Trust Companies* (1891–1894). The writer was unable to find any extended series of yearly statements of assets and liabilities.

investors in the complete sample resided in Great Britain or Ireland, with Englishmen in the overwhelming majority in this group. Most American investors were concentrated geographically in the middle and New England states. Although a list of investors—which included one of the indomitable Beechers and an English lord justice—possessed certain elements of distinction, it evidently included few individuals who were extremely wealthy. When discussing possible choices for the post of associate receiver, Watkins noted of one man that he was a millionaire. As such he was apparently an oddity among Watkins' clients. If the total number of investors at September 20, 1893, is divided into the gross sales of securities, we find that the average long-time investment per investor stood at just under $4,000. On the other hand, when the Girard Life Insurance, Annuity and Trust Company brought legal proceedings against the mortgage company in 1894, it did so on behalf of an estate which held more than $40,000 of securities obtained from the Lawrence agency.

X

LENDING IN THE NORTH, 1883-1893

WHILE the statesmen of the Republic had considered the area to the west of the Missouri as part of the Great American Desert, it had seemed the perfect spot to place the Indians living to the east. When the agitation to open the territory for settlement triumphed in the 1850's, the federal government had to extinguish the Indian title to a row of reservations stretching along the western boundary of Iowa and Missouri. For several decades the confusion which enveloped the title to land in portions of eastern Kansas and Nebraska testified to the way in which this was done.[1] In 1884 the J. B. Watkins Land Mortgage Company played a part in the final settlement of title to the Black Bob lands in Johnson County, Kansas.

Included in the various treaties which were negotiated between the United States and the Indian tribes of the Missouri Valley reservations was one of 1854, allotting a diminished reserve of 33,500 acres to a

[1] Annie Heloise Abel, "Indian Reservations in Kansas and the Extinguishment of Their Title," *Kansas Historical Collections,* VIII (1903–1904), 72–109, is an excellent treatment of this phase of land history in Kansas. See also Paul W. Gates, *Fifty Million Acres* (Ithaca, 1954), and Grant Foreman, *The Last Trek of the Indians* (Chicago, 1946).

band of Shawnees under the chief Black Bob.[2] This group lived on the reservation near Kansas City until 1861, when the depredations of the neighboring whites became so annoying that they moved to Indian Territory in the present state of Oklahoma. Hardly had the Indians left when rumor spread that the federal government was about to extinguish their title to the Kansas reservation by giving them equivalent lands elsewhere and to throw the reservation open to settlement under the pre-emption act of 1841. Squatters immediately moved in and settled on the choicest lands in the reservation.

To the consternation of the squatters a group of the Shawnees returned from Indian Territory and made individual selections on the reservation of 200 acres each. This they were entitled to do under their treaty with the federal government. The majority of these Indians immediately sold their selections to a group of land speculators in Leavenworth. The settlers saw the lands sold from under them. In a long-drawn controversy the settlers and a portion of the Indian band, who had not been willing parties to the transfer of the reservation lands to the speculators, hired attorneys who secured an act of Congress instructing the secretary of the interior to refuse to approve the sale until Congress could finally bring about an equitable settlement of the controversy. In the early 1880's the attorney general brought suit in the circuit court of the district of Kansas to clear the title. While the case was pending, the speculators and the settlers finally came to an agreement. At their request it was ratified by the court and the controversy finally settled during the spring of 1884.

Under the terms of the agreement between the settlers and the speculators the title of the latter was upheld. Settlers were entitled to deeds on the payment of $10.00 per acre in cash or in notes payable over a term of five years. If the settlers chose to buy on credit, they were to give their notes drawn at the rate of 8-per-cent interest and supported by mortgages on their farms. By the time of settlement the lands were valued at $50.00 to $60.00 per acre, lying as they did within twenty miles of Kansas City and considered to be among the most fertile in eastern Kansas.[3] Although the settlers had squatted on the lands some

[2] This account of the Black Bob lands is taken from the Olathe *Mirror-Gazette*, Apr. 3, 1884; T. H. Rudiger to E. M. Russell, Greenfield, Mass., July 30, 1884; J. B. Watkins Land Mortgage Company (E. F. S.) to Henry Dickinson, Aug. 6, 1884.

[3] T. H. Rudiger to Henry Dickinson, May 22, May 29, 1884.

twenty years previously, there were few of them who possessed the means to pay out immediately. The costs of litigation and the insecurity of their position had not encouraged them to accumulate funds. Nor did they wish to accept the credit extended to them by their adversaries. At this point they turned to the J. B. Watkins Land Mortgage Company and to other lending agencies.

After checking the title, the staff of Watkins' corporation offered to lend $50,000 at 7-per-cent interest plus a 4-per-cent cash commission to the settlers. It was agreed that the farmers of each neighborhood would come in together and act as appraisers for each other when submitting applications to a special agent sent by the mortgage company to Olathe.[4] The loans were negotiated late in May 1884. According to the local newspaper, the register of deeds and a special corps of deputies were kept busy recording deeds and making abstracts.[5] When A. L. Stanton of the Watkins company arrived in Olathe, he discovered that it would be possible to place $100,000 on the Black Bob lands. Since he did not wish to derange the finances of the company, he confined himself to lending some $60,000 and allowed the remainder to go to other agencies. The mortgages were drawn in the name of Henry Dickinson and sent east for immediate sale.[6] Peace had finally been restored to one more of the areas in Kansas where disputed titles had bred ill feeling and shiftless farming.

Early in 1884 Watkins decided to extend his lending field into the agricultural regions of Colorado. Apparently he wished to obtain applications for loans at a higher rate of interest than the company was then getting rather than merely to obtain a larger supply of applications.[7] At this time the company was placing funds in Missouri at 7-per-cent interest and a commission of 4 per cent. Local agents looked to the borrowers for their commissions. In Colorado, on the other hand, money was still being loaned at 10-per-cent interest plus commission.[8] Watkins hoped to close his agencies in Missouri and eastern Kansas if it was possible to carry on a safe business in Colorado.[9]

At Greeley, Colorado, Watkins visualized an office maintained by an inspector or two who would recruit local agents and supervise their

[4] D. M. Sprankle to John Hutchings, Olathe, Kans., May 16, 1884.
[5] Olathe *Mirror-Gazette,* May 22, 1884.
[6] T. H. Rudiger to Dallas office, May 21, June 11, 1884.
[7] D. M. Sprankle to J. B. Watkins, Mar. 28, 1884.
[8] *Ibid.,* Apr. 19, 1884. [9] *Ibid.,* Mar. 28, 1884.

efforts. The staff at Lawrence, however, was to attend to all of the clerical work.[10]

During the spring of 1884 D. M. Sprankle arrived in Colorado to establish the new inspector in his duties and was disturbed by the peculiar problems of the field. He learned that the success or failure of many farmers in Colorado hinged to a large degree on their water rights and privileges. Since the arable land controlled by one farmer was usually small, the amount of stock which he was grazing on the nonirrigable portion of his holding became of great importance as well. Sprankle suggested that the form of mortgage used in Colorado should bind these factors inseparably to the real estate security.[11]

Although work was begun at the Colorado office during the spring of 1884, the results were disappointing. In the older settlements of Colorado there were few farmers who were interested in borrowing money at rates higher than 10 per cent.[12] Higher rates were current along the newer irrigation projects, but the element of risk in lending was also much greater.[13] The territory in which loans could be made with safety proved too small to yield a large business. Finally, in the fall of 1884, Sprankle notified the Colorado inspector that work would be suspended at Greeley.[14] He believed that securities bearing rates of interest no less high than those in Colorado could be obtained in western Kansas with far less work and expense.

By 1880 J. B. Watkins had extended his lending operations in Kansas as far west as Edwards County, lying between the ninety-ninth and one-hundredth meridians. When he was forced to take over large amounts of land along the western fringe of his lending field, he withdrew to the counties of the ninety-eighth meridian. As early as April 1884 Sprankle, in the security department, argued that safe loans bearing a high rate of interest could be made on applications from western Kansas.[15] But in May 1885 Sprankle was still assuring agents that the company did not desire to extend its business beyond Harper County for the time being, concluding, "The great trouble in loaning in these new counties is, that although the land may be good security for the

[10] J. B. Watkins to Henry Diegel, Pueblo, Col., Feb. 16, 1884.
[11] W. J. Patterson to D. M. Sprankle, Apr. 14, 1884.
[12] D. M. Sprankle to J. B. Watkins, May 16, 1884. [13] *Ibid.*
[14] D. M. Sprankle to Henry Diegel, Sept. 22, 1884.
[15] T. H. Rudiger to D. M. Sprankle, Apr. 12, 1884.

money the parties have not sufficient start to enable them to pay interest. . . . We do not desire to loan for the purpose of taking the land in payment of the defaulted interest and the principal." [16]

As the need for additional applications became ever more apparent in 1885, Watkins approved an investigation of the counties in the extreme southwestern portion of Kansas. In March 1886 Sprankle reported that he had men exploring the possibility of lending in the counties of the upper Arkansas Valley, including Clark and Meade.[17] On the basis of their reports, the J. B. Watkins Land Mortgage Company moved into the counties of western Kansas lying beyond Edwards.

Under the direction of Sprankle and the field supervision of O. C. Stanton, lending operations had been extended to the Colorado boundary by the end of 1887. Despite the decision to enter the new counties of western Kansas, the company experienced sharp competition. In August 1886 the local agents in Clark County resigned, claiming that the business methods of the Lawrence agency did not allow them to compete with their rivals. Sprankle admitted to Stanton that he was

> aware that the privilege of paying the principal at any time after one year, and also that of paying over the money when the papers are signed, as is being done by other companies, is a hard thing to compete with, and we cannot understand how that can be done with any safety. It is all that we can do to keep on the safe side, and do business in our way that is by drawing the papers here and sending draft in payment of the loan with the papers.[18]

In January 1887 Sprankle admitted that officials of the company had considered allowing the local agents to write all papers and to draw on the company for the funds with which to close the loans but had concluded that the policy would not be wise. The possibility that breaking even hundreds would bring additional applications was also under discussion. Although the mortgage bonds of the company were written in even hundreds, such irregular paper could be used as backing for debentures.[19] In the end the company did nothing beyond disclaiming all control over the commissions taken by local agents after

[16] D. M. Sprankle to J. C. McCoy, Anthony, Kans., May 18, 1885.

[17] D. M. Sprankle to John Given, Mechanicsburg, O., Mar. 16, 1886, also to C. A. Fuller (no address given), Feb. 22, 1886.

[18] D. M. Sprankle to O. C. Stanton, Aug. 8, 1886.

[19] D. M. Sprankle to O. C. Stanton, to J. B. Watkins, Jan. 26, 1887.

prescribing the rates of commission and interest expected by the company and continuing an energetic attempt to recruit local agents.

In June 1887 Sprankle informed O. C. Stanton that few applications had been arriving at the office of the company and concluded:

The great trouble is the competition all over the state, not only in rates, but in the amounts which other companies are willing to loan and also the various privileges that they give or profess to give, but as you say if we cannot do a safe business we will quit, consequently you will have to use your best judgment without regards to what other companies are doing.[20]

In August Sprankle wrote: "There certainly is a line beyond which . . . land will not be sufficient security, and we think a great many of the loaning companies are already getting beyond this line, in other words they are loaning more money than the farms are sufficient security for." [21]

Lending rates in western Kansas actually varied little at this time from those which had been obtained along the western fringe of Watkins' lending field in 1881. In October 1881 farmers borrowing from Watkins in Kingman County, lying on the ninety-eighth meridian, were paying total charges amounting to slightly over 11 per cent annually.[22]

Stevens County is located on the Oklahoma border in the second tier of counties east of the Colorado boundary. Here the agent of the J. B. Watkins Land Mortgage Company was attempting to lend money at 11 per cent in March 1887.[23] Two tiers of counties to the east, in Kiowa County, the rate was 10 per cent.[24] If these agents were content with a commission of 3 per cent for their services, borrowers were obtaining funds from them at a total cost of 11 and 12 per cent per annum. Rates were dropping swiftly in southwestern Kansas during the spring and early summer of 1887, but they rallied and began to climb as the season proved to be one of drought. The total charges on the type of security desired by Watkins stood at 11 or 12 per cent per annum in the extreme southwestern corner of Kansas as the year ended.[25]

[20] D. M. Sprankle to O. C. Stanton, June 13, 1887.

[21] D. M. Sprankle to J. D. Miller, Lincoln, Kans., Aug. 5, 1887.

[22] J. B. Watkins to F. E. Gillett, Kingman, Kans., Oct. 11, 1881.

[23] D. M. Sprankle to O. C. Stanton, Scott City, Kans., Mar. 15, 1887.

[24] *Ibid.*, Garden City, Kans., Mar. 31, 1887.

[25] *Ibid.*, June 7, Oct. 19, 1887, to T. S. Moffett, Mullinville, Kans., Nov. 5, 1887, and to R. C. Carpenter, Ford, Kans., Nov. 5, 1887.

In 1887 the maximum rate obtained by the company was approximately the same as that obtained by Watkins in 1881, but it had been held up by lending on lands which were less improved and more recently settled than had been the case during the early 1880's. Such maximum rates were, of course, obtained on only a portion of the loans made by Watkins' agency. In the central third of Kansas where Populism was to develop its greatest strength,[26] the farmer with good security could obtain funds in 1886 and 1887 at 6 or 7 per cent, which with commission amounted to 8 or 9 per cent annually.[27] It is doubtlessly true that some agencies were obtaining higher rates than was the Watkins company. Sprankle instructed:

> We do not wish to place our money where the largest rates can be obtained, but where the best securities can be had, and borrowers having unquestionable security will take their loans where they can get the best rates; those having questionable security will take their loans where they can get them and this is the class of borrowers we wish to avoid.[28]

The motivation of the borrowers, the activities of the local agents, and the weather were all to play their part in the degree of success which the mortgage company experienced in western Kansas.

By and large Kansas, from Edwards County west, was opened up to settlement by farmers for the first time during the 1880's. Settlers who took claims with the intention of obtaining title and then cashing in their holdings immediately were common in newly settled areas.[29] Some years ago Professor James C. Malin used manuscript census data in an attempt to turn the spotlight of quantitative research on the behavior of farm operators in selected townships of Kansas. Had the set-

[26] Raymond C. Miller, "The Background of Populism in Kansas," *Mississippi Valley Historical Review*, XI (Mar. 1925), 467–489.

[27] See letters of D. M. Sprankle to agents in Arlington, Russell, Harper, Lincoln, Lyons, Iuka, Mankato, and Beloit, Sept. 23, 1886, setting rates of 6-per-cent interest and 6-per-cent commission to the company on loans of $500 or above, and 6-per-cent interest and 7-per-cent commission on loans of $400 and over.

[28] D. M. Sprankle to Burns and Combs, Montezuma, Kans., Nov. 18, 1887.

[29] The argument that there could be a speculative profit in land for the small holder was reiterated in the Kansas press during the late nineteenth century and can be found at least as early as Dec. 4, 1855, when the editor of the *Squatter Sovereign* (Atchison) proclaimed, "We have never known it to fail that when a claim was taken, and a cabin erected that the pre-emptor could at any time sell his rights for a handsome sum,—more than enough to pay him for his own labor. So there is a speculation to be made in lands here by those with a limited capital."

tlers been dominated solely by their desire to establish a home for themselves, the exodus of farm operators from pioneer townships should have been greatest in periods of economic depression. He found, however, little difference in the rate of turnover between periods of relative prosperity and periods of economic distress.[30] In good times settlers were seizing the opportunity to turn their bit of the national heritage into cash and to realize a profit from the rising value of land. In many cases Uncle Sam furnished the land, the settler contributed time and labor, and a mortgage company supplied operating capital from the funds of some eastern investor, church group, savings institution, or university. If drought came or the funds were exhausted before the settler found a purchaser, the mortgage company discovered that it had not made a loan but rather purchased a farm.

Undoubtedly, the local agents recruited by O. C. Stanton beyond the ninety-eighth meridian were neither better nor worse than were local agents of the company elsewhere or at other times. They were, however, presented with an unusual opportunity to pick and choose their sponsors. During 1886 and 1887 the flow of eastern and foreign capital into the western mortgage business was at its flood. Companies competed strenuously for agents. Greater powers of discretion were placed in the hands of these men than ever before. Greater opportunities for lending unhealthily large sums of money on inadequate security were also present. Although the mortgage companies had inspectors who checked the work of these local agents, it was impossible for them to examine the security behind every loan. In some cases local agents had done much poor work before the officers of the companies for which they were working realized the need for close control. If the traveling inspectors were too strict, the local representatives could easily find other companies with funds to loan, and the original sponsor would see its flow of applications diminish. That Stanton and Sprankle endeavored to keep their agents in line is undoubted; that they unconsciously were stampeded into some of the excesses of their competitors is probable. Sprankle argued in February 1888, "One year ago sub agents and borrowers run [*sic*] the loaning business in this state about to suit themselves."[31]

The weather also was to be of great importance in determining the

[30] James C. Malin, "The Turnover of Farm Population in Kansas," *Kansas Historical Quarterly,* IV (Nov. 1935), 339–372.

[31] D. M. Sprankle to J. B. Watkins, Feb. 15, 1888.

success of the company's operations in western Kansas. After a series of years in which adequate rainfall had allowed the settlers of western Kansas to produce crops of wheat and corn, the weather turned against the farmer. Eighteen eighty-seven was a year of drought. In the following year O. C. Stanton reported from Pratt County "that he could haul all the corn in his buggy that he saw in several miles driving . . . and that the people were leaving by scores." [32] Farther west the situation was even worse.

Watkins had obtained over 40,000 acres of land during the early 1880's when drought struck the pioneer counties of the ninety-eighth and ninety-ninth meridians—much of it he believed "sold" to him by petty speculators. Now the experience was to be repeated in the counties beyond Edwards. Actually, the company suspended lending in western Kansas during the spring of 1888. Various factors contributed to the decision. The unsatisfactory season of 1887 seemed ominous. But in addition, wrote Sprankle, "there is a strong probability of the Oklahoma country being opened for settlement. In which case it is our opinion that there will be a general stampede from that part and the country would be nearly depopulated." [33] Finally, there was the suspicion that many of the settlers in western Kansas had proved up their claims in irregular fashion, and the rumor that the commissioner of the general land office was about to cancel a large number of titles caused the Lawrence office staff some concern.

In April 1888 Watkins wrote to the Dallas office: "The loan business in Kansas is about played out. We are able to do but very little satisfactory business here." [34] During the previous two years Watkins had been considering extension of his business into both the Pacific northwest and other southern states in addition to Texas and Louisiana.[35] In May 1888 he informed Dart: "The loan business in this State is at an end. We will therefore have to do our entire business in the South hereafter. I am in hopes Texas and Louisiana will furnish us enough for the present and we . . . will gradually work into Arkansas, Mississippi, and portions of Alabama." [36]

In central Kansas lending was not halted completely. At Kinsley,

[32] A. L. Stanton to J. B. Watkins, Aug. 31, 1888.

[33] D. M. Sprankle to O. C. Stanton, Apr. 2, 1888.

[34] J. B. Watkins to Dallas office, Apr. 27, 1888.

[35] J. B. Watkins to M. J. Dart, Oct. 6, 1886, to D. M. Sprankle, Dec. 1, 1886, to H. G. Chalkley, Aug. 9, 1887.

[36] J. B. Watkins to M. J. Dart, May 19, 1888.

L. W. Higgins, holding the westernmost agency of the company, was allowed to lend funds on what he considered unimpeachable security in Edwards and Ford Counties during 1889. There was, too, a certain amount of business in renewals throughout the state.

There remained to the mortgage company the task of taking over title to the land secured by defaulted loans in western Kansas. In May 1888 Sprankle had informed O. C. Stanton: "By this time you no doubt can see about how these borrowers do. As soon as their loans are completed they abandon the land, if they can sell it to someone for a nominal sum above the mortgage they do so." [37] Early in 1889 he wrote, "We have not been pushing the foreclosure of our mortgages, for the reason that we desire to give the original borrowers all the opportunity that we can afford to to [*sic*] pay up their interest and hold their lands, but when we find that the original borrower has abandoned the farm we may as well foreclose." [38] Borrowers were encouraged to keep their lands where possible. When one settler offered to sell his deed to the mortgage company, he was told: "We do not pay anyone to make us a deed nor do we wish persons to deed their land to us anyway if it can be avoided. . . . Cant you pay part and square up later. . . . Better make one more effort to hold this land." [39]

Summing up in late 1891, Sprankle estimated that nine out of ten loans which had been made west of Edwards County were ending either in foreclosure or by the mortgagor deeding his land to the company.[40] In all, over 100,000 acres of land fell to the company in western Kansas. Still Sprankle maintained, "I believe that country is much better than it is credited for being. It is more on account of the class of settlers that went there than it is to climatic influences that the country did not prove a success." [41]

As drought and depression continued into the 1890's, considerable land was taken in central Kansas as well as in the western portion of the state. It became practice to offer a few dollars for the deed to mortgagors who were adjudged hopelessly in debt.[42] Yet there is no

[37] D. M. Sprankle to O. C. Stanton, May 21, 1888.

[38] D. M. Sprankle to J. F. Stone, Kirwin, Kans., Jan. 23, 1889.

[39] J. B. Watkins Land Mortgage Co. (Saxey) to Frank Coller, Kidderville, Kans., July 12, 1889.

[40] D. M. Sprankle to M. J. Dart, Aug. 8, 1891.

[41] *Ibid.*, Oct. 2, 1891.

[42] W. J. Patterson to W. M. Lauderman, Ulysses, Kans., Oct. 12, 1888; D. M. Sprankle to J. B. Watkins, Jan. 5, 1891, to J. J. Anderson, Feb. 1, 1892.

evidence that the mortgage company took the land willingly. In October 1891 Sprankle reported to Watkins:

I am and have been for the last 18 months or two years doing everything possible and making every effort to get new paper of some kind in order to prevent foreclosures. Where I can get new papers entirely, I do so. Where parties want extensions, in case of subsequent liens, or for other reasons, I grant them requiring them to pay up all arrears on present loan and a commission for the time for which the extension is to be made.[43]

When the mortgage company went into receivership in 1894, it held 116,000 acres of land in Kansas in addition to the farms lying west of Edwards County of which Watkins had assumed ownership.

Meanwhile, as they suffered continued depression and drought, many Kansans became highly critical of the transportation and marketing agencies, of the methods of public land disposal, and of the credit system. Such sentiment grew within the Farmers' Alliance and erupted openly into politics when aroused members of the Alliance and other dissident groups organized the People's Party in time to enter candidates in the acrimonious election of 1890 in Kansas. Watkins and his staff could not help but be interested in such developments, since they might have a very definite effect upon the fortunes of the company, and in turn company policy as interpreted by the agrarian radicals might well have political implications.

There was apparently no major effort made by the mortgage agencies in Kansas to hold a uniform rate after the attempt of the Kansas Loan Agents' Association in 1881. Undoubtedly, however, the loanbrokers did work together in later years in an attempt to defeat legislation of which they disapproved. In 1884 the Corbin Banking Company pointed out in a circular letter that a bill was before the House of Representatives of the United States designed to enlarge the consideration involved before a case could be brought into the federal rather than into the state courts.[44] W. J. Patterson admitted in his reply:

We with yourselves and all others in this class of business, are particularly interested in having such a bill defeated, as it becomes quite necessary for us in the protection of our interests very frequently to remove cases from the

[43] D. M. Sprankle to J. B. Watkins, Oct. 7, 1891.

[44] This amount was set at $500 in 1789. In 1883 Representative Culberson (Texas) began a campaign to have this amount increased: *Congressional Record,* 48th Congress, 1st Session, vol. 15, pt. 1, p. 118.

state to the federal courts. We presume there will be some organized and systematic effort made in this direction, and . . . [we shall] render whatever assistance we can in this direction.[45]

In 1886 one of Watkins' investors inquired nervously whether the legislature of Kansas might not levy a tax upon mortgages held by eastern investors. Patterson soothed the easterner by pointing out that there was a large and influential element engaged in the mortgage business throughout the state, whose influence would be thrown solidly against any bill levying on the investments of nonresidents.[46]

As the legislative session of 1889 opened in Kansas, numerous members of the Assembly announced that they would introduce bills dealing with the credit question. Stirred into action, the representatives of the loan companies met at Kansas City and organized. T. B. Sweet was given authority to take any steps which he thought necessary to check or amend legislation on farm credit. According to Patterson the representatives of the loan agencies generally believed that it would be easy to defeat any adverse legislation in the senate.[47] Only a Republican-sponsored amendment to the interest law was passed during the session.

By 1893 the issue of taxation was providing a basis for concerted action. By this time the mortgage companies or their receivers held large amounts of land in central and western Kansas. Since much of the land was bought in for less than the value of the judgment, personal judgments stood against many of the dispossessed debtors. The Watkins company received notice from the commissioners of Barber County that a tax had been levied on the judgments held by the company against residents of that county. Since officials were following the same practice in other counties, Patterson soon suggested to the attorneys of the Jarvis Conklin Mortgage Trust Company that the mortgage companies should work together to fight such levies. Beardsley and Gregory of Kansas City agreed with the suggestion heartily, arguing that judgments held by mortgage companies were taxable only in the companies' counties of residence. They added that some of the notices received by their company were, in effect, blackmail, since the county officers offered to refund the tax completely if the judgments

[45] W. J. Patterson to Corbin Banking Company, New York, N.Y., Nov. 22, 1884.
[46] W. J. Patterson to E. H. Perris, Albany, N.Y., Jan. 29, 1886.
[47] W. J. Patterson to J. B. Watkins, Jan. 18, 1889.

belonging to the companies were extinguished from the records.[48]

The mortgage men suspected that the lands of the mortgage companies were taxed heavily in order to lessen the burden of resident taxpayers. Sumner Whitson of the Southern Kansas Mortgage Company summed up, "We have for a long time been of the opinion that the taxes on lands in western counties, especially on lands owned by mortgage companies, are exorbitant and unreasonable; in fact, we believe that these taxes are in many cases illegal and cannot be collected."[49] Whitson pointed out that school taxes had been assessed and collected where there had been no schools maintained for three years past. Needless fire-guard taxes had also been levied and collected. These levies, Whitson claimed, had been collected and then divided up among the people of the district who used the funds to finance windmills and other improvements. Although he absolved the residents of some western counties of chicanery, he believed that such practices were widespread in many counties of western Kansas. Especially did he accuse the residents of Stevens County. In 1894 many of the mortgage companies which were still in existence or controlled by strong receivers worked together in the local districts to fight exorbitant assessments and the illegal use of tax money.[50]

As agrarian radicalism gained ground in the west during the 1880's, an increasing amount of criticism was directed at the activity of the mortgage agencies. Watkins was not completely hostile to such critics or to their proposals. When the judiciary committee of the Kansas House of Representatives submitted a bill designed to amend the collection laws of the state in 1891,[51] Watkins gave it limited approval. Perhaps, however, the provisions in it allowing foreclosure without recourse to the courts appealed to him much more than did the enlarged right of redemption which debtors were to enjoy under its provisions. In August 1891 he outlined the policy which he wished the editor of his newspaper, the Lawrence *Record*, to adopt toward the Farmers' Alliance:

> The Record should give support to the Alliance cautiously. We can afford to support the Alliance so far as their efforts are in the line of honest reform

[48] Beardsley and Gregory, Kansas City, Mo., to W. J. Patterson, July 25, 1893.
[49] Sumner Whitson, Wellington, Kans., to Lawrence office, Nov. 9, 1893.
[50] William O'Connor, Hugotan, Kans., to J. S. [*sic*] Patterson, Apr. 28, 1894.
[51] House Bill No. 540.

and no farther. We can not support anything championed by them that looks like a scheme to accomplish personal ends. We can support them in their efforts to make laws that will compel mortgage companies to treat borrowers fairly and honestly, but it is to the interest of the state to fight anything that looks like obstruction of actions or repudiation in any particular.

We should denounce anything tending to [endorse] the Sub-Treasury scheme or the government taking on burdens such as lending money to the farmers, operating railroads and telegraphs. The government has plenty to do now.[52]

In a letter to his British representative in the fall of 1891 Watkins further elaborated his opinion of the Farmers' Alliance:

The Farmers Alliance throughout this country is exerting every influence it possibly can against the mortgage business. In some respects it is doing harm and in another respect it is really beneficial. In this latter respect I have reference to the efforts the Alliance is making to get its members to pay off mortgages. Instead of making improvements, extending their operations and living extravagantly they are being urged to cancel their mortgages.[53]

Watkins' attitude toward the Alliance was obviously not one of complete opposition.

Nor did Watkins disagree completely with the Populist denunciation of the moneylender. He was prepared to admit that many of the mortgage companies were not above reproach. Indeed, as we have seen, he described the mortgage business in 1888 as "the most rotten branch of business that I have any knowledge of in this country."[54] A few days later he clarified his stand on the mortgage companies in a letter to his editor:

You sometimes go for mortgage companies generally on the ground that they are detrimental to the interests of the country. I am interested in a mortgage company and believe that it has been beneficial to the country at large. I do not care how much you go for mortgage companies in particular because I think there are many of them that are robbing both East and West and should be shown up.[55]

Watkins did not therefore defend the mortgage companies completely and was willing to let the agrarian judgment stand in part.

[52] J. B. Watkins to Col. H. M. Greene, Aug. 27, 1891.
[53] J. B. Watkins to H. G. Chalkley and Sons, London, Eng., Nov. 24, 1891.
[54] J. B. Watkins to H. G. Chalkley, London, Eng., Feb. 20, 1888.
[55] J. B. Watkins to Col. H. M. Greene, Jan. 14, 1890.

His position reflected his business interests. If his company could be sketched in colors of virginal purity against a background of sadly tarnished competitors, Watkins stood to benefit. When the Kansas legislators failed to revise the collection laws in 1891, Watkins inserted a new card in his eastern advertising media entitled "Kansas and the Alliance" which explained that eastern investors need fear neither hostile legislation nor careless supervision of their funds provided that they invested through the Lawrence agency.[56]

Early in 1891 Watkins and Sprankle discussed the possibility of again commencing an active lending business in Kansas. They decided that the time was not yet at hand. The widespread failures among the lending agencies of the state had given securities from Kansas a bad name. Watkins maintained, in addition, "There is such a large proportion of farms in the State mortgaged for more than they will bear, and a great many of these would be thrust upon us and we cannot exclude all; and to some extent we would be helping out defunct mortgage companies."[57] But also Sprankle argued that no further lending should be done until the criticism leveled by members of the Farmers' Alliance against moneylenders should die down. Again, as the summer of 1891 opened, the officers of the company discussed the future policy of the various departments with some care. At least once Watkins advised that foreclosures should be speeded up to counter the activity of the Alliance, and Patterson suggested that debtors might well be taking advantage of the company's proven leniency. As had been the case a few months earlier, the uneasiness which the credo of the agrarian radicals had aroused in the minds of eastern investors and the antipathy of Populist judges helped to convince Watkins and his staff that lending should not be expanded in Kansas for the time being.[58]

As early as 1890 investors had claimed that judges of Populist complexion allowed the attorneys of defaulting borrowers to use exaggerated tactics of delay in foreclosure cases.[59] Especially was this to be the case in Barber and Harper Counties, where Judge G. W. McKay pre-

[56] J. B. Watkins to D. M. Sprankle, May 16, 1891.

[57] J. B. Watkins to D. M. Sprankle, Mar. 18, 1891.

[58] Memorandum of D. M. Sprankle to J. B. Watkins, in late July, 1891; see also J. B. Watkins to D. M. Sprankle, Mar. 18, 1891.

[59] Editor, *American Investments,* Buffalo, N.Y. to J. B. Watkins Land Mortgage Co., Oct. 11, 1890.

sided over the sessions of the district court. In April 1892 Patterson reported his counter strategy:

> We have been baffled in our foreclosures in Barber and Harper counties for two or three years and have been utterly unable to do anything. In three or four cases which were large enough in amount I brought the suits in the . . . Federal Court after dismissing them in the state courts. . . . The same baffling tactics were attempted there by the defendants, but the . . . Circuit Court made short work of it by refusing to admit their answer as a defense at all, and not only that, but refused to give them further time to amend or take testimony, and in addition appointed a receiver to take possession of the land.[60]

The practice of transfer was not original with Patterson. Most mortgage brokers were aware that federal courts were less influenced by local prejudices and that federal judges were often better versed in the law and less tolerant of delay than those of the state courts.[61] Such advantages, however, were to an extent nullified because the federal judicial process was a more expensive one. Transferred cases made up a very small proportion of the foreclosures in any area.

[60] W. J. Patterson to J. B. Watkins, Apr. 4, 1892.

[61] C. M. Hawkes to S. N. Hawkes, Dec. 27, 1886. Hawkes Papers, Kansas State Historical Society, Topeka, Kans.

XI

TEXAS, 1883-1893

THE branch office which J. B. Watkins had established at Dallas under the management of Miles J. Dart in late 1881 expanded rapidly. By November 1887 Dart claimed to have invested over $3,000,000 in Texas real estate loans.[1] At about this time lending in Kansas was restricted to little more than renewing outstanding loans, and over the next few years the largest share of the mortgage paper handled by the mortgage company was obtained from Texas. In all, the company probably invested some $7,000,000 in Texas.[2] By November 1884 the Dallas office had a staff of six people, of whom two were stenographers. In addition, an attorney gave much of his time to checking titles. A network of some thirty local agents had been built up.[3] Eventually loans were made in at least fifty-six counties of Texas, but local agents were not active in all of them at any one time.

Dart discovered that mortgage law and lending procedure in Texas differed somewhat from that in Kansas. In Texas, as in Missouri, the

[1] M. J. Dart to G. R. Scott, Corpus Christi, Tex., Nov. 20, 1887.
[2] M. J. Dart to J. B. Watkins, Oct. 26, 1888.
[3] M. J. Dart to Henry Dickinson, Nov. 26, 1884.

deed of trust replaced the ordinary mortgage form used in Kansas and Nebraska. Under the terms of a trust deed, ownership of the property put forward as security was transferred to a third party who was empowered to sell it and to make restitution to the lender if the borrower defaulted upon his payments. In the course of Watkins' business this trustee was, of course, either Watkins or one of his employees. When borrowers defaulted on their payments, the trustee needed only to post notice that the property was to be sold as a preliminary to the sale. Most of the trust deeds used by the Watkins company stipulated that sale might be held twenty days after any default in the terms of the contract. When Watkins began business in Texas, it was not even necessary to place the notice of sale upon the door of the courthouse in the county seat of the debtor's county. Such notice could merely be posted at the courthouse in Dallas.[4] Texas possessed no stay or redemption law. It was, therefore, very simple for the moneylender to take over title to property.

Dart found a very strictly interpreted homestead law in operation in Texas. Two hundred acres of agricultural lands were reserved to every rural homesteader. The moneylender who loaned on a Texas homestead had no recourse in the courts if the debtor defaulted. To counter the provisions of the homestead law, the vendor's lien note was used extensively.[5] For instance, A might sell property to B and, in the deed which he gave to him, reserve a lien upon the property in order to guarantee payment of any purchase money which remained unpaid. The note arising from such a transaction was a vendor's lien note. A might sell this note to the mortgage company. The vendor's lien note was superior to all other claims on property with the exception of taxes. A trust deed was often written in support of a vendor's lien note in order to allow immediate sale in case of default. If the trust deed was not included in the transaction, the holder of the vendor's lien note was forced to resort to the courts for satisfaction.

Laws regulating the administration of estates in Texas differed from corresponding statutes in the northern states where Watkins had done business. In Texas the administrator had power to call in all mortgages against the property of a deceased debtor. The administrator could sell

[4] M. J. Dart to J. B. Watkins, Nov. 27, 1883; Texas, *Revised Statutes, 1879,* Title xxix, ch. 4, art. 1198, sec. 11.

[5] J. B. Watkins to Henry Dickinson, Apr. 22, 1889.

the debtor's premises subject to an existing mortgage or, if he so elected, could sell the premises and pay off the mortgage in full.[6]

In Kansas and Nebraska the county records contained a complete record of the condition of title on all property within the county. Both mortgages or liens against the property and judgments against the farm operators were recorded at the courthouse. In Texas the situation was somewhat different. Here a justice of the peace could issue an execution to a constable who might levy upon property by sale and not record the act at the courthouse. If a mortgage was given upon the property after such sale, the moneylender found himself in possession of worthless paper. Such idiosyncracies in the law of Texas put great responsibility upon the local agents of the mortgage company.[7]

As in other states, a usury law regulated the interest which creditors could demand from their debtors. During the 1880's "parties to any written contract were allowed to agree to and stipulate for any rate of interest not exceeding 12% per annum on the amount or value of the contract." [8] If a debtor could prove that interest had been exacted above the legal rate, all interest was canceled.[9] Evidence alleging usury, however, was not allowed in the trial of any case unless usury had been specifically charged and verified by the affidavit of the party wishing to avail himself of that defense.[10]

Upon his transfer to Texas, Dart applied himself energetically to building up an organization of local agents. Since the laws of Texas were more complicated than those of the northern plains states, Dart believed that it was necessary to exercise considerable care in picking such men. He wrote to Watkins, "One great thing here in the loaning business is to get good local men in the field and we must have none but those of the highest character as to *both integrity & ability.* Long residence in a community when the other qualifications are found is a good thing. Sly tricksters or 'boomers' must be avoided." [11] Again Dart wrote to his assistant, F. H. Banker, of the qualities to be sought in a prospective agent whom Banker was investigating:

[6] M. J. Dart to J. B. Watkins, Aug. 22, 1884; J. B. Watkins to Henry Dickinson, Aug. 26, 1887; Texas, *Revised Statutes, 1879,* Title xxxvii, chs. 12, 20, 22.

[7] M. J. Dart to F. H. Banker, Apr. 16, 1885, to J. B. Watkins, Apr. 22, 1885; Texas, *Revised Statutes, 1879,* Title xxxii, chs. 1–18.

[8] *Ibid.,* art. 2978.

[9] *Ibid.,* art. 2979.

[10] *Ibid.,* art. 2981; Texas, *General Laws, 1881,* ch. LV, sec. 3, amending art. 4665.

[11] M. J. Dart to J. B. Watkins, Sept. 20, 1884.

If he is a shirk, or tricky, we do not want him at all, but the fact that he is young will not hurt him any, if he amounts to anything. He says in one letter "I'll state that there has been plenty of rascality in lands through this section, but in case anything should arise to cast any suspicion whatever on the lands, I'll not send you any abstract of it!" That is of course good talk, and applies to a great deal of that western country.[12]

Wherever possible Dart attempted to obtain agents who would represent the J. B. Watkins Land Mortgage Company exclusively. This was not always possible. When one agent accidentally mixed his letters for the two companies for which he was lending, Dart wrote in protest. The agent, however, pointed out that he had a very good reason for representing another agency in addition to the Watkins company. The latter refused to deal in past-due vendor's lien notes and to purchase judgments. But there was much of this kind of paper available and the agent had found it profitable to handle it for his other principal. He assured Dart that he had always served the company from Kansas honestly and would continue to do so if given the opportunity.[13]

Watkins had not always been successful in finding honest agents in Kansas. Dart had his failures in Texas as well. In 1888 he sent a poster to Watkins which outlined the criminal career of E. T. Bunch, road agent. For some years Bunch had been one of Dart's best local correspondents. In 1887 Dart purchased a well-secured note from Bunch. When the note fell due, a year later, he discovered that there were three such notes in existence when there should have been only one. Dart concluded philosophically, "The fall of this man, in whom everybody once had confidence is depressing, yet it should have no further effect than to illustrate what may happen to a man not sustained by religion. As to its effect or influence on our business I do not consider it more than the flight of a bird."[14]

Local agents in Texas generally received a 2-per-cent commission on the loans which they negotiated for the mortgage company.[15] This rate was the same as that which the Kansas agents of the mortgage company received when their fees were paid by the company. The average loan in Texas, however, was larger in size than was the average loan in Kan-

[12] M. J. Dart to F. H. Banker, Mar. 2, 1886.

[13] Harrison and Williams, Gatesville, Tex., to Dallas office, June 21, 1888.

[14] M. J. Dart to J. B. Watkins, Nov. 19, 1888.

[15] Dallas office to Sewall Brown, Decatur, Tex., July 8, 1882.

sas by $1,000 or more. As in Kansas, the rate of commission was diminished for loans above $2,000 in size.[16] At a later date, Dart approved a 4-per-cent commission for local agents in the Texas Panhandle because they had little opportunity to negotiate a large number of loans.[17]

When Watkins transferred part of his business to Texas, his employees concentrated their attention on the farming land in the immediate vicinity of Dallas. In the fall of 1883 Watkins gave his opinion on the boundaries within which lending should be done in Texas:

It is my opinion that we *should not make loans* in Texas, west of the points where the land can be used for *agricultural* as well as grazing purposes. Should the native grass give out then we have land practically worthless. Our mistake in Kansas was making loans too far west where the climate or seasons was unreliable. We may come out these [*sic*] all right yet, but if we do, it will be owing to general advancement & improvement. We must not overlook the fact that the land was *sold* to us. While we can stand such transactions in small loans we could not well carry a few ten thousand dollar defaulted loans in Western Texas . . . our entire experience goes to show that the loans made in the oldest and best settled portions of the country, even on smaller margins, have given us the least trouble.[18]

The need for mortgage paper drove Dart to expand his field of operations beyond north central Texas. At an early date he had condemned some of the counties of eastern Texas as unsuitable for safe lending work. By 1886 one of the employees of the Texas office was using San Antonio as a base for his inspection trips. In that year Dart drew a deadline on the map of Texas excluding the southern and coastal counties of Brazoria, Matagorda, Calhoun, Refugio, Arkansas, San Patricio, Cameron, Hidalgo, Starr, Zapata, and Maverick from his field of operations. From east to west these counties stretched from Brazoria, lying east of the ninety-sixth meridian, to Maverick County, situated just west of the one-hundredth meridian. The remainder of the state, Dart believed, was safe territory in which to lend funds, with the exception of a few areas in some of the counties.[19]

While Dart extended his field into the south of Texas in the mid 1880's, he was also pushing into western Texas, including the counties of the Panhandle. In the face of widespread drought on this frontier

[16] *Ibid.* [17] M. J. Dart to D. M. Sprankle, Jan. 10, 1889.
[18] J. B. Watkins to Dallas office, Nov. 29, 1883.
[19] M. J. Dart to J. B. Watkins, Mar. 10, 1886.

during 1887 he concluded to withdraw and to do a larger amount of business in the southern portion of the state.[20] Out of this decision came a considerable number of loans on irrigated lands lying in the valleys of the Pecos and the Rio Grande del Norte.[21]

As in other plains states, there was intense speculation in land in Texas during the 1880's. It was a condition which emphasized the need for care in the lending business. In 1891 Dart described the reasons which had impelled him to cease lending in Tarrant County, of which Fort Worth was the county seat:

More than eighteen months ago [he wrote], we stopped making new loans in Tarrant County . . . because of inflated values and general demoralization. . . . What applies to the county outside of Fort Worth applies with double force to Fort Worth. Many of the principal merchants have failed, while Imboden, a leading money loaner, has been sent to the penitentiary for a term of years for forgery. One of the leading ministers of the gospel has also been sent to the penitentiary for forgery and another compelled to abandon his pulpit on account of serious family difficulties. Additions have been opened up in all directions, several miles from the center of business, and property handled at tremendously inflated values. A leading wholesale merchant was assassinated in cold blood a year or two ago by one of his clerks. . . . There are some good people there but on the whole it is a hurrah and unsubstantial town, something like Wichita, Kansas. I have no doubt but that the people there are willing to pay 12% if they can get money now.[22]

From 1882 to 1893 the difference in the rate of interest charged on real estate loans in Texas seems to have stayed at least 2 per cent above that realized in Kansas.[23] On certain varieties of mortgage paper the difference was undoubtedly greater than 2 per cent. In February 1886 vendor's lien notes in Texas were being written at 12-per-cent interest and the local agents obtained their commissions from the borrowers.[24] In

[20] *Ibid.*, Apr. 9, 1887. [21] *Ibid.*, Dec. 4, 1889. [22] *Ibid.*, July 20, 1891.

[23] M. J. Dart to G. M. Swink and Son, Estacado, Tex., Apr. 24, 1888; James O. Luby, San Diego, Tex., to Dallas office, Dec. 1, 1888; T. C. Green to J. B. Watkins, July 22, 1891; U.S. Census office, *Report on Real Estate Mortgages . . . 1890*, Table 69, p. 248, shows a smaller difference in the percentage rate:

	1880	1889	10-yr. avg.
Kansas	9.47	8.48	8.83
Texas	10.18	9.27	9.74

[24] M. J. Dart to F. H. Banker, Feb. 13, 1886.

Kansas during the same year mortgage papers were drawn to return between 8 and 9 per cent to the company. A variety of factors contributed to this discrepancy in interest rates.

The lands which lay unoccupied when Texas became a state were never contributed to the federal public domain. Although the administration of the public lands of the United States was not free from irregularities, it was less chaotic than the system of land disposal in Texas. Conflicting surveys and titles were abundant. Titles, therefore, required extremely careful investigation in Texas. The J. B. Watkins Land Mortgage Company began early a policy of forwarding a memorandum to investors which pledged merely that the title to security in Texas was unquestionably in the debtor; the abstracts were retained at Lawrence. This departure was intended in part to save postage, but it also prevented conservative investors from examining chains of title which might appeal to them much less than the simple Kansas abstracts.[25]

Texas was born in violence and the Texans seemed reluctant to forget their heritage. During the years of reconstruction lawlessness was widespread in the state. In 1883 Dart reported that fence cutting was widely prevalent in Pecos County. He alleged, however, that the governor and the better class of citizens were becoming aroused and that such troubles would be brought to an end before long. In the meantime, thought Dart, the less that was said about such "deviltry," the better.[26]

Dart found that the Texas borrower had his peculiarities. In many cases he had little grasp of business procedure. Dart wrote:

> Trying to get methods of neatness and clerical ability into the heads of Texas borrowers, is a matter we have long ago given over as a hopeless task. It is utterly impossible for you to comprehend the amount of errors in signatures, spelling, places of signatures, names, etc., which we are daily confronted with, and have to prune down in a manner as near satisfactory as we can before sending you. That we are not always successful only proves the fallibility of mankind.[27]

Nor were the borrowers of Texas always adverse to taking advantage of the laws of their commonwealth. In one such case, in 1885, a Texas farmer offered vendor's lien notes which he had received in payment for his homestead. When the company purchased the notes, the land

[25] T. H. Rudiger to Dallas office, Dec. 16, 1884.
[26] M. J. Dart to J. B. Watkins, Dec. 21, 1883.
[27] M. J. Dart to Lawrence office, Nov. 23, 1888.

was transferred back to the original owner, who claimed that the transfer had been merely a sham. The land, he argued, was his homestead and the mortgage company could not, therefore, enforce its claim.[28]

The question of competition is worth examining when rates in Texas are considered. Although the reports of the eastern state supervisors show that there were fewer companies offering securities from Texas in the northeastern states than there were agencies selling mortgages from Kansas,[29] many of the more important mortgage companies did enter Texas, including the Corbin Banking Company, the Equitable Mortgage Company, the Jarvis Conklin Mortgage Trust Company, and the Lombard Mortgage Trust Company. Dart regarded the Security, Mortgage and Trust Company of Dallas as the most dangerous competitor which he had to face. The board of this company was made up mainly of Texans and included two of the best-known insurance agents in Texas, the president of one Dallas bank, the cashier of another, two outstanding attorneys, an ex-president of the Texas and Pacific Railroad Company, and a wealthy wholesale grocer.[30] Competition among the lending agencies was keen by 1886 at least, and later the tactics of one rival in enticing away local agents led Dart to call him a "dirty dog." [31] By 1888 there was talk of combination to halt the decline in lending rates, but there was evidently no concerted action on this score.[32]

It appears evident that Texas was a more difficult field in which to work than was Kansas or Nebraska. This doubtless accounted for the fact that there were fewer companies in the field and for the discrepancy in rates between Texas and Kansas.

The Texas field differed in other characteristics from Kansas. The loans made to borrowers in Texas were considerably larger than those granted to borrowers in the northern state. Unless a loan was part of a vendor's lien transaction, a farmer must possess more than two hundred acres of land before the mortgage company would lend funds to him. This fact, plus the tendency to hold large units in the state, made loans

[28] Dallas office to M. J. Dart, Feb. 3, 1885; Dart to J. B. Watkins, Mar. 18, 1886.

[29] For example, there were ten licensed companies selling Texas securities in New York on Jan. 1, 1891, as compared to nineteen offering northern paper. New York, *Annual Report of the Superintendent of Banking relative to Foreign Mortgage, Loan, Investment and Trust Companies* (1891).

[30] M. J. Dart to D. M. Sprankle, June 10, 1889.

[31] M. J. Dart to J. B. Watkins, Mar. 23, 1887.

[32] M. E. Locke, Dallas, Tex., to M. J. Dart, June 7, 1888.

of several thousand dollars the usual thing in Texas. Whereas in Kansas an effort was made to loan no more than 40 per cent of the appraised value of a farm, Dart claimed that in Texas he must lend a higher percentage of the security's value.[33] A further variant from practice in Kansas was introduced when he began to lend on city property.[34]

The organization of an office in Dallas provided Watkins with problems in management. Orders from the English office and from the New York office and those sent directly by investors were all received at the Lawrence office. Here the orders to be filled in Texas were allocated to the Dallas office. Funds were sent to Dallas on a weekly quota basis which often lagged behind the amount of orders allocated to that office. When the mortgage company ventured into the debenture business, the technique was changed somewhat. Debenture securities were drawn in the name of a company official and then sent to Lawrence, where they were assigned to the Farmers' Loan and Trust Company. The office staff at Dallas forwarded as much debenture material as the supply of funds from Lawrence allowed. At the same time, however, some orders for the old type of mortgage bonds were being handled, and the backlog of such orders also played a part in determining the amount of funds allocated to debenture material.

Dart, in Texas, desired a relatively steady flow of funds allocated to his office. But the office staff at Lawrence occasionally cut down the size of the Texas quota of funds unexpectedly. When this occurred, Dart complained bitterly that his operations were disorganized.[35] Agents whom he had encouraged to send in applications must be put off and in disgust migrated to the service of other lending agencies. On the other hand, Watkins discovered that Dart at times carried a large balance in Texas. Such money, Watkins believed, could be used to better advantage than allowing it to stand in a Texas bank.[36] This problem of regulating the flow of funds was an outgrowth of the unevenness with which investment funds came to the company and was accentuated by the fact that the company was lending in other states than Texas. At times the difficulty was further complicated because Watkins temporarily diverted funds to his other enterprises.

[33] M. J. Dart to Lawrence office, Mar. 24, 1883.
[34] M. J. Dart to J. B. Watkins, June 25, 1883.
[35] *Ibid.*, Nov. 13, 1884.
[36] J. B. Watkins to M. J. Dart, May 11, 1888.

After a loan was completed by the mortgage company in Texas, the two offices exercised joint supervision over it. The principals of loans were generally paid in Dallas, but the interest payments of debtors in Texas were sent directly to Lawrence. When a debtor defaulted on two successive payments of interest his omission was reported to Dallas where his name was placed on a foreclosure list.[37] Confusion arose when a debtor on the foreclosure list paid his delinquent interest at Lawrence while the staff at Dallas was dunning him or preparing to sell him out.[38] Watkins suggested in 1887 that a duplicate foreclosure list be kept at Lawrence and that any changes upon it be reported to Dallas at thirty-day intervals.

A final problem in the relationship between the two offices was the character and personality of Miles J. Dart. An energetic and ambitious man, he did not take directions easily. Only from Watkins would he take advice, and as the latter's interests widened, Dart was increasingly allowed to make decisions without restraint.

At times Dart found the surveillance which the Farmers' Loan and Trust Company exercised over the securities placed in its custody almost more than he could bear. To his annoyance the officials of the trust company ruled that past-due vendor's lien notes were not suitable backing for debenture bonds. The criticism which officials of the Farmers' Loan and Trust Company leveled at irregularities in the format of securities from Texas was, in Dart's opinion, completely captious. In 1888 he wrote to Watkins:

> You have two or more times mentioned the fact that you have some securities in the vault that do not suit the Farmer's Loan and Trust Company. Getting some securities that may not pass that Co., is incident to the business and the J. B. Watkins Land Mortgage Company should expect it and prepare for it. What suits the Farmer's Loan and Trust Company one time does not suit them another, and *vice versa*. No man not gifted with the inspiration which closed with the death of John the Evangelist, can always tell just what will pass the Farmer's Loan and Trust Company.[39]

In 1886 Dart forecast to Watkins that the lending business in Texas had only some five years of profits remaining. By December 1889, however, he had revised his opinion. Prospects, he thought then, were no less favorable than they had been in 1886. Competition had increased,

[37] Lawrence office to Dallas office, Sept. 14, 1886.
[38] *Ibid.*, Sept. 9, 1887.
[39] M. J. Dart to J. B. Watkins, Oct. 26, 1888.

but the demand for funds was not showing much sign of slacking off.[40] How largely this estimate of Dart's was based on sober consideration and how largely it was based on his desire to retain a position of authority for himself in Texas, one can only guess. But apparently Dart became less careful in his administration of the business as his service in Texas lengthened. He was eager to expand his lending field into Arizona and New Mexico in 1889—a move which the more conservative Sprankle induced Watkins to veto.[41]

Dart's policy on collections is worth notice. He objected to granting extensions of time to debtors who found it impossible to make their interest payments. He wrote in January 1889 that extension agreements would tie his hands in case he found that it was necessary to begin proceedings and added, "Another objection to extensions is that it complicates the records and we desire to keep everything as simple as possible to prevent mistakes and misunderstandings. Another is that if it is the rule not to grant extensions, it prevents persons appealing to our sympathies, thus taking our time and annoying us." [42] It should be remembered, however, that lapses in the payment of interest were not reported to Dallas until some time after delinquency. At times also Dart allowed debtors extra time in which to meet their payments but refused to regularize the defaults by making formal extension agreements.[43]

An unusual type of trustee's sale grew out of the use of the vendor's lien. During the time that a vendor's lien note was in force, the property by which it was secured usually became the homestead of the debtor. If a vendor's lien note was renewed, the act was interpreted as lending upon a homestead. When a debtor who had been prompt in paying his interest notes found that he was unable to meet the principal of his note at maturity, Dart made the renewal in indirect fashion. As trustee he sold the land and had it bought in for the mortgage company. It was then immediately resold to the original debtor and vendor's lien notes taken.

Dart did not take full advantage of the stringent provisions in the trust deeds which the company used in Texas. He wrote in 1887, "We will state that not less than a dozen notices go to the borrowers after they are in default before notice of sale is posted and it is our universal cus-

[40] *Ibid.*, Nov. 23, 1889.

[41] D. M. Sprankle to J. B. Watkins, Aug. 14, 1889, to M. J. Dart, Oct. 23, 1889.

[42] M. J. Dart to Lawrence office, Jan. 28, 1889. [43] *Ibid.*

tom to send notices both to the borrower and agent when notice of sale is posted."[44]

As in Kansas, the years of depression during the early 1890's brought an ever-increasing number of defaults. In February 1893 Dart reported to Watkins: "With a considerable number of borrowers in a failing condition on hand, I got Wilkin, some weeks ago to assist me in tiding them over, and we are now trying to get new paper in lieu of the old, where the securities have depreciated and the men have become insolvent."[45] That this policy was not universally applicable is shown by the real estate holdings of the company in Texas when it went into receivership fourteen months later. The company held 116,000 acres of land in fifty-six counties. Although the corporation had holdings in Wheeler County, in the Panhandle, in Red River County in the northeast, and in Presidio County, which lies in the extreme southwestern corner of Texas, the great bulk of its land lay in a solid block of counties in north-central Texas extending from Grayson in the north to Milam in the south, and from Kaufman and Navarro in the east to Jones and Taylor on the west.[46]

In Texas as in Kansas competition led the mortgage companies to thought of co-ordinated action. Early in 1888 W. E. Locke of the Jarvis Conklin Mortgage Trust Company wrote to Dart:

> So many loan companies are now operating in Texas and new ones are coming in constantly, that the competition for business is getting very close. The percentage of profit must necessarily grow less in consequence, and the risk attending the business will increase in inverse ratio.
>
> It occurs to me that if the money lenders of this state were to meet and talk over the situation, means might be found to retard somewhat the downward progress of rates, and to lessen the danger of fraud or carelessness on the part of correspondents and abstracters.[47]

After asking Dart's advice on calling a general meeting, Locke offered to act as secretary for any organization which might be formed. No actual association, however, developed from Locke's efforts.

There is evidence of co-operation among the companies in 1890. A meeting of loan agents was held at Austin, Texas. One of the agents sub-

[44] M. J. Dart to G. R. Scott, Nov. 20, 1887.

[45] M. J. Dart to J. B. Watkins, Feb. 9, 1893.

[46] *Girard Life Insurance, Annuity and Trust Company* vs. *J. B. Watkins Land Mortgage Company,* Case 7083, filed in United States Circuit Court, District of Kansas, First Division, 1894.

[47] M. E, Locke, Dallas, Tex., to M. J. Dart, June 7, 1888.

mitted a set of resolutions on the relations between the agencies and their local representatives. He wished to eliminate the practice current among the mortgage companies of Texas under which the local agent received his commission from the mortgage company rather than from the borrower. He was unable to secure approval of his resolutions at the meeting, but later sent a copy of them to all agencies which were operating in the state. Dart could see no point in changing the existing arrangement.[48]

As in the home state of the Lawrence agency, the companies worked together in meeting the threat of unfavorable legislation. Samuel Kerr of the British and American Mortgage Company wrote to Dart in December 1890:

> The usual number of harassing measures aimed at money lenders will it appears be introduced at the coming session of the legislature. We were able, by employing parties "in the swim" to defeat or shelve many of those brought forward in previous legislatures.
>
> My own Company, . . . have agreed to give their usual subscription of $100 (or more if needed) to secure the services of a good man—or men—to watch the interests at stake and keep us advised. My friends representing other Companies have asked me to take charge of any fund subscribed as in former years and to write you asking you to aid the cause. The money will be judiciously expended and an account rendered at the close of the session showing what has been done with it. I hope you will send me your check payable to me as Treasurer of this fund, for such sum as you may see fit.[49]

A few months later Dart wrote to Watkins, "We have thus far succeeded in defeating unfriendly legislation in the committee rooms at Austin but whether we shall continue to succeed in this respect remaining [*sic*] to be seen, but I am of the opinion that we will succeed unto the end of the term." [50]

The mortgage companies, however, had not managed to keep all legislation pertaining to moneylenders off the statute books. In 1889 an act was passed which provided that all notices of trustee's sales should be posted on the courthouse door in the county in which the defaulting debtor lived.[51] A revised occupation tax law was also passed.[52] Corporations which were not organized within the state were required to file

[48] Francis Smith to Lawrence office, Dec. 24, 1890; M. J. Dart to Lawrence office, Dec. 29, 1890.

[49] Samuel Kerr, San Antonio, Tex., to M. J. Dart, Dec. 27, 1890.

[50] M. J. Dart to J. B. Watkins, Feb. 23, 1891.

[51] Texas, *General Laws, 1889*, ch. 118.

[52] *Ibid.*, ch. 32.

copies of their charter in the office of the secretary of state and to procure permits before they were allowed to transact business in Texas. The privileges of the courts of the state were denied to all corporations that disregarded the statute.[53] Obviously this act applied to more than merely the corporations which loaned money, and it was declared unconstitutional in short order.[54]

In 1891 the legislators of Texas passed one of the most controversial laws in the history of the state when they decreed that aliens would not be allowed to hold property in Texas.[55] An alien exclusion bill became law during the same year in Kansas, but the terms of the Texas statute seemed to prevent the foreign lender from even buying in land at foreclosure sale. Investors in the east as well as abroad regarded the act with foreboding.[56] A test case was introduced into the courts almost immediately and the law was declared invalid before the end of 1891.[57] When a substitute bill was passed in 1892, lenders were not in the least hampered in their operations.[58]

[53] J. W. Moore, secretary of state, to Dallas office, Apr. 29, 1889.
[54] Dallas office to Lawrence office, July 13, 1891.
[55] Texas, *General Laws, 1891,* ch. 62.
[56] J. B. Watkins to M. J. Dart, Aug. 10, 1891.
[57] J. B. Watkins to Lawrence office, Dec. 15, 1891.
[58] M. J. Dart to J. B. Watkins, July 15, 1892; Texas, *General Laws, 1892,* ch. 8.

XII

REAL ESTATE IN KANSAS

AT THE close of 1880 J. B. Watkins was holding some 8,000 acres of land in Kansas, Missouri, and Iowa which he had acquired through foreclosure and purchase. When he incorporated his business three years later, the acreage stood at 52,000. Although no more than 2 per cent of the loans negotiated during the mid 1880's ended in foreclosure, this figure represents an annual addition to the company's holdings of some twenty farms.[1] The drought years and low prices which plagued the plains states after 1887 combined to bring large amounts of land to the mortgage company. Despite sales, the corporation held some 225,000 acres of land in Texas, Kansas, Nebraska, South Dakota, and Missouri in April 1894. Over 100,000 acres more in western Kansas had been taken over by Watkins himself as a credit on claims which he held against the company.[2]

In the early years at Lawrence it is quite possible that Watkins was willing to obtain land by foreclosure. But the first large accessions of real estate by foreclosure between 1880 and 1883 apparently forced him

[1] T. H. Rudiger to Henry Dickinson, Feb. 27, 1895.

[2] J. B. Watkins to H. G. Chalkley and Sons, Feb. 9, 1894.

to change his attitude. A. L. Stanton described the policy which his employer worked out in these years. All land that could be sold without sacrifice was to be sold. Other farms were to be rented so that they might pay something toward taxes and a return on the money invested in them. Every mortgagor in default was to be visited and urged to pay up and to stay on the land.[3] Watkins' activity in Louisiana proved that he still had faith in land as a form of investment. But the cost of his southern holdings was but a few cents per acre. Land, which came into his possession by foreclosure in the northern states, usually represented an outlay of some $3.00 to $5.00 per acre.[4] Nor was such land so located that it could be administered and sold as part of a co-ordinated development project.

By 1880 A. L. Stanton was in charge of the land department at Lawrence, a position which, in Dart's opinion, required a nice combination of oiliness and mental endurance.[5] Operating through southern Kansas and stationed at Hutchison was a field man. Shortly after 1880 a second inspector was added who made Beloit his base. After 1888 these field men worked directly from the Lawrence office, and for a time in the mid 1880's they were expected to check the work of local loan agents as well as to sell and rent land. Stanton's technique was simple; he endeavored to learn as much as possible about every farm and then have it sold or rented on terms which were as favorable as possible to Watkins. He was to remain in charge of the land department long after the company had ceased doing an active mortgage business.

The farm inspectors visited real estate as soon as possible after it had been foreclosed or deeded to the mortgage agency. They submitted a written description and a map of each farm to the Lawrence office. Along with the description went an estimate of the farm's value and a note of any special characteristics which it might possess.[6] The field men kept careful watch over changes occurring in the various communities that might affect the value of real estate. When railroads were built, land values along the line invariably rose.[7] The location of a county seat near a farm was sufficient to raise appraisals also.[8] But if the farmers of a township taxed themselves heavily for local improvements, land val-

[3] A. L. Stanton to M. J. Dart, Aug. 15, 1882.

[4] A. L. Stanton to J. B. Watkins, Aug. 16, 1882.

[5] M. J. Dart to J. B. Watkins, Sept. 1, 1884.

[6] A. L. Stanton to Bruce Robinson, Hutchinson, Kans., Apr. 19, 1884.

[7] *Ibid.*, June 1, 1886.

[8] *Ibid.*, Larned, Kans., Oct. 12, 1885.

ues sometimes dropped. Bonds voted for bridges, schoolhouses, or even for constructing sugar factories, might well represent a commendable desire to improve the community, but they also involved higher taxes.[9] Inspectors were urged also to report on business conditions generally in the area which they visited, including whether or not large numbers of farmers were mortgaging their chattels.[10]

The frequency with which the inspectors visited the regions over which they had supervision depended upon the state of the land market in those regions.[11] If real estate was booming in a district, visits were frequent and values were constantly revised. At the home office Stanton used the reports of his traveling men as a basis for the price lists which he sent to real estate agents and other interested parties in both western and eastern states.

From his earliest days at Lawrence, Watkins had a firm belief that widespread advertising was an invaluable aid in selling land. As early as 1877 he had advertised "Homes in Kansas" in a number of Chicago papers and at the same time had begun to advertise his holdings in the eastern states as well.[12] An effort was made to contact real estate men in the east. Such men were encouraged to get up excursions of land seekers and to send them west. In 1879 Watkins arranged with the railroads of central Kansas to prepare excursion tickets for him. Watkins or a representative would meet land seekers at Atchison and from there escort them on what he termed a "grand circuit." From Atchison, the excursionists would travel west to Clyde, thence southwest to Junction City, Emporia, and Chanute. From Chanute they would return to Kansas City, after traveling some 460 miles through the "garden of the state." [13]

These early efforts of Watkins to have eastern agents send settlers west to prearranged meeting points were not outstandingly successful. In 1881 Stanton wrote to a real estate agent in Antrim County, Michigan:

> It seems very difficult for our agents to succeed in getting purchasers to come direct to our office. There is such an effort being made by railroad agents

[9] *Ibid.*, Dec. 5, 1885; W. W. Fulton to W. J. Patterson, Oct. 29, 1890.

[10] A. L. Stanton to Bruce Robinson, Sept. 13, 1884.

[11] *Ibid.*, Apr. 25, 1885.

[12] J. B. Watkins and Co. to N. W. Ayer and Sons, New York, N.Y., Aug. 23, 1877.

[13] J. B. Watkins and Co. to Isaac D'Isay, Fort Wayne, Ind., Oct. 31, 1879, to Northing and Huddle, Tiffin, O., Oct. 31, 1879.

and other land sharks along the line that it is almost like running the gauntlet for a man to get through, and in nine cases out of ten he is gobbled up by someone on the road. We do not wish to discourage your efforts, but these are facts, and having mentioned them, we will leave you to dispose of them. We felt at first rather sanguine as to the results of efforts that were being made by our eastern agents for the sale of our farms, but out of nearly 300, only one man has succeeded in furnishing us with a purchaser.[14]

Nevertheless Stanton was still organizing and accompanying excursions in the fall of 1882.[15] At the time Stanton could offer such excursionists a choice of more than 150 farms on terms which gave several years credit after a down payment of some $200 to $500.[16]

While in Europe during the summer of 1880, Watkins attempted to work up a market for his lands amid the citizens of the continent. In Hamburg he made contacts with representatives of the Denmark and American Line and with officials of the Guion Lines of Christiana, Norway. On his return to America he sent circulars to these companies which advertised Kansas farmlands in the Danish and Norwegian languages. Similarly Louis Scharlach and Company of Hamburg were entrusted with the task of distributing circulars in Germany. The net result of such European advertising, however, seems to have been small.[17]

The circulars formed an integral part of Watkins' advertising in the United States as well as abroad. They extolled the merits of Kansas in considerable detail. Here the skies were bluer, the children better educated, and insanity less common than in other states. In the booklets successful Kansans described the ease with which they had obtained a competence. Prospective settlers learned that government lands and railroad lands were not the only ones within the reach of men of small means. J. B. Watkins offered them improved productive farms at a price little higher than that asked for wild lands by other agencies—or at least so Watkins claimed. Down payments were small and the purchaser was allowed five years' time in which to make his deferred payments. Each

[14] A. L. Stanton to H. T. Alcott, Bellaire, Mich., Dec. 22, 1881.

[15] A. L. Stanton to Bruce Robinson, Nov. 8, 1882; T. H. Rudiger to J. B. Watkins, Nov. 28, 1882.

[16] A. L. Stanton to J. W. Corwin, Loveland, O., Jan. 12, 1882.

[17] J. B. Watkins to Morris and Co., Copenhagen, Denmark, Jan. 6, 1881, to F. Bennett, Christiana, Norway, Jan. 8, 1881, to Louis Scharlach and Co., Hamburg, Germany, Jan. 8, 1881.

circular contained a list of farms along with a detailed description and the price of each one.[18]

In 1884 A. L. Stanton prepared a circular advertising the Kansas lands of the J. B. Watkins Land Mortgage Company which were situated in the counties of Mitchell, Jewell, and Lincoln. Stanton wrote that he had three main purposes in mind when he drafted the circular.[19] First of all, he wished to head off "the mania that seems to possess so many for going to Dakota." Secondly, he hoped to direct all the purchasers possible into the counties of Jewell, Lincoln, and Mitchell. Finally, he attempted to dissuade them from taking either government or railroad land. A few such circulars were mailed to the rural post offices of eastern states such as Pennsylvania with instructions that the postmaster should hand them out to anyone who would be interested.[20]

Stanton endeavored to keep a close check on the activities of the railroads and other land companies with farm real estate for sale. If such agencies began an advertising campaign in an area where the mortgage company owned land, Stanton co-ordinated his advertising efforts with theirs.[21]

The most important figure in the mortgage company's organization for selling farms was the local real estate agent. Stanton made a special effort to keep local real estate agents supplied with lists and circulars in which the holdings of the mortgage company were given. At times an attempt was made to provide special incentives for the local agents to sell the farms of the Lawrence agency, and larger commissions were given to them if they managed to sell on particularly favorable terms.

The field men of the mortgage company were advised to make arrangements with neighboring farmers to protect the Watkins farms from depredation. Occasionally such men were able to sell farms as well. When they made sales they received a commission of from 1 per cent to 2½ per cent of the sale price or about half the commission paid to professional realtors.[22]

[18] See *Farms in Sunny Kansas* in the J. B. Watkins Papers, University of Kansas.

[19] A. L. Stanton to J. B. Watkins, Jan. 2, 1884.

[20] A. L. Stanton to Dallas office, Apr. 16, 1886.

[21] A. L. Stanton to B. McAllister, Kansas City, Mo., Sept. 29, 1883; J. B. Watkins to Lawrence office, Feb. 13, 1888.

[22] A. L. Stanton to Mills and Mace, St. John, Kans., May 19, 1885, to Bruce Robinson, Aug. 17, 1886.

Sometimes Stanton ordered cloth notices posted at each farm which the field men believed to have a good chance of sale. Buyers were directed to apply to one of the local contact men for further particulars.[23]

Occasionally circumstances decreed that special arrangements should be made in the sale of real estate. Among the farms acquired in 1881 and 1882 were some on which careless loan agents had loaned sums equal to the full market value. Where these farms could be sold, Stanton tried merely to have the buyer assume the old mortgage.[24] When foreclosed farms had in time been mortgaged either by Watkins or by the mortgage company and the securities sold or in later years used as backing for debenture bonds, an effort was made to have the buyer assume payment of the mortgage as part of the purchase price.[25] The remainder of the purchase price was taken either in cash or in the form of a note secured by a second mortgage.

Special inducements were held out to special groups at times. In 1883 Watkins offered improved farms to the agent of a Belgian colonization society. Although he could not offer a solid block of farms, he maintained that he could provide enough farms in some districts of Kansas so that the settlers would actually form a close-knit Belgian settlement. Watkins discouraged the agent from sending out settlers who had no means whatsoever, but he concluded an account of the negotiations, "We know the character of the Belgians, and are willing to furnish them land upon a very small payment—as low as $100—if they will go upon it and have a team and implements to go to work with. We are certain that they will meet their obligations. They are a thrifty class of people." [26]

Consistently Watkins and his staff attempted to discourage speculators from buying their lands. Speculators bought land only if they believed that there was a margin of profit between the cost price and the price at which they themselves could sell the land. By constant surveillance and frequent revisions of his price lists, Stanton attempted to keep his prices at a level at which only actual farmers would buy.[27]

Stanton's achievements in selling real estate during the greater part of the active life of the J. B. Watkins Land Mortgage Company are

23 *Ibid.*
24 M. J. Dart to Herman Fist, Clay Center, Kans., Nov. 15, 1882.
25 D. M. Sprankle to L. W. Higgins, Kinsley, Kans., Dec. 17, 1892.
26 J. B. Watkins to Henry Dickinson, Sept. 11, 1883.
27 A. L. Stanton to F. T. Woodard, Beloit, Kans., Apr. 18, 1885.

digested in Table 7, although the data for the year 1884 are not available. There was an active land market in the west during the mid 1880's. Stanton and his agents succeeded in selling 153 farms for $231,113 in the three years 1885–1887. Thereafter sales dropped sharply, and over nine years but 307 farms were sold for a total return of $426,262.[28] From this last figure, of course, must be deducted any commissions obtained by local real estate agents.

Table 7: Farm sales in Kansas, 1885–1893.

	Farms sold	Sales revenue
1885	43	$69,990
1886	53	77,795
1887	57	83,329
1888	14	11,475
1889	12	10,499
1890	15	13,880
1891	25	30,545
1892	49	69,470
1893	39	59,280
Totals	307	$426,263

Evidently many of the farms brought prices well above the investment in them. But the farms which were sold between 1885 and the end of 1893 numbered somewhat less than the holdings with which the company began its course. Although the cash receipts from land sales represented no small sum, sales gained upon accessions only in the mid 1880's. As depression deepened after 1888, they fell far below the number of farms acquired by the company. In 1891 D. M. Sprankle sharply criticized the sales policy which the company had followed during the mid 1880's.[29] He claimed that prices on company farms had been held to a level which retarded sales. Better, he thought, to have sold at somewhat lower prices and thereby have released frozen capital rather than to carry a large amount of real estate into a period of acute depression. Even if we discount a tendency of Sprankle to play Cassandra, there was doubtless truth in his criticism. Although Stanton was nominally

[28] This material was taken from the company land books still in the possession of Mr. Dick Williams of Lawrence. See also J. B. Watkins to Rev. Dr. J. W. B. Clark, Haverhill, Mass., July 21, 1884 and a memorandum on land sales 1888–1892, dated Aug. 1, 1892, in the J. B. Watkins Papers.

[29] D. M. Sprankle to J. B. Watkins, June 2, 1891.

in charge of the land department, Watkins exercised sufficient supervision that the sales policy should be deemed his rather than that of his employee.

Real estate accumulated charges for taxes and the interest on the capital invested in it. In 1882 Watkins instructed his staff, "Let each farm be as near self-sustaining as possible." [30] If rented, the farms not only ceased to be a drain upon operating capital, but the cultivated land did not revert to sod. Renting also helped to solve the problem of guarding improvements. In southwestern Kansas the houses on farms taken by foreclosure often disappeared.[31] When neighboring farmers wrote in to report that farmhouses were being demolished and asked to buy the remaining improvements, Stanton, through sad experience, came to suspect that the informants had themselves begun the looting to convince the mortgage agency that the improvements should be sold.[32] Where timber was growing on Watkins' farms constant surveillance was necessary to protect the wood.[33] In preventing such depredations and trespassing, the representatives whom the field men obtained among local farmers performed their greatest service to the mortgage agency.[34] Renting, however, was a better solution to the problem.

At times the field men added improvements to the farms if they believed that a new granary, a fence, or a new roof on the house would aid in attracting tenants.[35] For a time Watkins attempted to take part of the rent in improvements. In this way, he believed, the value of the farms would increase more rapidly than otherwise. The experiment, however, proved to be a failure.[36] In one way or another, tenants contrived to evade their obligations. Only in one respect were the farm inspectors successful in taking improvements instead of cash rent. They discovered that agreements could be made successfully with tenants to break out additional prairie for cultivation.[37] It was easy to measure broken land and there was little danger that tenants could misinterpret the terms of a breaking contract.

[30] J. B. Watkins to Lawrence office, Aug. 30, 1882.
[31] J. B. Watkins to Lawrence office, Dec. 28, 1882.
[32] A. L. Stanton to F. E. Gillett, Kingman, Kans., Feb. 13, 1882.
[33] J. B. Watkins and Co. to E. H. Nehlsen, Greenleaf, Kans., Aug. 21, 1877.
[34] A. L. Stanton to D. M. Sprankle, Feb. 17, 1882.
[35] J. B. Watkins to Bruce Robinson, Feb. 4, 1881.
[36] A. L. Stanton to Z. A. McComber, Kinsley, Kans., Feb. 27, 1882.
[37] A. L. Stanton to R. M. Pratt, Waushara, Kans., Mar. 7, 1882.

Contracting to receive rent in kind also proved to have disadvantages. It was a system which tenants were apt to abuse, Stanton found. He wrote to his field man in 1883:

> It appears to us that if W. H. Clements does not make a success in Pratt Co. it will not be for want of cheek. He hauled off our share of the wheat without our consent and used the money. He now sets his own time for paying us for it, his own price for hauling and asks us to pay him $5 for storing the grain, when we gave him the privilege of putting it into one of our own granaries or into his own. We presume he put it into his own granary that it might be more convenient for him to haul it away. However, if he agrees to pay by Dec. 1, and you think that it is best for us to wait on him, can you not get him to give a note for the amount, to be secured by chattel mortgage? [38]

Another farmer "allowed his sheep to gather the greater part of the corn." [39] When accounting came at the end of the season, the mortgage company received a small share of this farmer's total crop.

After experimenting with crop rent for some years, Watkins decided in 1885 to demand rent in cash if at all possible. A. L. Stanton explained the fundamental reasons for the change in a letter to one of the field men. He pointed out that it was almost impossible for the mortgage company to care for its share of the crop even when it was delivered. The company did not have crib or granary facilities. It was an "endless task" to market the crops, and by the time all expenses were paid there had been little profit left. Stanton added, however, that in some cases it would be preferable to take rent in grain rather than to allow the farms to stand idle. Here the field man was to use his own judgment. Stanton suggested that the farms should be graded and valued acre by acre as a preliminary step in calculating rent. The custom of the neighborhood would govern rental charges in part, but Stanton urged his field man to raise the rents in areas where they were exceptionally low.[40]

In renting farms Stanton leased only the improved land. If renters wished to use the unbroken prairie land on the farms for pasture, they must pay additional rent. Stanton explained that this practice of reserving the grasslands allowed him to give immediate possession of part of

[38] A. L. Stanton to Bruce Robinson, Aug. 17, 1883.
[39] *Ibid.*, Mar. 12, 1885.
[40] A. L. Stanton to F. T. Woodard, Beloit, Kans., Aug. 5, 1885.

a farm to its purchaser.[41] Where wheat was the main crop, leases ran from August 1 to July 31 in the following year.[42] Renters could take possession immediately after the first of August and have sufficient time to sow a crop of wheat for the next year. Similarly, the crop would be harvested well before August 1 and the renter could give up possession without inconvenience by the end of July. In eastern Kansas and Missouri, where corn was the standard crop, the calendar year was used, but leases specified that the crop should be harvested by November 15.[43]

At times the land department of the mortgage company furnished seed wheat to the settlers renting its land. This was not regular practice, but where a succession of dry years had so impoverished the settlers that they had no funds with which to buy seed, the mortgage company helped them. Actually such assistance in Pratt County during the early 1880's was quite profitable.[44] Settlers paid for the seed wheat by giving one half of the harvest to the mortgage agency.[45] During the mid 1880's such aid to the tenants became unnecessary.[46] But as the decade drew to a close many of the settlers beyond the ninety-eighth meridian were destitute. Again the land department advanced seed in some cases.[47]

Where tenants were notoriously reluctant to meet their obligations, it was the practice of the land department to take a chattel mortgage in support of the rental agreement. But the company did not follow a ruthless policy in demanding rents. When the settlers were hard pressed, the mortgage company extended their notes. Stanton sketched the difficulties involved in such a policy for his brother, who was on inspection tour in the field during 1888:

> A number of parties write us for an extension of time on the payment of their notes, and in most cases we presume it is a necessity with them in asking this indulgence. Of course we do not wish to encourage anything of this kind, or do we believe it is best for the parties themselves to make this extension in cases where they can possibly pay, as it only seems to encourage them to go in debt still deeper, and when the time comes around which they

[41] A. L. Stanton to O. C. Stanton, June 14, 1886.
[42] A. L. Stanton to J. E. Graham, Kirwin, Kans., July 30, 1886.
[43] A. L. Stanton to E. Cockerel, Noborne, Mo., Apr. 7, 1882.
[44] A. L. Stanton to J. B. Watkins, Aug. 31, 1888.
[45] A. L. Stanton to J. W. Ellis and Son, Iuka, Kans., July 6, 1881.
[46] A. L. Stanton to Bruce Robinson, Sept. 5, 1884.
[47] A. L. Stanton to O. C. Stanton, Aug. 31, 1888.

have fixed for payment, they are no nearer able to make it than when the promise is given. This is why some of our notes have been running for two or three years, and parties sometimes leave the country without paying. In all such cases where you can do so, we would like to have you take some adequate security from the party, so as to ensure payment on the time fixed.[48]

In 1889 Stanton tried a new departure in renting when he offered 10 per cent of all the rents which he could collect from the farms of the mortgage company in Edwards County to L. W. Higgins of Kinsley.[49] Higgins was to assume complete supervision, drawing rental agreements, carrying out all inspections, and directing any litigation which might prove necessary. A real estate agent of more than ordinary ability, Higgins had long been associated with the company as a local agent and an inspector on a part-time basis. Apparently Stanton was unable to find many representatives to whom he could offer similar arrangements.

By 1889 Stanton's field men were operating from the home office. In the fall of that year he sent out George F. Soxman on a trip through western Kansas. A letter of instruction to Soxman outlines the policy of the land department in that area during the late 1880's.[50]

Soxman was urged to arrange for cash rents wherever they could be obtained. If it was impossible to obtain cash in advance, he was to obtain a satisfactory note for the rent drawn at 10-per-cent interest. Failing this arrangement, he could rent for a share of the crop. But there were restrictions upon the crops which the mortgage company would accept. Corn, flax, castor beans, and wheat were satisfactory crops. But Stanton had learned from experience that the mortgage company received little return when the tenants grew oats, millet, or sugar cane. If a tenant wished to raise these crops, he must pay cash rent. When a tenant grew spring crops, Stanton desired that he should be obligated to sow wheat in the fall. If renters persisted in offering very low cash rents for wheat land, Stanton preferred to have the rent taken in kind, rather than in cash. If tenants would not agree to pay one-third of the wheat crop, delivered on the premises, Soxman was allowed to cut the rent to a quarter of the crop delivered on the market. This was a rather dubious concession, but it sounded well.

[48] *Ibid.*, Sept. 12, 1888.

[49] A. L. Stanton to L. W. Higgins, Kinsley, Kans., July 9, 1889.

[50] A. L. Stanton to G. F. Soxman, Nov. 22, 1889.

Soxman was instructed to take "personal" notes, where rent was to be paid at the end of the season. If it was necessary to take a chattel mortgage, Stanton warned Soxman to be sure that the crops to be mortgaged were already in the ground. The wife of the renter must sign the chattel mortgage in such cases as well as the lease. Farmers were allowed to rent land for more than one year at a time if they agreed to surrender possession at the end of any year in which the property was sold and accept fair compensation for any seeded wheat. If such tenants had placed improvements on the farms in the expectation that they could use the land for a term of years, they would be allowed to remove them or would be given fair compensation.

Soxman learned that he should pay out as little money as possible for the repair of buildings, for sinking wells, or for building fences. But when a small outlay for such accommodation would rent a farm, Stanton believed the company should make such improvements.

Stanton warned Soxman that many of the farms in southwestern Kansas had not been rented in the year 1889. Where he discovered farmers on such property, he was to treat them as trespassers unless they consented to pay rent. If they refused to settle up and refused also to vacate, Stanton gave Soxman authority to hire a local attorney and to evict them. But the local attorney was to understand that he was at all times subject to the law department of the mortgage company. When settlers in a district had been stealing or destroying buildings on company land, Soxman was urged to search out the guilty parties and to bring them to justice. A few cases, vigorously prosecuted, thought Stanton, would put a stop to such pilfering.

Finally, Soxman found that he should seek out responsible farmers in each locality and entrust the supervision of the company farms in the district to them. These men could hardly be trusted to draw up rental agreements, but they could carry out any supervision which was necessary. Where Soxman found a farm which as yet had not been placed on the sale lists of the company or was still in the process of foreclosure, Stanton asked that he forward sketches and an appraisal of the farm's value.

A special problem of the early 1890's was that of breaking the land on the newly acquired farms in western Kansas. For the most part the settlers had occupied the farms but a few years before they gave them up to the mortgage company. There was often only enough land in cultivation to convince the officials of the local land office that the requirements of settlement had been fulfilled. Seth Humphrey, traveling as a mortgage company inspector through western Nebraska and Dakota Territory during the same period, tells of farm after farm on which only some five or ten acres of land had been brought under the plow.[51] To render the farms of the J. B. Watkins Land Mortgage Company in western Kansas more salable, Stanton attempted to break out more land. Some of the mortgage companies paid cash for such work, but Stanton sought to make more profitable arrangements. Where other companies gave complete use of the newly broken land to the farmers who broke it out or even paid $1.50 to $1.75 cash per acre, Stanton offered four-fifths of the first crop on freshly broken land. This, he argued, was equivalent to a cash payment of $1.50 per acre.[52]

How successful was the mortgage company in realizing an income from rents? During the mid 1880's a high proportion of the farms in Kansas were rented. Rents in central Kansas stood at some $2.00 an acre for broken land by the early 1890's.[53] But few of the company farms could have returned an income of more than $150 per year. Much of the land acquired in the western third of Kansas after 1888 stood unrented until the receivership of the company in 1894. In these years it was difficult to obtain renters. The turnover among farm operators was always high in frontier areas, and in times of depression there was no inflow of population to balance the outflow. Many of the settlers in western Kansas trekked back over the ninety-eighth meridian to their "wives' folks." Others moved on to join in the Oklahoma runs. In large portions of western Kansas and Nebraska there was partial depopulation. On a trip through Clark, Meade, Seward, Stevens, Morton, Stanton, Grant, and Gray Counties in the summer of 1892, L. W. Higgins reported to Stanton that there were not enough settlers in the country to farm the land which had been put in cultivation during the boom.[54] Even so, Stanton later reported that the farms of the mortgage company, administered from Lawrence, produced a rental of $34,000 in 1892 and $14,200 in the following year.[55] This revenue was derived for the most part from the farms in central Kansas. When it is remem-

[51] S. K. Humphrey, *Following the Prairie Frontier* (Minneapolis, 1931), p. 104.
[52] A. L. Stanton to P. A. Hallowell, Belleville, Kans., Mar. 4, 1892.
[53] A. L. Stanton to F. P. Hill, Stockton, Kans., Apr. 20, 1892.
[54] A. L. Stanton to J. B. Watkins, July 5, 1892.
[55] *Ibid.*, June 25, 1894.

bered that the total tax bill of the company in Kansas was over $30,000 during those same years,[56] it becomes apparent that the rents derived from the company's real estate brought little return on invested capital, at least in times of depression. Rents, however, did help materially in meeting the tax bill.

The activities of the agrarian radicals influenced the policy of the land department to some extent. In Morton County the Watkins agency was confronted with something perilously close to a tenant strike as the farmers renting the lands of the loan companies became unwilling to pay their rent. Finally A. L. Stanton of the land department decided to invoke the courts and sent instructions to a local attorney:

> We understand that there is a very strong feeling with your people, against paying rents to loan companies for use of their lands. While we are not disposed to be exacting, much less exorbitant, in the amount of rent which we claim from parties who farm our lands, yet we do not consider it either good business policy for ourselves, nor to the interests of a community, to allow our lands to be farmed unless we can get something out of them in the way of rents. In conducting these cases, we want it understood that we wish to deal with these people in a way to preserve good feelings as far as practicable, and we wish to bring them to see that we are asking nothing more than what is reasonable and right in the matter of rents.[57]

In response to the demands of their constituents the legislators of 1893 passed a redemption law allowing the debtor eighteen months in which to redeem his land after foreclosure sale. The delay which this act would cause in regaining title when purchasers defaulted on terms along with the discrimination which the company met in the courts caused Sprankle to write:

> Stanton and myself have decided that we will not be justified in parting with the title to our farms unless we receive as the min [*sic*] amount one-fourth the purchase price in cash where the consideration is $1,000 or upwards. . . . Our law dep [*sic*] insisted after the passage of the recent act that we should have one-half cash in all sales, but a ruling of this kind would debar us from selling much land.[58]

[56] M. J. Dart to J. B. Watkins, June 29, 1893.
[57] A. L. Stanton to G. Porter Craddock, Richfield, Kans., July 9, 1892.
[58] D. M. Sprankle to J. B. Watkins, May 8, 1893.

XIII

EASTERN REGULATION

WHILE the real estate fever of the 1880's held the west in its invigorating grip, the western farm mortgage reached great heights of popularity among eastern investors. Businessmen who had utterly no conception of western land values or of the risks involved in the mortgage business eagerly pressed their funds on the mortgage broker.[1] Guaranteed mortgages were purchased with but little attempt to check on the standing of the companies which made the guarantee. In testimony to the gullibility of investors stood Perkins' Western Farm Mortgage Company of Lawrence.[2] Although the unusual manner in which this company had been organized was well publicized, its officers were able to obtain sufficient business to keep it out of receivership for eleven years. Nor was it the only one using doubtful business methods. As L. D. Richards, the president of a Nebraska loan company, remarked piously of a rival agency, "If the truth was known, it was conceived in

[1] Read, for instance, the Backus Papers, Yale University Library, New Haven, Conn. Cited by permission of the Yale University Library.

[2] See above, Chapter 7.

fraud."[3] There were other companies of which the same could be said.

As the decade of the 1880's drew to a close, the knowledge spread that the western farm mortgage was not a completely fool-proof investment. Actually, it had never been free from some criticism. During the 1870's Watkins had believed it necessary to combat the activities of critics by explaining the failure of the loan agent from Illinois, Corydon Weed, in a circular and by sending letters to the press. The eastern promoter who saw investment capital flowing westward beyond his reach, the eastern observer who distrusted the rapidity with which land values were rising in the west,[4] and the investor who had been unfortunate in his choice of a western agent were all willing and eager to stress the danger in western mortgages.

In the mid 1880's J. B. Watkins himself contributed to the distrust which western mortgage brokers encountered in some quarters. He pointed out that the business was a corrupt one and long since ready for the weeding out which the insurance companies had undergone a decade previously.[5] By 1887 the Western Farm Mortgage Company of Lawrence had worked itself by reckless, if not corrupt, methods into a position where it owed considerable sums to both eastern investors and western borrowers.[6] Well remembering that this company had been founded through the treachery of a former employee, Watkins set himself to render a *coup de grâce.* He bombarded both western and eastern newspapers with accounts of the company's origin and manner of business.[7] Although the company was saved by a union of Watkins' enemies in Lawrence and some of the eastern stockholders who reorganized it as the Western Farm Mortgage Trust Company,[8] the pub-

[3] L. D. Richards, Fremont, Neb., to John and Ira Davenport, Dec. 21, 1891, Davenport Collection, Collection of Regional History, Cornell University, Ithaca, N.Y.

[4] See, for instance, Frank Wilkeson in New York *Times,* Dec. 27, 1887, Jan. 23, Feb. 6, and Feb. 11, 1888.

[5] J. B. Watkins to C. H. Robertson, Grand Forks, D.T., July 12, 1887, to J. A. Bennet, New York, N.Y., May 18, 1888.

[6] J. B. Watkins to R. J. Waddell, Ottawa, Kans., July 13, 1887, to H. G. Chalkley, Dec. 6, Dec. 27, 1887; R. J. Waddell to J. B. Watkins, July 15, 1887; Henry Dickinson to J. B. Watkins, Nov. 28, 1887.

[7] J. B. Watkins to Tri-State Association Press, Kansas City, Mo., Nov. 25, 1887, to Albany *Argus,* Nov. 21, 1887.

[8] H. F. Dow, Syracuse, N.Y., to J. B. Watkins, Nov. 8, 1887; J. B. Watkins Land Mortgage Co. (Miller) to G. W. Hare, Philadelphia, Pa., Nov. 28, 1887; J. B. Watkins to D. A. Hunter, Philadelphia, Pa., July 10, 1889.

licity served in part, at least, to discredit all mortgage companies.

Finally, the governments of the eastern seaboard states began to take an interest in the affairs of the western mortgage companies. The fiscal officers of these states saw the citizens of their commonwealths investing large sums of money through financial institutions over which they had no supervision. The investors of Massachusetts alone were sending between $8,000,000 and $12,000,000 westward annually during the mid 1880's.[9] The investors of New York and Connecticut were but little behind in the amount of similar investments.[10]

In 1887 the legislators of Connecticut initiated state regulation by requiring the mortgage companies to submit semiannual business statements to the banking commissioners of the state.[11] These officials made the statements public in their annual departmental reports. Investors could now examine the records of the mortgage companies and restrict their business to those which appeared to be in the strongest financial position. In the following year Vermont followed the lead of Connecticut and passed an almost identical statute.[12] In 1889 a somewhat more complicated law was placed on the statute books of Massachusetts.[13] Finally, in 1890, the state of New York passed the most comprehensive of the laws designed to regulate the business done by the mortgage companies.[14]

Under the authority of this law, the superintendent of the banking department of the state obtained supervisory authority over all of the mortgage loan, investment, and trust companies doing business in New York and organized under the laws of other states. If they disregarded the law, companies were liable to a fine of $1,000. The superintendent, or his proxy, was empowered to make an annual examination of the companies. In addition, the companies were required to submit semiannual reports to the banking department.

If the superintendent decided that the business affairs of a company were in sound condition, he issued a license which allowed the cor-

[9] Massachusetts, *Annual Report of the Commissioner of Foreign Mortgage Companies* (1890), p. 6.

[10] If the investments of the Hartford insurance companies were included, Connecticut would undoubtedly have led the other two states, since these corporations alone were sending several times the Massachusetts figure west annually.

[11] Connecticut, *General Statutes, 1888,* ch. CXIII, secs. 1853–1857.

[12] Vermont, *Public Acts, 1888,* No. 16.

[13] Massachusetts, *Acts, 1889,* ch. 427.

[14] New York, *Laws, 1890,* ch. 506.

poration to do business within the state for one year. Within thirty days after licensing, company officers were required to submit a list of the agents who handled their securities in the state. By proper resolution the company appointed the superintendent of banking to be their attorney, empowered to receive service of legal proceedings brought by any resident of the state against their corporation with the same effect as if the company itself was so served.

If the superintendent decided that a licensed company was carrying on a reckless business, he could order the officials of the company to desist from their reckless practices on the pain of losing their license. When the New York official decided to revoke a license, he informed the home office of the licensee, all agents serving the company within the state, and he might also, at his discretion, publish the reasons for his action in the official paper of the state at Albany.

In the year ending on October 1, 1891, the superintendent of banking in New York directed the examination of fifty-seven companies. The officers of eighteen were unable to prove that they were doing a safe business. Accordingly, the superintendent refused to grant licenses to them. Permits were issued to the remaining thirty-nine. Some $3,350,000 of the capital stock in these thirty-nine companies was held by New Yorkers. The licensed companies listed nearly 800 agents in the state and had sold almost $6,500,000 of mortgages and debentures to investors of the commonwealth during the previous year.[15]

From the annual reports of the eastern fiscal officials and from their letters in answer to the inquiries of investors, the businessmen of the northern seaboard states learned that there were some irregularities at least in the operations of the western farm mortgage companies.[16]

The state examiners found irregularities in the way in which debenture bonds were issued by some companies. Occasionally they found the trustee, who was custodian of the mortgage securities against which the debentures were issued, to be an officer or stockholder of the company selling the debentures. Nor did the trustees guarantee the

[15] New York, *Annual Report of the Superintendent of Banking relative to Foreign Mortgage, Loan, Investment and Trust Companies* (1891), p. 8.

[16] The following account is based on the *Annual Reports* of the Connecticut Bank Commissioners (1888–1895), of the Massachusetts Commissioner of Foreign Mortgage Companies (1890–1895), of the New York Superintendent of Banking relative to Foreign Mortgage, Loan, Investment, and Trust Companies (1891–1896), and of the Vermont Inspector of Finance (1889–1893).

quality of the securities behind the debenture series, but instead merely certified that they were of the same face value as the debenture bonds issued against them. Sometimes the securities backing the debentures were not assigned to the trustee. At times company officers removed mortgages from the possession of the trustee in order to foreclose them and did not replace them, thereby leaving less than 100-per-cent backing behind the bonds. One company was found to have deposited its entire capital stock as a base for debentures. This procedure, as the inspecting officer pointed out, was merely an attempt to secure the payment of one obligation by pledging another. At times, also, examiners found debentures issued against very irregular securities. Tax certificates and second mortgages occasionally were placed behind debentures, and an examiner discovered one company which had included past-due interest coupons in its supporting paper.

To remedy such digressions from sound financing, the eastern supervisors suggested that trustees should be sound financial institutions in all cases, rather than individuals. They suggested also that such trustees should carefully scrutinize the securities which were deposited with them. The New York superintendent of banking believed that debentures should be backed by mortgages showing a total of 125 per cent of the face value of the bonds. Mortgages could then be drawn out for foreclosure without reducing the backing of the debentures below face value. Such a policy would, in addition, leave a margin to cover any loss from litigation or from imperfect securities.

The inspectors also discovered imperfections in the ordinary mortgage business of the companies. At one time the companies had, with few exceptions, advertised their offerings as farm mortgages. The examiners, however, discovered that some of the companies were lending on city property in the little boom towns of western Kansas, Nebraska, and other plains states. In other cases the examiners found that the mortgages handled by the loan companies were not really mortgages on improved farm property, but were instead backed by land which the mortgage companies or their officers owned. Even when the loans were made to bonafide farmers, inspectors believed that some companies had loaned excessive amounts on poor security.

Examining officers reported that some loan companies paid taxes for mortgagors and much later forced mortgagees to redeem the tax certificates at the high rate of redemption called for by the laws of western states. At times, too, the mortgage companies foreclosed second, or commission, mortgages, thereby taking possession of the security while the mortgagee held his first mortgage undisturbed. Examiners of the eastern states reported that the claim of the first mortgagor was thereby cut off. Actually, such foreclosures did not have this effect. Sometimes the agents of the mortgage companies did not record the assignment of mortgages to eastern investors but left them standing on the county books in the name of the mortgage companies. It was argued, therefore, that mortgagees could not foreclose such loans themselves, but must obtain recourse, if necessary, through the mortgage companies. This charge was also founded on a misunderstanding of real estate law, since easterners were possessed of the documents necessary to record their own assignments if they so desired.

The inspectors reported that the financial administration of some companies was reckless. They suggested that companies were paying dividends at a higher rate than prudence would advise. It was pointed out that the large dividends came in part from the practice common among the companies of reckoning profits on the basis of commission notes secured by second mortgages. Actually, these notes should have been included as income only as they were paid in cash. One company which collapsed in the middle of 1890 had paid a dividend on its capital stock of 40 per cent during the previous year. Sometimes company officials handed out capital stock recklessly to investors to encourage investment in the company. The manager of one lending corporation issued certificates of capital stock to himself which he promptly deposited as collateral for personal loans. Some of the companies were engaged in other enterprises little related to the mortgage business or carrying on an extensive brokerage business in the stocks and bonds of western municipalities and development projects.

The eastern examiners found much fault with the manner in which the companies administered their real estate. As the 1880's drew to a close, the amount of such holdings rose at an alarming rate. Sometimes the mortgage companies hid the amount of land which they had taken by forming a subsidiary real estate company. Then the capital stock of this company was placed in the stock and bonds account of the mortgage company when statements were submitted to the eastern state authorities. The lands of the subsidiary company were remortgaged as soon as they were obtained and the mortgages placed behind debenture issues.

The administrative officers of some companies drew high salaries. The commissioner of foreign mortgage companies of Massachusetts described other companies that "pay large salaries to their officers and small dividends to their dupes."[17] In a few cases there was outright chicanery and the officers absconded with company funds.

As depression deepened in the west, the debtor class became vociferous in its demand for relaxation of the collection laws. Much of the interest in the legislature of 1891 in Kansas centered on the attempt to pass a redemption law. In that same year an alien law was passed in Texas which was so worded that a foreigner who loaned money in Texas was unable to bid in the land securing his loan at foreclosure sale.[18] A justice of the supreme court of Nebraska was widely quoted when he supposedly promised that he would not approve foreclosures which were the result of crop failure.[19] Finally, in 1893, a new redemption law was passed in Kansas.[20] The supervisory officials of the eastern states helped to keep their investors fully informed of the achievements of "those who would persuade the farmers of the West that it is their right, and for their interest, to cheat their creditors in the East."[21]

Without access to the examiners' reports on which were based the published reports of the supervisory officials, it is impossible to calculate the frequency with which they discovered the abuses sketched here. Some of the criticism was patently ill founded, and other practices, stigmatized by the examiners, need not have been fatal to the well-being of the companies, but obviously the investigations of examiners from New York, Massachusetts, and Connecticut did reveal grave abuses. It is wrong to assume, however, that the failure of most of the western mortgage companies during the early 1890's proves that they were all corrupt or recklessly administered. It is very probable that the officers of many companies which failed during the years between 1889 and 1894 were guilty of no greater sin than overoptimism.

Yet if the examiners from the eastern states exposed the transgressions of the mortgage companies, they were not completely unsympa-

[17] Massachusetts, *op. cit.*, 1892, p. vii.
[18] Texas, *Laws, 1891*, ch. 62.
[19] New York, *op. cit.*, 1891, p. 21.
[20] Kansas, *Laws, 1893*, ch. 109.
[21] Massachusetts, *op. cit.*, 1892, p. v.

thetic toward them. One official pointed out that the business had expanded very rapidly. It was hardly surprising that some unorthodox practices and unreliable companies should be discovered. The reports of the loan company inspectors did, however, disabuse investors of the idea that they had found a kind of mother lode among investments in the western mortgage which demanded but little care or supervision and yielded superlative returns. As the 1890's opened, the investors of the east were scrutinizing the claims of the mortgage companies with a new carefulness.

XIV

RECEIVERSHIP

IN AUGUST 1893 the J. B. Watkins Land Mortgage Company suspended payment on the principal of its obligations then due. On April 5, 1894, the company was placed in receivership.[1] It is not difficult to sketch the factors which contributed to the failure of the mortgage company, but it is less easy to assign the proper weight to these contributing causes.

There were elements of weakness in the original organization of the company. Watkins subscribed a capital of $750,000 in return for which he took over the complete issue of stock and then sold a portion of it to investors. The $750,000 was made up as follows:

315 farms (52,000 acres)	valued at	$456,200.00
Business and franchise	" "	291,109.47
Office fixtures and furniture	" "	2,690.53
Total		$750,000.00

[1] *Girard Life Insurance, Annuity and Trust Company* vs. *J. B. Watkins Land Mortgage Company*, Case 7083, filed in United States Circuit Court, District of Kansas, First Division, 1894.

On the date of the incorporation the real estate advanced to the company was encumbered by mortgages totaling $155,500. Watkins assumed payment of this sum, and adding it to the business franchise and fixtures, he calculated that $449,300 of the capitalization had been subscribed in cash.[2] Possibly Watkins did not overvalue the assets which he placed in the company, but the item of cash was a polite fiction. Had he not deposited $100,000 with the company, it would have had no cash with which to begin business. As time passed, the supply of funds used in the mortgage business was enlarged, but much of it was obtained by borrowing, as in the case of the arrangements with Brown Brothers and with Barclay and Company or of the short-term loans from banks in Kansas City, New Orleans, and New York for six months' time or less. From the beginning, therefore, the J. B. Watkins Land Mortgage Company was compelled to earn interest on much of its working funds before it could return dividends to its stockholders.

Down to 1891 the mortgage company returned a dividend of 10 per cent per annum to its shareholders and had accumulated a surplus of some $450,000. But this surplus was not a liquid one. Despite sales, the amount of land held by the mortgage company steadily mounted. Totaling 52,000 acres at the date of the company's organization, the land holdings of Watkins' company stood at almost 86,000 acres by May 1886. Over the next two years sales gained on accessions, but the company's real estate increased rapidly in amount after 1888. Such land was not carried at the value of the loan and the costs of foreclosure and taxes, but was marked up to its current market value when obtained. During the mid 1880's land values rose swiftly in Kansas. The company sometimes revalued its real estate every six months.[3] It was not an increase in the operating funds of the company which pushed up the surplus during the 1880's but rather the accessions of land and the method of revaluation. As long as land values continued to rise and there was no call to turn the land into immediate cash, the company was not endangered by the practice. Such a surplus could be of little use, however, if land values in the plains states were to take a sudden turn downward or the company was forced to meet sudden demands for cash.

During the 1880's Watkins became interested in an increasing number

[2] T. C. Green to J. B. Watkins, Oct. 23, 1891.

[3] T. H. Rudiger to J. B. Watkins, July 9, 1885; J. B. Watkins to Henry Dickinson, Mar. 30, 1889.

of enterprises in addition to the mortgage company. Early in the decade he obtained a controlling interest in the Lawrence Canning Company. In 1887 he established the Watkins National Bank at Lawrence with a capital of $250,000. Watkins was president and held approximately one-fifth of the stock in this institution. In 1889 he obtained ownership of the Lawrence *Record*—an independent Republican newspaper.

But Watkins' greatest interest came to lie in the south. In 1882 he combined with English investors to organize the North American Land and Timber Company, which purchased some 900,000 acres of land in the southwestern portion of Louisiana. In this company he served as American manager, and he himself held one-third of the stock. At the same time he bought some 600,000 acres of adjacent lands for himself. Much of this 1,500,000-acre purchase was swampland which had been granted by the federal government to the state; the price paid by Watkins was an extremely low one. To perform a general banking business and to act as his financial agent in the region, Watkins established a private bank, the Watkins Banking Company, at Lake Charles, Louisiana, in 1884.

Watkins turned much of his attention to opening up the southwestern portion of Louisiana so that he might realize on his land speculation. Professor Alexander Thomson of Iowa State Agricultural College—Watkins' brother-in-law—and Seaman Knapp, president of the same institution, were hired to demonstrate the feasibility of agriculture in the area. They opened up lands for rice and sugar culture and tended extensive herds of livestock. Watkins joined in lobbying activities at Washington to have the harbor improved at Calcasieu Pass. He planned the Kansas City, Watkins, and Gulf Railroad to stretch from Kansas City through his southern holdings to the gulf, and during the early 1890's built the section between Lake Charles and Alexandria in Louisiana. In 1888 he purchased the New York *American* and transplanted it in Louisiana to serve as an advertising organ in the work of publicizing southwestern Louisiana. In the new decade a railway car full of the products of Louisiana was sent on tour through the north central states.

With the exception of the Watkins National Bank and the Watkins Banking Company, Watkins' new ventures demanded outlays with little immediate return. To a large extent the mortgage company provided him with the funds for these expenditures. More than 90 per cent of the $75,000 dividend which it declared yearly went of course to Watkins.

When the debenture bond was adopted Watkins mixed large quantities of bonds secured by his lands in Louisiana among the securities backing the debenture series. Under the agreement with the Farmers' Loan and Trust Company, Watkins was allowed to place $20,000 of such paper behind each debenture series. He considered these securities as lent to the mortgage company. On $200,000 of such land bonds, however, he accepted a commission of 2 per cent for providing the securities and apparently paid no interest on them.[4] This transaction appears to have been a questionable one, although the writer has been unable to find Watkins' own rationalization for it. Watkins was to draw vendor's lien notes on other portions of his property in Louisiana and inject them into the debenture series as well. But on these securities drawn against land in Louisiana, Watkins was charged with interest as were other borrowers of the company. Nevertheless, some debenture series included more than $20,000 of Louisiana securities. In addition to the Louisiana paper Watkins sometimes placed another $20,000 or more of securities behind the debenture series which were secured by the lands of Watkins or of the mortgage company in Kansas or Texas. Although mortgage paper drawn on Watkins' southern holdings, or on the real estate of the company, did provide debenture paper, there was no income from commissions and the interest was a charge against either Watkins or the mortgage company.

One must understand that Watkins thought in long-range terms. He had entered the loan business when the returns were high. When competition threatened to cut his margin of profit, he determined to seek another field where substantial rewards awaited the pioneer. He believed that the undeveloped lands of Louisiana provided an opportunity. By 1888 he foresaw the time when he would withdraw from the mortgage business. In May of that year he informed an investor:

> The probabilities are that in the future we shall make very few loans in any of the Western States, and our business in the Southern States will be of moderately short duration. It is my determination to close up this business with as good a record as we have sustained in the past, and to do so we are compelled to use greater caution than in years gone by.[5]

Late in 1891 Watkins wrote to his British representative:

> It is my intention to take advantage of a revival of prosperity in this country to get rid of our lands and largely curtail efforts in the mortgage business.

[4] T. C. Green to J. B. Watkins, July 22, 1891, May 7, 1892, Sept. 5, 1893.

[5] J. B. Watkins to Dr. J. A. Bennet, New York, N.Y., May 18, 1888.

We have in the railway and landed interests in the South ten fold more to look forward to than in the mortgage business, and there is where I shall devote most of my energies.[6]

Watkins undoubtedly hoped that by 1893 he would have the lands in Louisiana opened to settlement and be obtaining revenue from land sales which would pay the interest and help to retire the principal of the indebtedness which he had placed upon his southern holdings.[7]

While Watkins was committing himself heavily in the south, depression struck the plains states during the late 1880's. The real estate holdings of the company multiplied. A source of revenue in good times, such land became parasitic, eating up between $30,000 and $40,000 in taxes yearly in Kansas alone, while freezing up many times that amount of working capital.

As the real estate holdings of the company increased swiftly during 1889 and 1890, Watkins decided to assume ownership of all the farms which were acquired in Kansas to the west of a line drawn south from the northwest corner of Phillips County to the southwest corner of Edwards County and from there jogging east to include Kiowa and Comanche Counties. Taking the lands at their cost to the company, Watkins became owner of between 400 and 500 farms, totaling roughly 100,000 acres. The purchase price of some $250,000 was subtracted from the debt which the company owed to him in uncollected dividends and in exchange for Louisiana securities. Watkins explained that the transfer would relieve the company of a portion of its real estate and of its indebtedness, but the effect of the move on the condition of the company is debatable. Yet only an optimist at this time would have argued that the farms in western Kansas were undervalued at $2.50 per acre.

Since the record of the loans made under Watkins' direction over the twenty-year period between 1873 and 1893 is not complete, it is impossible to arrive at the exact percentage of the loans which ended in failure. Evidently some 2,500 farms were obtained by foreclosure, and this number represented between 10 and 20 per cent of all the loans made to bonafide farmers.[8] It was not the long-run foreclosure rate, however, which brought disaster to the company, but rather departure from the

[6] J. B. Watkins to Chalkley and Co., Nov. 24, 1891.

[7] M. J. Dart to J. B. Watkins, Apr. 10, 1893.

[8] The estimate of the number of farms acquired is based upon reports made by Green and Stanton in 1893 and 1894, the number of farms sold during the 1880's and the real estate holdings of the company at various points in its history.

rate of foreclosure experienced prior to 1888. D. M. Sprankle estimated that the rate of failure on loans in western Kansas was 90 per cent.[9] It was less of course in central Kansas, but of all the mortgages made by all borrowers in one township of Edwards County during 1886 and 1887, 45 per cent ended in default.[10]

Despite the problems of the mortgage business which were apparent in 1890, Watkins began construction of the Alexandria–Lake Charles section of the Kansas City, Watkins, and Gulf Railroad. Since he intended to raise money for construction of the road in the money markets of the eastern United States and Europe, it was of great importance that investment funds should remain easy of access while construction proceeded. But in the fall of 1890 the money market in New York began to show definite signs of tightening. By the spring of 1891 it was evident that business was in a state of recession. Customers for mortgage securities were, therefore, urged to buy railroad securities instead. The mortgage company lost the revenue from commissions when investors switched from mortgage securities to railroad paper.

The depression of 1891 was fatal to many of the mortgage and loan companies. Between 1888 and 1891 some fifty or sixty Kansan loan agencies slipped into receivership.[11] Watkins sketched the condition of the mortgage business in the eastern states early in 1891 for Sprankle's benefit:

> From all sources the information comes of a horrible condition of affairs, many times worse than I had ever supposed. Dickinson reports that all through the region he visited it is generally understood that all Eastern agencies have quit, given up their offices and gone out of business. No effort is being made now to send money West. Throughout New York State everywhere, we hear of mortgage negotiators having abandoned their business, and the holders of mortgages are trying to take care of them themselves, and they are about distracted; everybody losing money and denouncing Western mortgages.[12]

The losses which eastern investors experienced and the publicity which the financial press and the eastern fiscal officials gave to the failures of the companies convinced many investors that they should withdraw

[9] D. M. Sprankle to M. J. Dart, Aug. 8, 1891.

[10] See study of Kinsley Township, Chapter 16.

[11] New York, *Annual Report of the Superintendent of Banking relative to Foreign Mortgage, Loan, Investment and Trust Companies* (1891), p. 14.

[12] J. B. Watkins to D. M. Sprankle, Mar. 18, 1891.

their capital from the west. During 1890 the investors of New York sent $6,500,000 west for investment in farm mortgages.[13] In the following year the figure was cut in half.[14]

Although the J. B. Watkins Land Mortgage Company weathered the financial crisis of 1891, it was not without difficulty. Investors became reluctant to reinvest the principal of maturing loans or to send fresh funds into the west. Through 1891 the mortgage company slipped behind on orders as Watkins channeled the investment funds at his command into the enterprises which appeared to need them most. In July 1891 there were unfilled orders for mortgage securities dating back to July 1889. On July 18, 1891, the company had not yet allocated mortgage securities to cover some $400,000 already submitted by investors.[15] Some lag between order and delivery was, of course, normal, but certainly not one of such size. At the same time collections in the west slowed to a mere trickle. On August 11 Watkins noted that the Lawrence office had collected less than $50,000 of the $227,000 of principal and interest due from debtors on that date.[16] In the face of the financial stringency, Watkins decided to forego his portion of the June dividend.

It was in the summer of 1891 that Watkins began to order drafts to be drawn on the New York accounts of the company when there were no funds in them and then to telegraph funds to cover the drafts at the last possible moment.[17] There was nothing reprehensible in such practice, but Watkins had never found it necessary to cut corners so sharply before. To add to the problems of the company, Brown Brothers canceled the agreement under which they advanced up to $100,000 against the security of debenture bonds deposited with them. Operating capital was, therefore, reduced at a critical time.

It was in 1891 that the examiners from the eastern seaboard states began to criticize the financial condition of the mortgage company. The examiner from Connecticut was comparatively mild in his criticism. He merely pointed out that no list was kept of the second or commission mortgages held by the company.[18] The examiners from the state of New York were more critical.[19] They wished to know the reason why the

[13] New York, *op. cit.*, p. 8. [14] *Ibid.* (1892), p. 10.

[15] T. C. Green to J. B. Watkins, July 18, 1891.

[16] J. B. Watkins to Lawrence office, Aug. 11, 1891.

[17] *Ibid.*, Sept. 21, 1891. [18] T. C. Green to J. B. Watkins, May 29, 1891.

[19] D. M. Sprankle to J. B. Watkins, July 7, 1891; J. B. Watkins to Lawrence office, Oct. 1, Dec. 18, 1891.

company had been incorporated in Colorado. They did not believe that the transfer of some 100,000 acres of land beyond the ninety-eighth meridian to Watkins was of any advantage to the mortgage company. At the same time they maintained that the land holdings of the corporation were much too large for safety. Finally they pointed out that there were far too many of Watkins' own obligations included in the backing of the debenture series. To the inspector from Massachusetts the business of the mortgage company appeared to be too closely interwoven with the affairs of its president.[20] Should either Watkins or the company become financially embarrassed, the other would be in grave danger of being pulled down also. To the skilled observer the mortgage company was beginning to show definite signs of weakness.

During the late summer of 1891 at least one of the officers of the company believed that it stood faint chance of pulling through. In mid September, Sprankle wrote to Watkins:

> It appears to me that the situation is getting pretty serious. We are and have been for a long time paying more than we can collect and cannot sell anything, nor use personal mortgages only to a limited extent. What are we to do? When debenture bonds begin to mature I am afraid it will be worse. I cannot see how we are to get through. Can you? [21]

But even as Sprankle made his gloomy forecast, the pressure on the company was beginning to ease. Watkins wrote that confidence was being restored in the east. He forecast that withdrawals would diminish and that it would soon be easier to obtain new investment funds.[22] By late October 1891 the clerk in charge of the interest department at Lawrence reported that a good harvest had improved collections in the west.[23] By the middle of February 1892 Watkins could write that the company was in better shape than it had been for some ten months.[24]

The company apparently held its own through 1892. In September of that year the unfilled orders stood at $400,000.[25] This was the same figure at which they had stood in July 1891. In the meantime Watkins had almost completed the essential Alexandria–Lake Charles link in the

[20] T. C. Green to J. B. Watkins, Nov. 20, Nov. 27, 1891.
[21] D. M. Sprankle to J. B. Watkins, Sept. 17, 1891.
[22] J. B. Watkins to D. M. Sprankle, Sept. 21, 1891.
[23] A. E. Saxey to J. B. Watkins, Oct. 20, 1891.
[24] J. B. Watkins to M. J. Dart, Feb. 17, 1892.
[25] T. C. Green to J. B. Watkins, Sept. 26, 1892.

Kansas City, Watkins, and Gulf Railroad. Although Miles Dart realized the importance of the Louisiana lands in Watkins' over-all plan, he pointed out that the $1,500,000 used to build and to begin operating the railroad had been obtained at the expense of the mortgage company, which had thereby lost heavily on commission account.[26] Although the staff at Lawrence found itself hard pressed to obtain mortgage paper to replace the maturing securities behind the debenture series, the company was still solvent.[27] Perhaps renewed prosperity in the business world and a revival of land sales would bring it safely back to a sound financial condition.

In November 1892, Superintendent Hall of the New York banking department refused the company a license to operate in that state during 1893.[28] Undoubtedly the main reason behind Hall's decision was the large amount of land which the company had been forced to take. Watkins suspected, in addition, that his enemies in Lawrence had applied pressure to the examiners.[29] By preparing a summary of the company's land sales in the past, Watkins managed to convince the officers of the banking department in New York that real estate had not been a cause of loss, but rather one of gain to the company. With reluctance the superintendent renewed the license.[30]

By May 1893 Watkins was preparing to catch up on the outstanding orders, which still stood at a dangerously high figure. He was drafting a new agreement with the Farmers' Loan and Trust Company which would relax the restrictions which this corporation placed upon the mortgage paper supporting the debenture series. Under the new agreement Watkins hoped to mortgage additional amounts of his Louisiana lands. With the securities obtained in this way he believed that the open order account could be brought down to reasonable dimensions.[31] No one can gainsay, however, that the method by which he hoped to achieve the reduction was anything but a stop gap. Complete safety could be achieved only if large amounts of land were sold at profitable prices.

[26] M. J. Dart to J. B. Watkins, June 14, 1892; Watkins to Dart, Aug. 19, 1893.

[27] D. M. Sprankle to J. B. Watkins, May 9, 1892.

[28] Charles Hall, Albany, N.Y., to Lawrence office, Nov. 12, 1892.

[29] J. B. Watkins to D. M. Sprankle, Nov. 14, 1892, to W. F. Presby, Nov. 17, 1892.

[30] D. M. Sprankle to J. B. Watkins, Nov. 26, 1892; T. C. Green to J. B. Watkins, Dec. 12, 1892.

[31] J. B. Watkins to M. J. Dart, May 29, 1893.

In June business conditions deteriorated rapidly. The flow of funds to the east, which had been going on since 1891, was accelerated. Texas, claimed Dart, was drained dry. In the west land values dropped rapidly but buyers could not be found. It was now impossible to mark up the value of the lands which were owned by the company. Profits of even this paper variety were impossible. Collections in the west diminished seriously. Late in July it became evident that the company was not going to be able to meet its obligations on the first of August.

On that date a circular was sent to all investors to whom principals were owing. In part the statement read:

> Today including interest and principal about $300,000 of our mortgage obligations are due. Because of the stringent times it is impossible to collect much more than enough to pay the interest. At this season farmers have not much to turn into cash, and are not able to borrow a dollar locally to carry them over until the marketing of crops. Even if farmers have money, they will not entrust it to local banks to be transferred to New York. It is impossible to sell products on hand; dealers cannot get the cash to handle them. . . .
>
> In three years our mortgagors have reduced their indebtedness nearly $2,500,000 in response to demands by the investor. They have done nobly but just now they must be shown some leniency. Give them time to turn their crops. It would be unjust to ruin them by sacrificing their securities.[32]

This circular gave the inability of western borrowers to meet their obligations as the reason for suspending repayment of principals owing to investors. This was hardly the whole story. In a letter to Watkins on the same date, Green, the cashier of the company, analyzed the finances of the company. Green pointed out that the company had outstanding some $4,100,000 of debenture obligations on which an average rate of 5½-per-cent interest was paid. To secure these bonds the company had the following securities:

Louisiana bonds	$ 320,000
Louisiana mortgages	640,000
Mortgages on the farms of Watkins and the company in Kansas and Texas	610,000
Deeded mortgages	410,000
Regular loans	2,200,000
	$4,180,000

[32] Letter dated Aug. 1, 1893, sent to all investors with principals due.

Of the regular loans, however, some $200,000 were in foreclosure suit or were badly in arrears. There were, according to Green's analysis, only $2,000,000 of income-bearing securities to pay the interest and principal payments on debentures amounting to more than $4,000,000. At the same time there were open orders to at least the amount of $300,000 on which the company was paying interest although the investors had not yet received securities. Finally Green pointed out that at least $2,000,000 was invested in 1,200 farms which were bringing in almost no income.[33]

For a time it appeared that Watkins' enterprises must tumble in the early fall of 1893. It seemed impossible to raise the $4,000 necessary to meet an acceptance of the Lawrence Canning Company.[34] Watkins, however, succeeded in obtaining the funds to meet the acceptance, and receivership was postponed. Of the mortgage companies which had thus far remained solvent, the Lombard Investment Trust Company and the Jarvis Conklin Mortgage Trust Company passed into receivership during September. These companies had dominated the western mortgage business during the late 1880's, and their failure was a sickening blow to eastern investors who had thus far retained confidence in the western farm mortgage.

Watkins, however, managed to keep his company out of receivership during 1893. In England, H. G. Chalkley and Sons were instructed to sell 5½-per-cent gold debentures. Since the rate on such securities was ½ per cent above the market rate of interest on long-term obligations, Watkins hoped to obtain new supplies of money from England. An effort was made both in America and in England to have lenders renew all securities which matured. Watkins involved himself further in the financial difficulties of his company by personally guaranteeing the payment of the securities renewed by the more reluctant investors.[35] In the west a desperate attempt was made to collect as large a share of delinquent collections as possible and to sell land.

To make matters even more difficult for Watkins, the officials of the Farmers' Loan and Trust Company decided to regulate more carefully the securities which their corporation held as trustee for the debenture series. In August some 38 per cent of the securities behind the $4,100,-

[33] T. C. Green to J. B. Watkins, Aug. 1, 1893.

[34] William R. Willcox, New York, N.Y., to M. Summerfield, Lawrence, Feb. 8, 1898, along with Green's draft of a reply is helpful in understanding the connection between various branches of Watkins' business.

[35] J. B. Watkins to Alexander Thomson, Mar. 2, 1894.

000 of debentures were drawn on land owned by either Watkins or the mortgage company. In some series the percentage stood at considerably more than 40 per cent. In the fall of 1893 the officers of the trust company decided to establish 20 per cent as the percentage of Louisiana paper which might be included in the debenture series. This still further limited the ability of the mortgage company to obtain debenture paper.

To add to the difficulties facing the company, there were some $100,000 of short-term loans owing to banks in Lawrence, New Orleans, and to the Bank of Commerce in New York.[36] These were refinanced during the fall of 1893 with the greatest of difficulty. By the end of 1893, however, Watkins believed that the fortunes of the mortgage company were definitely improving and left New York for Louisiana. But W. F. Presby, who had been with the company for thirteen years, summed up the necessity of selling land when he wrote to Watkins:

> I hope a great deal of Louisiana land will be sold this Winter. That, it seems to me, is the only salvation; but I have feared, and still do, that not much will be accomplished at present prices; that a heroic cut will have to be made before much will be done. I think you have been too inclined to see the bright side of Southwest Louisiana, and that has caused you to keep raising your ideas of the value of land there; and every time you go there you continue to see the bright side and think land is 'rapidly advancing' and up go the prices again. For this reason I sincerely hope that this time you will see the dark side of Louisiana, its drawbacks and disadvantages, and come home discouraged as to fancy prices ever being realized. Such a discouragement on your part will in reality be the first ray of light through the cloud that has been gathering over us for a number of years and is now very black. I would begin to hope that even now at the eleventh hour there is a possibility of escape.[37]

The revival of business which Watkins hoped for in the fall of 1893 did not materialize in time to save his company. Land could not be sold either in the plains states or in Louisiana. Investors refused to entrust more funds to his care. Collections improved somewhat, but as Green's analysis demonstrated, collections alone were not sufficient to save the company. On April 5, 1894, the company was placed in receivership in the United States Circuit Court at Topeka.[38] Watkins was named as re-

[36] J. B. Watkins to H. G. Chalkley and Sons, Feb. 9, 1894.
[37] W. F. Presby to J. B. Watkins, Oct. 19, 1893.
[38] See balance sheet which follows.

ceiver. Within a few months he had a plan of reorganization approved and the receivership was terminated. Business was still stagnant, however, and the company was returned to receivership after but a few months of operation. The second receivership lasted until 1900 and was terminated only as a step in winding up the mortgage business.[39] With its first receivership the J. B. Watkins Land Mortgage Company ceased to be an active lender in the plains states.

It is an intriguing question to ask whether or not the mortgage company could have retained its solvency had Watkins concentrated solely on the western farm mortgage business. Had the accumulation of assets which he built up in the twenty years of activity as a mortgage broker been preserved as a liquid reserve, the company could no doubt have weathered the storm of the 1890's. The judgment is, of course, hindsight. The scale and the nature of the western mortgage business during the late nineteenth century were unique. Its promoters had little in the way of precedent to guide them. Failure to turn over land promptly once it had been acquired during the 1880's contributed in a measure to the failure, and it was impossible to do so during the next decade.

Despite allegations by some groups of investors during the second receivership, the writer does not believe that Watkins' course was marked by patent dishonesty. Underlying his whole policy was an over-optimistic estimate of the value of his lands in Louisiana as well as a misunderstanding of the immediate agricultural potential of the western portion of the plains states. That Watkins may have led investors astray by innuendo is possible. He had in the beginning sold mortgages on western farms only. The fact that paper backed by unimproved land was placed behind the debenture bonds was never specifically stated to investors, although the writer has been unable to find any letters in which it was denied to an investor that such was the case. Watkins was quite sincere, undoubtedly, in his estimate of the value of his Louisiana holding. It is difficult, however, to explain creditably Watkins' action in ac-

[39] *Girard Life Insurance, Annuity and Trust Company* vs. *J. B. Watkins Land Mortgage Co.*, Case 7370, filed in United States Circuit Court, District of Kansas, First Division, 1896. The liquidation of the J. B. Watkins Land Mortgage Company was carried out under agreements between the principals to the liquidation dated, May 12, 1896, Dec. 9, 1896, Mar. 30, 1897, June 29, 1897, Sept. 30, 1898, June 14, 1899, Dec. 2, 1903, July 24, 1903, and June 30, 1908. See agreements in J. B. Watkins Papers under dates, also File 1497, Farmers' Loan and Trust Co. in files of City Bank Farmers' Trust Co., New York, N.Y.

Table 8. Balance sheet of the J. B. Watkins Land Mortgage Company, Apr. 5, 1894.

ASSETS:	
Cash on Hand,	$240.89
Cash on Hand, N.Y. Office,	220.63
Cash, Watkins National Bank,	197.51
" J. B. Watkins L. M. Co., Dallas, Texas,	4,221.53
" Barclay & Co., Bankers, London,	13,349.55
Interest due from Borrowers,	123,912.31
Second Mortgage Notes, taken for commissions,	48,291.07
Notes taken for Rent of Company's Lands,	10,291.65
Due from Borrowers—Past Due Mortgages,	67,800.00
First Mortgage Loans, Deposited as Security for Debenture Bonds,	4,789,690.00
First Mortgage Securities,	94,398.52
Farm Lands in Kansas, Missouri & Texas,	2,446,517.96
Office Building, Fixtures & Furniture,	102,988.14
Deposit for costs in foreclosure cases,	2,806.75
Taxes paid for Borrowers,	3,574.83
Tax Title to lands in process of foreclosure,	1,744.88
Tax Certificates,	5,864.99
County Warrants,	143.99
Livestock,	763.00
Miscellaneous Items in Suspense, pending Distribution to proper accounts,	18,145.08
The Lawrence Canning Company,	20,197.07
J. B. Watkins, Trustee,	11,575.00
Due from sundry persons,	2,427.93
	$7,769,363.28

LIABILITIES:	
Capital Stock,	$ 750,000.00
Surplus Fund,	395,360.02
Funds awaiting investment in Mortgages,	188,500.00
Accrued Interest on above to April 5,	4,208.55
Funds awaiting Investment in Debenture Bonds,	12,915.47
Accrued Interest on above to April 5,	653.15
Mortgages Collected—Past Due—Unpaid,	102,992.27
Accrued Interest on above to April 5,	1,622.05
Debenture Bonds—Cancelled, Unpaid,	11,335.85
Loans paid by Borrowers,	34,017.35
Coupons paid in advance by Borrowers,	4,164.01
Debenture Bonds outstanding,	4,242,213.28
Bills Payable,	80,691.10
Mortgages outstanding on Company's lands,	1,167,916.70
Time Deposits,	7,040.46
Saving Certificates,	1,615.00
National Bank of Commerce Over-Draft,	4,188.26
Outstanding Checks, New York,	865.91
Loans from Barclay & Co., Bankers, London, secured by Debenture Bonds,	97,500.00
Kansas City, Watkins & Gulf Railway Company,	92,812.42
J. B. Watkins,	568,751.43
	$7,769,363.28

cepting commission and failing to pay interest on $200,000 of Louisiana bonds. But his later course in sacrificing personal assets to meet the obligations of his companies and his determination that investors should be paid back at least the face value of their investments is proof that he was no irresponsible pirate. He was to devote much of the remainder of his life to realizing on the assets of the company to the best of his ability.

Two years after Watkins' death in 1921 an agent of his estate could write that "the holders of debenture bonds issued by the Mortgage Company have had their principal amount paid in full. The interest [agreed upon under the second receivership] is being paid gradually and will be paid in full because the Mortgage Company has sufficient assets to insure this. The stock holders will receive something on their stock."[40] By installments the bond and mortgage holders received $4,860,865, the face value of securities issued in cancellation of the original obligations of the company. They obtained, also, more than $1,500,000 simple interest on these obligations, calculated at two-thirds of the rate called for in the debentures and guaranteed mortgages prior to the original receivership—5 per cent and 6 per cent. Various miscellaneous creditors were paid off as well. But the stockholders did not share formally in the remaining assets of the Watkins company. J. B. Watkins' old claim of $568,751.43 against the company was held to be superior to those of the stockholders, and Mrs. Watkins as his legatee acquired the residue assets valued at $230,000 by decision of the district court of Douglas County in 1928. Of course it must be remembered that Mrs. Watkins held some 93 per cent of the stock of the company at this point. Not until 1928 were the accounts of the J. B. Watkins Land Mortgage Company closed on the books of the Farmers' Loan and Trust Company in New York City, and as late as 1932 Watkins' widow bought the claims of a small investor who had not presented his securities previously.[41]

So successful a liquidation was not carried out without difficulties. It is hard to conclude that the three sons of H. G. Chalkley did not use their influence with investors to plunder the assets of the mortgage com-

[40] F. H. Miller to W. E. Mitchell, South Britain, Conn., Apr. 7, 1923.

[41] D. P. Condon, Registrar, City Farmers' Loan and Trust Co. to Lawrence National Bank, Nov. 27, 1928, in Farmers' Loan and Trust Co., File 1497; File 1497 also contains a copy of the final liquidation agreement dated Mar. 9, 1928.

pany and Watkins' southern enterprises. In 1911 Watkins estimated that the mortgage company had suffered losses aggregating millions of dollars through their machinations.[42] T. C. Green, who was never one to mince words or to judge Watkins' actions in adulatory fashion, referred in 1909 to "the fact that certain ones have come into the Company and taken out of the concern or its assets, about $250,000 or $300,000." [43] This was somewhat less sweeping than Watkins' estimates but certainly the statement indicates there might have been a solid foundation for his charges.

Despite the problems of liquidation, Watkins was by no means ruined by the failure of the J. B. Watkins Land Mortgage Company. Prior to the crash of 1893 he had acquired in his own right large land interests in the south and in western Kansas as well as organized the prosperous Watkins National Bank. Although unquestionably backed to the wall during the 1890's, Watkins saw his position improve with the upturn in real estate values after 1900. By the date of his death in 1921 he was indisputably a millionaire once more.

[42] J. B. Watkins to Rev. A. J. Allen, New York, June 22, 1911; see also Watkins to Henry Tatnall, Philadelphia, Pa., Oct. 4, Oct. 22, Dec. 30, 1910, to F. W. Walker, Roselle, N.J., Feb. 16, 1911.

[43] T. C. Green to J. B. Watkins, Sept. 17, 1909.

PART 3

LAND CREDIT IN THE WESTERN TOWNSHIP

THERE are few studies in which a detailed analysis of the county mortgage records has been combined with other sources of information to give a clear picture of the processes of agricultural land credit in pioneer western townships.[1] They require laborious

[1] Those interested in the technique of mortgage studies should read: Arthur F. Bentley, *The Condition of the Western Farmer as Illustrated by the Economic History of a Nebraska Township* (Johns Hopkins University Studies in Historical and Political Science, 11th ser.; Baltimore, 1893, nos. vii–viii); Robert Diller, *Farm Ownership, Tenancy, and Land Use in a Nebraska Community* (Chicago, 1941); Eleanor H. Hinman and J. O. Rankin, *Farm Mortgage History of Eleven Southeastern Nebraska Townships: 1870–1932* (University of Nebraska, Agricultural Experiment Station Research Bulletin, 67; Lincoln, 1933); William G. Murray, *An Economic Analysis of Farm Mortgages in Story County, Iowa, from 1854 to 1930* (Research Bulletin, 156, Agricultural Experiment Station, Iowa State College of Agricultural and Mechanical Arts; Ames, 1933); David Rozman, "Land Credit in the Town of Newton, Manitowoc County, Wisconsin, 1848–1926," *Journal of Land and Public Utility Economics*, III (Nov. 1927), 372–384; U.S. Census Office, *Report on Real Estate Mortgages in the United States at the Eleventh Census, and Report on Farms and Homes at the Eleventh Census, 1890.* Since 1930 various agricultural economists have published mortgage studies dealing with the recent history of farm mortgage loans in restricted areas. An excellent example of the techniques used is provided by Joseph Ackerman and L. J. Norton, *Factors Affect-*

research and careful evaluation of data. The sample studies, in the following chapters, of Kinsley Township in central Kansas and of Pebble Township in eastern Nebraska it is hoped, bring out aspects of pioneer farm credit that have hitherto been neglected.

These studies differ from earlier ones in their concentration on the pioneer period and in their greater emphasis on the success or failure of borrowers with different backgrounds. Access to the land records of the Atchison, Topeka and Santa Fe Railroad Company and of the Union Pacific Railroad Company allowed a comparison of the credit history of railroad land with that of land which settlers obtained directly from the government. A greater variety of sources has been used than in most of the earlier studies. Excellent document collections proved to be of help in the study of both townships.

---

ing Success of Farm Loans (Illinois Agricultural Experiment Station Bulletin, 468; Urbana, 1940).

XV

PIONEER PEBBLE

BOUNDED on the south by the Platte River, Dodge County lies in the second tier of counties west of the eastern boundary of Nebraska. The county seat is Fremont. Receiving some thirty inches of rainfall annually and enjoying an average frost-free growing season of about 160 days, the county is situated within the portion of eastern Nebraska which agricultural geographers include in the corn belt of the United States. In the last "type-of-farming" study, produced by the Experiment Station of the University of Nebraska College of Agriculture, the northern half of the county was included in the intensive livestock production area of northeastern Nebraska, while the south half was placed in the region of general farming which stretches southward from the Platte. The annual yields of corn, oats, alfalfa, and winter wheat, as well as the value of the cattle and of the pig crop, stamp the county as one of the most productive in the state. The average valuation of farmland in Dodge County, returned for the Agricultural Census of 1950, was somewhat higher than that of most of the surrounding counties.[1]

[1] Nebraska Department of Agriculture and Inspection *et al., Nebraska Agricultural Statistics, Annual Report, 1951* (Lincoln, 1953); L. F. Garey, *Factors Deter-*

Pebble Township is township 20, north of the base line, range six, east of the sixth principal meridian in the federal survey, and lies between Webster and Cuming Townships against the northern boundary of Dodge County. Since some of the sections in the township are fractional, the total area is only some 22,745 acres. The topography is rolling rather than hilly. The Elkhorn River meanders through the eastern side of the township, passing through sections 3, 2, 10, 14, 13, 24, and 25. Pebble Creek converges upon the course of the Elkhorn from the northwest, cutting through sections 6, 7, 17, 18, 19, 20, 21, 28, 27, 34, 35, and 36.

The dominant soil type in the township was mapped by the United States Soil Survey in 1916 as Marshall silt loam, an upland soil of loessial origin. Lying mainly between the river and the creek and occurring again in the southwest corner of the township, this soil type predominates in some fifteen of the thirty-six sections. When the areas of Waukesha silt loam, a terrace type, and of Wabash silt loam, the typical soil of the stream bottom, are added to those of Marshall silt loam, some seven sections are left. These are made up, for the most part, of Waukesha fine sandy loam, Sarpy very fine sandy loam, and Cass very fine sandy loam. All of the major soil types found in the township are excellent corn soils.[2]

Pebble Township fell within the boundaries of the land grant given to the Union Pacific Railroad Company in 1864.[3] Land in the sections designated by odd numbers, therefore, became the property of that corporation to be sold in aid of construction of its line. The land in sections bearing even numbers was eventually allocated directly to individuals

---

mining Type-of-Farming Areas in Nebraska (University of Nebraska College of Agriculture Experiment Station, Bulletin 299; Lincoln, 1936), and *Systems of Farming and Possible Alternates in Nebraska* (*ibid.*, Bulletin 309; Lincoln, 1937); Arthur F. George, *Annual Farm Business Report, 1951, Eastern Nebraska, 38 Farms* (Extension Service, University of Nebraska College of Agriculture *et al.;* mimeographed; Lincoln, 1952); U.S. Bureau of the Census, *U.S. Census of Agriculture, 1950,* Vol. I, "Counties and State Economic Areas," pt. 12 (Washington, 1952), Table 1.

[2] U.S. Department of Agriculture *et al., Soil Survey of Dodge County, Nebraska* (Washington, 1918). This publication was written by B. W. Tillman and H. C. Mortlock. Field surveys were carried out in 1916.

[3] Nelson Trottman, *History of the Union Pacific: A Financial and Economic Survey* (New York, 1923), p. 18. Pebble Township lay beyond the limits of the original grant of 1862.

by the federal government with the exception of sections 16 and 36, the state school lands. In this chapter the land transferred to individuals by the federal government will be referred to as government land.

The tract books of the United States Land Office identify the settlers who sought to obtain title to government land.[4] In 1859 Thomas Parks pre-empted 160 acres in section 12. No further entries were made from the township until 1866, when five settlers entered land under the homestead act. During 1868, 1869, and 1870 settlers recorded 118 entries at the district land office from Pebble Township, as the land passed rapidly into the hands of claimants. When William McClintock homesteaded eighty acres in section 12 in 1879, the government lands in Pebble Township were exhausted. Title, as represented by the final certificate of the district land office, passed to the settlers between 1872 and 1878 for the most part. Twenty-four settlers obtained certificates in both 1873 and 1875, and eleven settlers obtained evidence of title in 1874, 1876, and 1877. The process of alienation was completed in 1885 when McClintock obtained his final certificate. In all, 114 individuals received title to 121 parcels of government land in Pebble Township. These figures represent 71 per cent of both the number of settlers from the township whose names appear on the tract books, and of the number of entries which they filed at the district land office (see Table 9).

One hundred and seven settlers obtained title to government land in Pebble Township under the terms of the homestead laws. This number includes seven who commuted their homestead rights and purchased their claims at $2.50 per acre.[5] Only seven of the successful homesteaders obtained holdings of more than eighty acres. Settlement in the township was well under way before it became lawful for veterans of the Civil War or their heirs to acquire 160 acres within the confines of a railroad land grant and was almost complete when it became lawful for the ordinary settler to do so. A large proportion of the pioneers in the township, however, probably could not have qualified for an additional

[4] Duplicate sets of land office tract books for the state of Nebraska are held in the Nebraska State Historical Society, Lincoln, and the Department of the Interior, Washington, D.C. Pebble Township fell in the territory of the district office at Omaha until 1868 and was then included in the Grand Island district.

[5] The word "homestead" will be used hereafter to refer to land either acquired by its owner under the terms of the various federal homestead acts or to land in the process of thus being acquired without recourse to commutation. In the legal sense, of course, a homestead is a holding which its owner holds free from the claims of creditors under certain conditions.

eighty acres as veterans. Eighty-two of the 114 settlers who obtained government land bore German or Bohemian names. Many of these were recent immigrants who had not served in the forces of the Union. Of the homesteaders, one also pre-empted land. Seven settlers obtained tracts under the pre-emption act of 1841 alone.[6]

Table 9. Disposal of government land in Pebble Township.

Year	Successful entries	Unsuccessful entries	Final certificates
1859	1	—	1
1866	5	—	—
1867	5	2	—
1868	35	17	3
1869	20	8	1
1870	23	15	5
1871	11	4	3
1872	7	1	9
1873	6	—	24
1874	4	—	11
1875	1	—	24
1876	1	—	11
1877	—	2	11
1878	1	—	9
1879	1	—	2
1880	—	—	5
1882	—	—	1
1885	—	—	1
Totals	121	49	121

The eighteen odd-numbered sections in Pebble Township which fell within the land grant obtained by the Union Pacific Railroad Company embraced 11,401 acres. To this total must be added forty acres in section 10, which the Union Pacific acquired in 1872 as part of an indemnity list to replace tracts in the grant which had been occupied by settlers before Congress set it aside for the use of the company.

The portion of the land grant lying in Pebble Township was offered

[6] A summary of most of the acts under which title was transferred from the government in this township will be found in Thomas Donaldson, *The Public Domain* (Washington, 1884). The specialist of course will use the *U.S. Statutes at Large* as well.

for sale in the spring of 1870. Between that date and the year 1884, when the last railroad land in the township was sold, seventy-one sales were made to fifty purchasers.[7] The Union Pacific Railroad Company offered to sell its lands on cash or on time. Despite the discount of 10 per cent for cash, only 640 acres in two sales were purchased on such terms. Deeds were issued on the remainder, sold by land contract, from 10 to 134 months after sale. During June 1870 the land department of the Union Pacific advertised in the Fremont *Tribune* that all sales on credit thereafter would be written for periods of five years. Buyers would pay one-fifth of the principal at the date of purchase, but only interest on the remaining principal at the end of the first year. At the end of the second, third, fourth, and fifth years, one-fifth of the principal was to be paid along with interest on the unpaid portion to that date at 6 per cent per annum.[8] Some of the contracts drawn after this announcement, however, ran for ten years.

The Union Pacific accepted its land grant bonds in payment for land. During the early 1870's these bonds sold at a discount, enabling purchasers to realize a saving on the cost of land obtained from the railway. In August 1869 the Fremont *Tribune* announced that one bond house had begun to take orders from small purchasers whose payments did not amount to $1,000—the smallest denomination in which the bonds were printed.[9] When orders totaled the price of a bond, the bond house purchased one and tendered it to the railroad company on behalf of a group of small purchasers. Thus, some of the savings which could be derived from using land grant bonds in payment for railroad land was to be passed along to the small buyer. A private banker and real estate agent acted as the representative of the brokerage firm in Fremont. When the officials of the railroad ruled that clubbing was no longer acceptable in 1873, the *Tribune* indignantly stigmatized the edict as "Another Public Outrage and Private Steal." [10]

[7] These and later statistics bearing on the sale of railroad land in Pebble Township were taken from the tract books of the Union Pacific land grant in the possession of the company at Omaha, and from the Deed Registers of Dodge County in the office of the Register of Deeds, Fremont, Neb. All purchases made by one individual in 1870 were counted as one sale, since in the first rush of buying, individuals buying large amounts of land often received contracts bearing several dates. Thereafter, purchases by the same individual in any year were counted separately if they bore different dates.

[8] Fremont *Tribune,* June 30, 1870. Used in the office of the newspaper at Fremont.

[9] *Ibid.,* Aug. 20, 1869.

[10] *Ibid.,* Aug. 1, 1873.

Table 10. Quotations on "Union Pacific Land Grant 7's."*

July 2, 1870	76	Dec. 27, 1873	74½
Dec. 24, 1870	58½	July 11, 1874	81
July 1, 1871	85½	Dec. 26, 1874	90
Dec. 30, 1871	80	July 3, 1875	100
July 6, 1872	82	Dec. 25, 1875	101
Dec. 28, 1872	79	July 1, 1876	101
July 5, 1873	69½	Dec. 30, 1876	101

* Taken from the *Commercial and Financial Chronicle* (New York) of the dates given.

The Union Pacific sold some 82 per cent of its land in Pebble Township during 1870 and 1871, when 9,400 acres were transferred in nineteen parcels. Sales thereafter were made from the remaining 2,040 acres and from tracts which were returned to the railroad company after purchasers had defaulted on their contracts. Of the successful buyers, those who obtained forty- or eighty-acre units were most numerous, but John Davenport of Bath, New York, acquired 6,678 acres, which amounted to more than one half of the railroad land in the township. Two other nonresidents of Nebraska obtained a total of 360 acres. Thus over 7,000 acres of the 11,441 acres of railroad land in the township were sold to nonresidents who held the land for resale rather than for farming purposes. Certain of the purchases which were made by residents of Omaha and Fremont were obviously of this type as well. In total, speculative purchases accounted for 68 per cent of the railroad land in the township.

Table 11. Total purchases of forty-two successful buyers.

Acres	Buyers	Acres	Buyers
40	14	200	1
80	10	320	1
120	8	480	1
160	5	640 or more	2

Twelve, or 24 per cent, of the buyers defaulted on land contracts. Four of the twelve, however, paid out on a portion of the land which they had purchased. Forty-two, or 84 per cent of the fifty buyers, were, therefore, successful in completing all or part of their purchases from the Union Pacific. In terms of acreage a little less than 10 per cent of the railroad lands were sold a second time. At least twelve purchasers assigned land contracts to other individuals. Five of these assignees purchased additional railroad land on their own account.

Of the fifty who purchased land from the railroad, thirteen had obtained land from the government within Pebble Township by homesteading or pre-emption. This group represented 11 per cent of all the individuals who obtained government land and 26 per cent of the purchasers of railroad land. These thirteen individuals, of course, purchased far less than 26 per cent of the land grant in the township.

Table 12. Union Pacific land sales: Pebble Township.*

Year	Total sales	Acres	Cancellations
1870	19	9,000	1
1871	3	400	—
1872	4	240	1
1873	14	720	6
1874	3	120	3
1875	2	120	2
1877	1	40	—
1878	5	400	—
1879	10	480	—
1880	3	120	—
1881	1	40	—
1882	2	160	—
1883	3	400	—
1884	1	40	—
Totals	71		13

* All acreages sold to one buyer on the same day and having the same date of deeding were counted as one sale.

The twelve buyers who failed to make good all or part of thirteen purchases are worth some attention. Twelve of the thirteen repudiated purchases were made in the four years 1872–1875 and represented 54 per cent of the sales of those years. All of the cancellations involved tracts of 40, 80, or 120 acres. Three of the purchasers lived nearby in eastern Nebraska, and one gave Omaha as his address; the remaining eight were undeniably residents of Pebble Township. Five of the latter had homesteaded government land. The price of the land embraced in the canceled contracts of the eleven residents of Pebble or adjacent points may well have had some significance. The Union Pacific sold most of its land in the township for prices which ranged from $4.00 to $6.00 per acre, but in seven of the twelve cancellations made by local men the consideration was either $10.00 or $12.00 per acre.

In all, some 68 per cent of the railroad land in Pebble Township was sold to speculators who did not live in the township. This finding contradicts the contention that the land grant was sold to resident farmers only. Actually, if the experience of the land department of the railroad in Pebble Township is at all typical, it would not even have been good business to limit sales to actual residents. Twelve of the thirteen cancellations occurred on tracts falling within the 32 per cent of the land grant in the township which was sold to actual residents of the immediate locality. In Pebble Township, at least, the railroad company would apparently have experienced a much higher rate of cancellation in the sale of its land had an effort been made to sell only to residents of the area.

During 1870 and 1871 John Davenport and his brother Ira purchased almost 18,000 acres of land in Dodge County from the Union Pacific Railroad Company. For the most part this land lay in the northern tier of townships, and over one-third of it lay in Pebble Township. Ira Davenport did not at first agree with his brother that the land purchase was a wise one. He was to write, referring to a tract of land in Pebble Township, "I bought the other half the section myself after my brother had bought the other half in our large purchase and I had gone out to Nebraska to see what had made him crazy enough to buy so much land. My buying the half section and a couple other pieces I picked up was a practical answering of myself." [11]

The Davenports bought their land on five-year contract. Title was obtained during 1875 and 1876. The 6,678 acres which lay in Pebble Township included all or a portion of fifteen sections. Seven dollars per acre was paid for 640 acres, while the remainder was obtained at a price of $5.00 per acre.[12] The total purchase price of the land was $38,265. To this must be added over $6,000 of interest payments which were made

[11] Ira Davenport to Richards and Reynolds, Fremont, Neb., Nov. 29, 1877.

[12] Purchase and sale data are to be found in the land book of the Davenports, labeled "Fannie Davenport Ledger" in the Davenport Collection.

over the term of the contracts. The Davenports, however, paid for their land with land grant bonds of the Union Pacific and realized a sizable discount as a result. In 1871 the resident of Cedar Rapids, Iowa, who had entered the land for John Davenport received $500 for his services.

Contractors assumed the payment of taxes immediately after making their purchases. The Davenports had disbursed some $4,500, at least, in taxes by the end of 1879. The rapidity with which charges accumulated against land was a sobering feature of land speculation to Ira Davenport. Late in 1876 he wrote, "We are loaded to the water's edge with lands & I frankly say with our trouble with loans & lands I wish I had never seen Nebraska. . . . Look at the rate int & taxes are rolling up on our lands & ask yourself if you believe the investment likely to prove as paying a one as a good seven per cent Eastern bond." [13]

Late in 1877 the Davenport brothers placed their land in Dodge County upon the market through the real estate agency of L. D. Richards of Fremont. They placed a minimum price of $10.00 per acre on a list of lands about which Richards had received inquiries. If buyers so desired, they would be given credit of five or ten years with interest on the deferred payments reckoned at the rate of 10 per cent per annum. The brothers cautioned Richards against publicizing the price of their lands if he believed that potential buyers might be frightened away and concluded, "It may be deemed high. But the good crops & decreasing rates of interest must affect land also." [14]

The land nearest to the town plat of Scribner (in 31, T20N, R7E) was held off the market in expectation that prices would rise there to a greater extent than elsewhere in the township. Farmers owning lands adjacent to the lands of the Davenports were given preference over other buyers. Care was taken lest the first purchaser in a tract should obtain all of the best land. Where an eighty-acre holding was to be divided into parcels of forty acres, the more fertile land was to be divided between the two. Contracts were drawn "payable at Bath" so that the purchaser would pay the cost of exchange. Interest was compounded when contractors were late with their payments. An interest rate of 10

[13] Ira Davenport to E. O. Crosby, Fremont, Neb., Nov. 22, 1876.

[14] John and Ira Davenport to Richards and Reynolds, Aug. 29, 1877; see also *ibid.*, Nov. 14 and 29, 1877, Jan. 8, 1878; Richards and Keene, Fremont, Neb., to John and Ira Davenport, Mar. 6, 1883, and Nov. 10, 1887.

per cent on deferred payments was held until 1883, when it was lowered to 8 per cent. This rate in turn was dropped to 7 per cent during the early 1890's.

In selling the Davenport land, L. D. Richards obtained as large a down payment as possible and divided the remainder of the principal among any number of years up to ten, but usually five or ten. Often, however, the first payment was one-fifth or one-tenth of the principal. Contracts specified that the premises were sold "for improvement and cultivation" and that all improvements placed upon the premises by the contractor must remain there until title was surrendered by the Davenports. Purchasers assumed the payment of taxes immediately on signing the contracts. If a buyer failed to make his payments when due or broke other conditions of the contract, the Davenports could declare the agreement broken and resume full possession of the land without legal proceedings. Nor were the brothers obligated to compensate defaulting contractors for payments already made. On the other hand, if the Davenports so desired, they could allow the contract to remain in force, provided that interest was paid on the overdue interest and principal.[15]

During the first few years of sales, Richards assured purchasers that they could pay out on their contracts before they became due if it was their wish to do so. Early in 1880 Ira Davenport decided that contracts thereafter should run through until maturity.[16] Possibly Davenport made this decision because the brothers were obtaining a better rate of interest on land contracts than could have been obtained in other avenues of investment.

No land was sold in the township of Pebble during 1877, but in 1878 eleven tracts were sold which totaled 480 acres. Nine tracts were sold during the following year, but 1880 was to be the year in which occurred the greatest turnover of Davenport land. Thirty-four tracts, embracing 1,721 acres, were sold. Also, 1882 and 1883 were years of active selling. By the end of the latter year 69 per cent of the lands held by the Davenports in the township had been sold. In 1886 the brothers

[15] The canceled contracts used in Dodge County are not among the Davenport papers. Many examples of the form used elsewhere in Nebraska are available and one purchaser of Davenport land in Pebble Township filed an identical contract at the office of the Register of Deeds. See Dodge County, Miscellaneous Records, B, pp. 156–158.

[16] L. D. Richards to Ira Davenport, June 10, 1880.

took their remaining lands off the market, and only three sales were made between 1885 and 1891. Between this year and 1904 the residue was fed slowly into the market. When Ira Davenport died in 1904, only forty acres, on which the original contractor had defaulted, remained unsold.

The revenue from the sales of Davenport land in Pebble Township totaled slightly more than $122,000 by 1905, well over twice the sum which had been invested in the land by the end of 1876. The average sale price per acre was $18.00 as compared to an average purchase price of less than $6.00. Such totals and averages are apt to be misleading, however, unless one realizes that allowance must be made for accumulating taxes and sales commissions and that, contrary to other types of investment, no yearly dividends had been received with the exception of the occasional rent payment. When these factors were taken into consideration and the per-cent return per year calculated, the results were less striking.[17]

The yearly average return on the funds invested in lands which were sold before 1885 varied from 9 per cent to 13 per cent, although returns on individual tracts fell as low as 6 per cent, and one quarter section returned 15 per cent. After 1885 the average return on the lands sold each year fell sharply, reflecting the sharp decline in western land values after the collapse of the western real estate boom in 1887–1888. The last forty-acre tract sold under Ira Davenport's administration in 1904 for $75.00 per acre returned 12 per cent on the invested capital. This land had been rented almost continuously after 1881, and the

[17] The yearly allowances for taxes used in calculating per-cent return per annum on invested capital were based on the actual tax bills for the Dodge County railroad lands as noted twice in correspondence with Richards, on the taxes which the brothers paid over extended periods on foreclosed land in the county, and on the taxes which they paid on behalf of those who purchased railroad land from them and became delinquent in their payments. These tax estimates may well have been a little exaggerated but were not seriously so. Richards usually collected his sales commission by deducting 2½ per cent at date of sale and one per cent from all principal and interest payments thereafter. In calculation he was credited with a flat 3½ per cent at date of sale. From rentals the agent obtained 10 per cent from the first payment and one per cent for subsequent payments on the same lease. The actual discounts at which the Davenports purchased Union Pacific bonds were found for only two years. These corresponded closely with the July quotation in the *Commercial and Financial Chronicle* for those years, and as a result the Davenport land payments in other years were scaled down by the amount of the quoted discount.

rents raised the yearly returns by 4 per cent. Seventeen other tracts were rented for varying periods of time, producing in some cases an upward revision of one or 2 per cent in the annual return on the invested funds. The total revenue obtained from rents in Pebble Township between 1880 and 1904 was $6,121.

Table 13. Davenport land sales: Pebble Township.

Year	Sales	Acres	% return per annum
1878	11	480	12
1879	9	359	9
1880	34	1,721	9
1881	5	190	13
1882	18	1,031	11
1883	16	863	10
1884	4	236	11
1885	3	120	12
1888	2	80	8½
1890	1	40	7
1891	7	357	9
1893	3	120	5
1894	5	196	7
1895	1	80	5½
1896	4	160	6
1897	1	80	4
1899	4	240	5
1900	6	280	5
1901	1	40	default
1904	1	40	12

In his study of the Diller community in southeastern Nebraska, which he described as "fairly typical of the prairie part of the Middle West" and which was settled at about the same time as was Pebble Township, Robert Diller wrote of the land speculators, "It is sad to think how poorly they were paid." [18] Such may well have been the case in Diller, but the experience of the Davenports shows that not all speculators were poorly rewarded in eastern Nebraska.

[18] Robert Diller, *Farm Ownership, Tenancy, and Land Use in a Nebraska Community* (Chicago, 1941), pp. 7, 21.

In 1883 the brothers lamented that they had placed their lands in Dodge County on the market too soon.[19] Actually, as events developed, they were not able to obtain returns equal to those of the early years of sales on the lands held past the mid eighties. Perhaps a good part of the credit for the profitable returns should be given to L. D. Richards, who constantly revised the price lists in an attempt to keep the prices on the Davenport lands in step with rising land values. In 1899 he summed up, "Your prices have been always a little higher and at a figure quite often above that of fairly improved farms in the same neighborhood. The favorable terms, of course, are an inducement to buy your lands." [20] Aside from the sale price, it must be remembered that most of the Davenport lands were sold on credit and that the land contracts returned a relatively high rate of interest on the unpaid principal.

John and Ira Davenport sold 136 tracts of land in Pebble Township to 81 individuals—fewer purchasers than the 114 settlers who obtained government land and more than the 42 who were successful in purchasing land from the Union Pacific. Of the 81 who purchased land from the Davenports, 33, or 41 per cent, had already obtained land from the government as homesteaders or pre-emptioners. Six, or 7 per cent, had purchased land directly from the railroad company. Others were quite obviously the second generation descendants of the original settlers. Most of the purchases were made in forty-acre units, and it was common for the same purchaser to buy several tracts over a period of ten or fifteen years. Hans Martens, for instance, purchased five parcels of land—one eighty-acre unit and four forty-acre tracts—between 1878 and 1886. Martens was the most frequent customer of the Davenports, but other farmers made two or three purchases. A high proportion of the purchasers took advantage of the credit offered by the New Yorkers. The Davenport land book shows that only two purchasers defaulted on their contracts and that one of these successfully completed another contract.

With this summary of the way in which the land in Pebble Township entered private ownership, let us examine its role as mortgage security in a pioneer western township.

[19] John and Ira Davenport to Richards and Keene, Sept. 27, 1883.

[20] L. D. Richards to Ira Davenport, Feb. 15, 1899; Richards, Keene and Co. to Ira Davenport, Sept. 23, 1902.

Of the 114 persons who obtained government land in the township, 60, or 53 per cent, did not mortgage their land. Fifty-five, or 47 per cent, did encumber all or part of the land which they obtained from the government. Of the 106 parcels to which title was obtained under the homestead laws without commutation, 49, or 46 per cent, were eventually encumbered by the settler. Fifty-seven tracts, or 54 per cent of the whole, were not mortgaged by the settler. Four out of 7, or 57 per cent of those who commuted their homestead rights, mortgaged their land. Of the 8 pre-emptors only 3, or 38 per cent, encumbered their holdings.

Table 14. Date of encumbering government land.

	Homesteads		Preemptions		Commutations		Combined totals	
Mortgaged	*No.*	*%*	*No.*	*%*	*No.*	*%*	*No.*	*%*
Within 6 months after title	15	31	2	67	1	25	18	32
Between 6 months and 1 year after title	7	14					7	13
Between 1 year and 2 years after title	6	12					6	11
Between 2 years and 3 years after title	7	14					7	13
Between 3 years and 5 years after title	7	14	1	33			8	15
More than 5 years after title	7	14			3	75	10	18

Of the 49 encumbered homesteads, 15 were mortgaged within six months of the date on the settler's final certificate. Another 7 were mortgaged within the next six months. In other words, 45 per cent of the encumbered homesteads were put up as security for a loan within the first year after title had passed from the government to the settler. Over half of the encumbered homesteads were mortgaged within the first two years after the settler obtained title.

Of the 4 commuted homesteads which were encumbered, only one was mortgaged within six months after the final certificate was obtained. The other 3 tracts were not mortgaged until between the sixth and fifteenth years after the government had surrendered title.

Table 15. Mortgage debt in Pebble Township.

Year	First mortgages			Second mortgages		Total	
	No.	*Amount*	*Acres*	*No.*	*Amount*	*No.*	*Amount*
1869	1	$ 4,600	43	—	—	1	$ 4,600
1870	3	3,700	440	1	400	4	4,100
1871	1	400	80	—	—	1	400
1872	3	1,150	240	—	—	3	1,150
1873	3	850	240	1	400	4	1,250
1874	11	6,387	1,000	—	—	11	6,387
1875	10	3,717	958	—	—	10	3,717
1876	23	6,154	1,840	—	—	23	6,154
1877	7	2,183	760	2	707	9	2,890
1878	13	6,910	1,320	—	—	13	6,910
1879	13	6,525	1,160	—	—	13	6,525
1880	7	3,297	520	1	100	8	3,397
1881	14	9,150	1,327	5	890	19	10,040
1882	6	4,775	480	5	1,832	11	6,607
1883	17	15,255	1,660	3	1,767	20	17,022
1884	9	8,775	700	3	1,056	12	9,831
1885	14	10,883	1,380	7	1,935	21	12,818
1886	20	11,500	1,340	6	975	26	12,475
1887	7	7,318	700	4	1,860	11	9,178
1888	13	21,655	1,330	3	536	16	22,191
1889	10	10,210	760	6	3,732	16	13,942
1890	11	15,025	1,228	1	425	12	15,450
1891	11	12,086	955	2	4,500	13	16,586
1892	13	20,975	1,350	4	3,359	17	24,334
1893	10	12,235	847	2	2,650	12	14,885
1894	12	11,308	1,158	1	300	13	11,608
1895	8	10,700	960	5	3,777	13	14,477
1896	6	6,305	640	—	—	6	6,305
1897	10	10,800	890	3	805	13	11,605
1898	11	19,990	1,250	1	542	12	20,532
1899	11	24,650	1,406	1	350	12	25,000
1900	12	19,850	900	—	—	12	19,850
1901	12	26,854	1,238	2	9,089	14	35,943
1902	11	26,600	1,370	1	1,200	12	27,800
1903	6	11,600	480	1	2,000	7	13,600
1904	10	31,665	1,081	3	1,840	13	33,505
1905	8	14,852	720	—	—	8	14,852

One of the 42 successful buyers of railroad land mortgaged his property within six months after the railroad had given him his deed. Two of the 12 assignees mortgaged similarly. Four others among the original 42 encumbered one or more parcels of land at dates extending from six and one-half to thirteen years after they had obtained title. Thirteen, or 16 per cent of the individuals who purchased land from the Davenports, mortgaged all or part of their holdings within six months after acquiring title. Another 8, or 9 per cent, mortgaged their purchases eventually.

Between October 2, 1869, and December 31, 1905, lenders recorded 367 first mortgages to the value of $420,889 and 74 junior mortgages worth $47,027 on the agricultural land of Pebble Township.[21] The mortgage history of the township began in 1869 when J. B. Robinson filed a mortgage to secure a loan of $4,600 to H. J. Robinson, another member of his family. In certain respects the mortgage was irregular. H. J. Robinson mortgaged his half interest in forty-three acres of section 36. This was school land on which the state did not issue a deed to Robinson until January 1871. The high valuation reflected the efforts of the Robinsons to promote a town site in section 36.

No more than three first mortgages were filed from the township in any of the years before 1874. In this year 11 first mortgages were filed. Two years later, 23 first mortgages were filed. Not for another ten years did the total again rise as high as 20. In the 19 years after 1886 the fluctuation in the number of first mortgages diminished in contrast to the earlier years as the number stabilized between 6 and 13.

The total amount of funds loaned annually to the farmers of the township, however, made a somewhat different pattern. The yearly totals fluctuated in amount, but the over-all trend was steadily upward. If fewer first mortgages were filed after 1887, they represented larger amounts. The 23 first mortgages of 1876 represented loans totaling $6,154; the 12 first mortgage loans of 1901 totaled $26,854.

Table 16 shows the total first mortgage debt on farms in Pebble Township at intervals of five years. The debt of $8,324, divided into 15 loans encumbering 1,430 acres in 1875, had risen by 1905 to $103,244, divided into 45 loans secured by 5,947 acres of land. The greatest increase in the first mortgage debt occurred between 1885 and 1890,

[21] Mortgage statistics were compiled from data taken from the Dodge County Mortgage and Deed Registers in the office of the Register of Deeds, Fremont, Neb.

when the total rose from \$37,945 to \$64,493. Although the total debt rose, the number of loans outstanding declined after 1890, when the figure stood at 69; by 1905 the equivalent figure was 45. The percentage of agricultural acres which were encumbered in the township rose until it stood at 29½ per cent in 1900, but it declined thereafter to 26.2 per cent in 1905.

Table 16. First mortgage debt at five-year intervals.

	No. of first mortgages	Value of first mortgages	Encumbered acres (agricultural)	Percentage of acres (agricultural)
Jan. 1, 1870	1	\$ 4,600	43	—
Jan. 1, 1875	15	8,324	1,430	6.3
Jan. 1, 1880	49	22,774	4,598	20.3
Jan. 1, 1885	51	37,945	4,607	20.3
Jan. 1, 1890	69	64,493	6,038	26.7
Jan. 1, 1895	68	69,490	6,341	28
Jan. 1, 1900	61	90,893	6,672	29.5
Jan. 1, 1905	45	103,244	5,947	26.2

In eight years the amount of funds borrowed on junior mortgage totaled over 20 per cent of the mortgage debt contracted in that year. Three of these years fell within the five-year span 1887–1891. Small non-interest-bearing second mortgages which had been accepted by loan agents as their commission appeared in some years but seldom represented a majority of the second mortgages.

What motives impelled the pioneer landholders of Pebble Township to mortgage their land? The records show 51 first mortgages during 1874, 1875, 1876, and 1877. Of these, 15, or 29 per cent, formed part of real estate transactions or were negotiated to refinance mortgages which were coming due.[22] But 36 first mortgages, or 71 per cent, cannot be explained in this manner. During the years between 1873 and 1877, however, the settlers obtained final certificates on 81, or 67 per cent, of the tracts in the township which were acquired directly from the federal government. There were thus during the mid 1870's a large number of pioneers who for the first time had real estate to advance

[22] When a mortgage was recorded within six months after purchase of the property by the mortgagor it was assumed that the indenture represented part of the purchase price. Undoubtedly the assumption leaves a margin for error.

as security. Many of the mortgages drawn between 1874 and 1877 undoubtedly represented the efforts of settlers to convert an interest in their property into supplies, stock, machinery, and other farm equipment.

In 1878 for the first time the first mortgages growing out of real estate transactions and refinancing formed more than 50 per cent of the number recorded. In only two years thereafter, 1879 and 1883, did these two categories of mortgages together make up less than 50 per cent of the total, while the average was 64 per cent, and in the eight years 1898–1905, 75 per cent. For a five-year period from 1893 to 1897, however, refinancing and transfer mortgages totaled more than 60 per cent of all mortgages recorded in only one year. In the other four years such indentures made up a bare 50 per cent of the first mortgages. These were years of agricultural depression in the district, if the letters of L. D. Richards accurately mirror conditions. Mortgages growing out of economic distress, therefore, may well have formed a larger proportion of the mortgage total than usual.[23]

It has been pointed out in other studies that hard-pressed settlers often commuted their homesteads with borrowed funds. As soon as such settlers had evidence of title, they secured their loan with a mortgage and used any surplus in the loan above the land office price for family living. Such mortgages, it is inferred, were born of desperation, or of the desire to obtain speculator's profits by a quick sale as soon as the settler had obtained title. Similarly, the pre-emption law was used to obtain title quickly.[24] No definite conclusions can be based upon such a small sample as that provided by Pebble Township, but two settlers, or 25 per cent, of those who pre-empted land did mortgage it within six months, as did one of the settlers, or 14 per cent,

[23] Precipitation fell below twenty-five inches in sections of eastern Nebraska in 1870, 1887–88–89, 1890–92–93–95–97 and 1901, while in 1894 it fell below twenty inches. Statement based upon Eastern Division Averages in Nebraska Legislative Reference Bureau, *Nebraska Blue Book* (Lincoln, 1938), p. 468, and on the figures given in the yearly *Report of the Chief of the Weather Bureau* (Washington, D.C.) and, for Omaha and Fremont, in *Senate Document 115*, 51st Congress, 1st Session (1889–1890).

[24] Charles Lowell Green, *The Administration of the Public Domain in South Dakota* (South Dakota Historical Collections, XX; Pierre, 1940), 204–225, and Harold Hathaway Dunham, *Government Handout: A Study in the Administration of the Public Lands, 1875–1891* (Ann Arbor, 1941), pp. 188–190. Actually Pebble Township was settled for the most part before the abuses of the commutation clause of the homestead act became most widespread.

who commuted their homesteads. In comparison, 15 per cent of all homesteaders mortgaged their land within six months. The two settlers who pre-empted and then mortgaged almost immediately did dispose of their holdings within a few years, but the homesteader who commuted his homestead right to cash and then mortgaged did not alienate his land.

The mortgage appears to have played a small role in financing the purchase of land from the Union Pacific, since only one of the forty-two successful purchasers mortgaged his land within six months after completing his purchase. To the farmers who bought land from the Davenports the mortgage was more important. Thirteen, or 16 per cent, of them mortgaged a portion of their land almost immediately after obtaining title. Of this thirteen, three had paid cash; the remainder had purchased on credit. On the average, the ten who purchased on credit received their deeds seven years after they had purchased the land. Since the Davenport brothers were anxious to grant ten years' credit, this group evidently preferred to pay up with borrowed money in order to obtain a deed rather than to take full advantage of the terms offered to them. Since the rate of interest specified in the land contracts of the Davenports was usually somewhat above the rate charged for first mortgage funds at the same time, such a decision is understandable.

Turning briefly to the junior mortgages, twenty-seven out of seventy-four, or 36 per cent of the total, represented the commission on first mortgage loans. Seventeen, or 23 per cent, arose from the purchase of real estate, leaving the motivation underlying 41 per cent of the second mortgages unexplained.

From 1870 to 1877 capital from other midwestern states and from the northeast provided more than 50 per cent of the funds loaned on first mortgages in all but one year. Between 1878 and 1884, however, sources of credit within Dodge County were more important than nonresident funds with but one year of exception. During the three years 1885, 1886, and 1887 nonresident capital was again dominant, supplying at least 84 per cent of the funds advanced on the security of first mortgages in the township in each year. In four of the eight years from 1888 to 1895 more than 50 per cent of the capital invested in first mortgages was of local origin. But from 1896 on, local lenders became unquestionably the most important source of funds. In only two years did nonresident capital finance 50 per cent of the first mortgages which were drawn on the security of land in Pebble Township. In the thirty-seven years studied, however, the percentage of first mortgage funds from nonresident sources was less than 30 per cent in only five years and those well scattered. To the very end of the period the funds of nonresidents played a significant role in financing the farmers of Pebble Township.

Table 17. Percentage of nonresident capital loaned on first mortgages in Pebble Township: 1869–1905.

Year	%	Year	%	Year	%	Year	%
1869	—	1879	58	1888	29	1897	50
1870	84	1880	36	1889	53	1898	34
1871	100	1881	20	1890	66	1899	27
1872	52	1882	19	1891	41	1900	48
1873	35	1883	30	1892	42	1901	33
1874	93	1884	39	1893	38	1902	41
1875	75	1885	93	1894	83	1903	52
1876	63	1886	84	1895	79	1904	34
1877	82	1887	100	1896	30	1905	49
1878	41						

Undoubtedly the yearly variations in the amount of capital obtained from outside sources were linked in part to the availability of that capital. Thus the four years 1874–1877, in which nonresident capital entered the township in large amounts for the first time, marked the entrance of the first of the large western mortgage agencies into the township. The three years between January 1, 1885, and December 31, 1887, were the years in which these agencies reached the height of their popularity in the eastern states and had the largest supply of funds at their disposal. After 1896 the percentage of nonresident capital disbursed in the township was kept up by several eastern insurance companies that replaced the private eastern investors and the western mortgage agencies of the previous twenty years.

In 1870 two mortgagees gave New York as their state of residence. In the following year, John and Ira Davenport recorded their first mortgages on land in the township. Aside from their land speculations, the brothers loaned some $5,500,000 on first mortgage in the states of Michigan, Illinois, Iowa, Kansas, and Nebraska between 1868 and 1905. By 1905 they had extended thirty-two first mortgage loans to

Pebble Township farmers, totaling $26,325. For a time the brothers concentrated their lending activities in Nebraska in districts where they held real estate for sale.[25] Their motive was a simple one. Credit was necessary before the holdings of the settlers established in these townships could be developed adequately. If credit was supplied, the improvements which the settlers made would be reflected in rising land values. Such an increase, however, would enhance the value of the unimproved lands held by the Davenports as well. Other noncorporate investors from the northeastern United States also loaned money in the township, but none on a scale to compare with the Davenports.

Numerous western mortgage companies were organized during the late 1870's and particularly during the early 1880's.[26] The first of these agencies to appear in Pebble Township was the Corbin Banking Company of New York. In all, this company negotiated twelve of the thirty-three mortgages recorded from the township during 1875 and 1876. Other companies followed the lead of the Corbin agency during the late 1870's and the 1880's, including the Western Trust and Security Company of Fremont, the Iowa Mortgage Company of Muscatine, Iowa, and the Dakota Mortgage Loan Company of Boston, Massachusetts. During 1885–1887 the mortgage companies brought in over 74 per cent of the funds loaned on first mortgage. In nine other years between 1875 and 1898 the equivalent percentages ranged from 19 to 47 per cent. Although most of the western mortgage companies had failed by 1894, the Western Trust and Security Company continued after some reorganization, while the Phoenix Mutual Life Insurance Company supported the Security Investment Company of Lincoln when most of the other mortgage companies found their operating capital drained away by the necessity of making great numbers of foreclosures.[27] All of the loans in the township of Pebble after 1892 which

[25] Ira Davenport to E. O. Crosby, July 7, 1874.

[26] The *Annual Reports* of the Connecticut Bank Commissioners (1888–1895), of the Massachusetts Commissioner of Foreign Mortgage Companies (1890–1895), of the New York Superintendent of Banking relative to Foreign Mortgage, Loan, Investment and Trust Companies (1891–1896), and of the Vermont Inspector of Finance (1889–1893) provide the most satisfactory catalogue of the more important western mortgage companies of this period.

[27] For information on this phase of the history of the Security Investment Company I am indebted to the officers of the Farm Loan Division of the Phoenix Mutual Life Insurance Company who opened the early mortgage registers of that company to me in August 1948.

were negotiated by mortgage companies were written by these two agencies, and all of those drawn by the Security Investment Company were negotiated on behalf of either the Aetna Life Insurance Company of Hartford, Connecticut, or of the Phoenix Mutual of the same city.[28]

These life insurance companies, along with the Connecticut Mutual Benefit Life Insurance Company of Hartford, the Union Central Life Insurance Company of Cincinnati, and the Northwestern Mutual Life Insurance Company of Milwaukee formed the most important group of nonresident lenders after the year 1889. From 1890, when the Connecticut Mutual loaned $5,400 in four loans, to 1905, these companies negotiated thirty-three loans, totaling $57,800.

Local banks were never very important directly as sources of land credit in the township. In all, three banks located in Dodge County appeared as mortgagee in seven first mortgages amounting to $6,973 and in eight second mortgages totaling $8,803.32. All of these indentures were filed after 1886.

Most important of the banks which appear on the mortgage records was the Merchants and Farmers Bank of Scribner. Lying in a village just across the eastern boundary of the township adjacent to section 36, this bank stood as mortgagee in four first mortgage loans to the amount of $4,203 and in all of the eight second mortgages negotiated by local banks. Two of the second mortgages were securities for commissions owing to the bank in return for its services in obtaining first mortgage loans.

These banks ranked far behind such investors as the life insurance companies or the Davenport brothers in the actual amount of funds which they placed at the disposal of Pebble Township farmers on the security of their farms. The importance of the local banks, however, did not end with the loans which they negotiated in their own name. The Merchants and Farmers Bank of Scribner acted as the local agent for a mortgage company. Although the national banks in Fremont ostensibly played no part in farm mortgage financing in the township, these institutions were important in that their officers sponsored two mortgage companies which were active in Dodge County as well as farther to the west. Of these, the more important was the Western Trust and

[28] The *Annual Reports* of the Connecticut Insurance Commissioner contain much information on the lending activities of the Hartford companies. See particularly those published in 1875 and 1876.

Security Company, organized by L. D. Richards and other directors of the Fremont National Bank.[29]

Making it still more difficult to assess the role of banking institutions in the farm mortgage field was the activity of the noncorporate private banker. Since they seldom used a firm name which distinguished them as bankers and infrequently appeared as mortgagee in any considerable number of mortgages, it is easy to overlook the work of such individuals. Yet their activities were undoubtedly of great significance in total. Preferring to use their own limited supply of funds in more remunerative fields than first mortgage farm financing, they served as local agents for the mortgage companies or for individual eastern investors. A. P. Hopkins, for instance, a private banker of Fremont, negotiated more than 500 loans for the Davenport brothers during the late 1870's and early 1880's. At least one private banker was located at Scribner during the 1880's, acting as the agent of a mortgage company.

The provisions in the mortgages filed on land in Pebble Township varied in their complexity. When the mortgagees were local men, the indentures were usually simple and short—a mere transfer of the security in case the terms of the notes should be broken. The mortgages filed by eastern investors or their agents were much longer and filled with a greater variety of terms which were designed to safeguard the mortgagee.

Clauses which were designed to nullify the effect of the collection laws of the state were common in the forms used by eastern investors. Although the code of Nebraska allowed attorney's fees to be assessed against mortgagors in foreclosure cases during only the years intervening between the legislative terms of 1873 and 1879,[30] mortgages containing clauses authorizing such practice were filed in later years. Stay and appraisal laws were specifically waived in many of the mortgages as in the concluding paragraph of the form used by the Corbin Banking Company: "The said parties of the first part do hereby expressly waive an appraisement of said real estate, should the same be sold under execution, order of sale, or other final process, and do further waive all benefits of the stay, valuation or appraisement laws." [31]

[29] Incorporation of this company was noted by the Fremont *Tribune*, Sept. 9, 1885.

[30] Nebraska, *General Statutes, 1873*, p. 98, and *General Laws, 1879*, p. 78.

[31] Mortgage Register H, p. 320.

Most mortgages recorded on behalf of nonresident mortgagees named a place of payment in the eastern United States, thereby insuring that the mortgagor would pay the cost of exchange.

The first four mortgages recorded from Pebble Township backed notes drawn at 10 per cent. Then, during the next three years, 12 per cent became the prevalent rate. From this figure the average rate on all first mortgages slumped, with some fluctuation until 1905, when the average rate specified in seven notes was 4.9 per cent.[32]

Table 18. Average interest rates in Pebble Township.

	First mortgages		Second mortgages			First mortgages		Second mortgages	
Year	No.	Rate—%	No.	Rate—%	Year	No.	Rate—%	No.	Rate—%
1869	1	10	—	—	1888	12	6.8	1	9
1870	3	10	—	—	1889	8	7	3	8.6
1871	1	12	—	—	1890	11	7.1	—	—
1872	3	11.3	—	—	1891	11	7.6	2	9
1873	3	12	1	12	1892	11	7.5	3	8.6
1874	11	11	—	—	1893	10	7.2	2	9
1875	10	10.8	—	—	1894	11	6.7	—	—
1876	23	10.8	—	—	1895	7	6.3	4	8
1877	6	12	1	12	1896	6	8.2	—	—
1878	13	10.8	—	—	1897	10	7.5	2	8.5
1879	12	9.7	—	—	1898	11	6.5	1	10
1880	5	9.6	2	9	1899	10	5.7	1	8
1881	14	9.4	2	10	1900	12	5.6	—	—
1882	6	7.8	1	9	1901	11	5.4	2	6.5
1883	16	9	4	8.7	1902	11	5.2	1	5
1884	9	8.3	2	6.5	1903	6	5.2	1	5
1885	13	7.9	1	9	1904	10	5.5	3	6.6
1886	19	7.8	2	8.7	1905	7	4.9	—	
1887	7	7.6	1	8					

In the years when comparison is possible the rate on funds loaned by residents was equal to the nonresident rate in four years, less than the nonresident rate in eight years and greater than the nonresident rate in twenty-two years. Seven of the twelve years, when the resident

[32] Occasionally the interest rate specified was not given in the recorded mortgage. The annual number of the mortgages given in Table 10 does not always coincide with the yearly total in Table 7.

rate was below or equal to the rate charged by out-of-state lenders, fell before 1880. Evidently the nonresident rate tended to be lower than the local rate after 1880 because the commission of the mortgage agent was usually not included in the rate given in the note and mortgage. Had the commission been added, the resident and nonresident rate would have been more nearly equal.[33]

Why, however, was the local rate usually below or equal to the out-of-state rate during the 1870's? Part of the explanation may be found in the usury legislation of the state of Nebraska. Interest was regarded as usurious, before 1879, if the mortgagor had paid more than 12 per cent in one year, and after the legislative session of that year, if he paid more than 10 per cent to lenders on new loans. If local mortgage brokers could be proven to be the agents of eastern lenders, their commissions were counted as part of the interest rate obtained by such investors. The supreme court of Nebraska interpreted the word "agent" more broadly than did the courts of adjacent states.[34] Nonresident lenders, therefore, adopted the policy of writing notes at the legal maximum and paying the local agent from interest payments. Under such conditions the resident and the out-of-state rate were equal unless, among the local lenders, friends or kinsfolk gave special accommodation to borrowers or unless a canny real estate salesman offset a high sale price by a lower rate of interest in the note accepted as partial payment in a real estate transaction; then, the local rate might fall below the nonresident rate. During the 1880's, however, the market rate of interest dropped well below the upper limit set by the usury law. There ceased to be as much danger that the agent's commission, when combined with the interest rate, could bring a charge of usury, and the number of lending agencies which took their commission above the interest rate increased.

Although the rate of interest was often not given in the junior mortgages filed from the township, figures were obtained from forty-two of seventy-nine such indentures. In all but a few years the rate stood above that of the average on all first mortgages. Since the junior mort-

[33] The difference between the average local and the average nonresident rate was less than one per cent in twenty years and reached 2 per cent in only three years.

[34] Ira Davenport to Wilson and Hopkins, Fremont, Neb., Aug. 31, 1877; see also *Philo* vs. *Butterfield, Nebraska Reports*, III, 256, *Cheney* vs. *White, ibid.*, V, 261, and *Cheney* vs. *Woodruff, ibid.*, VI, 151.

gage is less satisfactory as a claim on security, it is natural that it should return a higher rate of interest than do first mortgages. Sometimes, however, relatives or friends take second mortgages as security for loans, and then the rate may well be no higher or even lower than the going rate for first mortgages.

Over the period covered by this study, the percentage of loans written for one year declined. In most years before 1879 at least a third of all the first mortgages drawn on agricultural land in the township specified maturities of twelve months or less. After 1883 the percentage of such mortgages was never greater than 18 per cent, and in nine of the twenty-two years there were none recorded. Evidently the pioneer used his land to provide short-term financing to a much greater extent than did his successors in the township.

Once large amounts of nonresident funds were available to the farmers of Pebble Township, the average length of time between the recording of the mortgage and its release stood generally between four and six years, although the mortgages recorded in 1887, 1895, and 1902 all enjoyed an average life span of between ninety and one hundred months.

The mortgage first recorded from the township specified that repayment should be made in installments. Such clauses became rarer as the years passed, although the insurance companies allowed the repayment of principal when the interest became due, if the mortgagor so wished.

The farmers of Pebble Township were generally successful in their use of land mortgage credit during the pioneer period. In all, eleven owners appear to have entered unsuccessfully into first mortgage contracts. Creditors foreclosed the mortgages of eight farmers, and three owners deeded their security to the mortgagees. There is some doubt whether one of the latter should be regarded as failing, since he deeded for a consideration of $900 only three years after borrowing $400 on the security of eighty acres. Even had he neglected all interest payments, a judgment could hardly have amounted to $900. With this reservation the mortgagor was included among the unsuccessful debtors. In addition to the group of eleven whose first mortgages were closed out disastrously, three junior mortgagors deeded their interest in real estate to the mortgagees. These men had all purchased land on which a first mortgage already stood. As part of the purchase price of the land they gave a second mortgage to the original mortgagor and assumed the payments on the first mortgage. Eventually they deeded back their interest in the land to the original owner and mortgagor. The failures of these three men did not represent unsuccessful first mortgages, but did evidently involve the failure of farm operators. Reduced to percentages, 3 per cent of all the first mortgages recorded on Pebble Township land in the period between 1869 and 1905 were terminated either by foreclosure or by the mortgagor deeding the real estate to the mortgagee. Three second mortgages, or 4 per cent of all second mortgages, were closed out by deeding.

Of the eleven owners who failed to complete first mortgage contracts successfully, four belonged to the group of one hundred settlers who had homesteaded government land. Thirty-six per cent of those who lost their land were, therefore, homesteaders, but this group actually represented only 4 per cent of all those who had homesteaded in Pebble Township. One of the eleven was listed among the purchasers of land from the Union Pacific, but the security which he deeded to his mortgagee represented only one-quarter of his purchases from the railroad. Four others failed to extinguish mortgages which they had given as part of the purchase price of their holding. Neither of the two remaining unsuccessful mortgagors were residents of the county; one gave his residence as Wisconsin and had obviously inherited the land which he gave up, while the other resided in Cuming County, Nebraska.

Five of the eleven defaulted first mortgage contracts were filed before 1877, two were recorded during the 1880's and one in 1905. Of the five filed before 1877, four were placed on the mortgage rolls during 1876. Seventeen per cent of the twenty-three first mortgages filed in that year ended therefore in failure.

The contractors who deeded away their equity to the holders of second mortgages signed these indentures in 1876, 1887, and 1891.

Of the warranty and sheriff's deeds which terminated the title of the fourteen unsuccessful mortgagors, six had been written by the end of 1880 and eight by the close of 1887. Five were recorded in the years 1889–1905 and one in 1910. The evidence is clear. Mortgagors in Pebble Township made the greatest number of unsuccessful loans during the 1870's or early period of settlement rather than during the late 1880's and the 1890's when the Alliance movement and the Populist agitation were at their peaks.

In all, the eleven defaulted first mortgage loans were backed by 1,000 acres of land as security, or some 5 per cent of the total land area of the township which was used for agricultural purposes. Despite the predominance of the upland soils in the township, only three of the eleven failures occurred on these soil types. These three parcels embraced, in all, 280 acres, or 28 per cent of the land on which first mortgage loans terminated unsuccessfully. With the exception of eighty acres of the more droughty type of terrace soils, the remainder was found in the bottoms. In proportion to its total area, therefore, far more bottom land was sacrificed than either terrace or upland soil. This finding perhaps reflects the drainage problem which was a very real one in the bottoms during the pioneer period.[35]

[35] Dan V. Stephens, "Soil and Drainage of Dodge County," in William H. Buss and Thomas T. Osterman, *History of Dodge and Washington Counties, Nebraska and Their People* (Chicago, 1921), I, 128–132.

XVI

PIONEER KINSLEY

LYING in the valley of the Arkansas River between the ninety-ninth and the one-hundredth meridians is Edwards County, Kansas. The administrative township of Kinsley is situated in the northwest quarter of the county and lies, but for portions of six sections, to the north and west of the Arkansas River.[1] In round figures the township embraces 29,000 acres of land. Kinsley, the county seat, is located in the township. Of this town a correspondent of the Atchison *Champion* said, "For a long time it was the westernmost town that really aimed to get a respectable living [in the Arkansas Valley]. Dodge was further on, but Dodge, in those days, lived on the Government and its own wickedness." [2]

[1] This study was designed to supplement work which Professor James C. Malin had already published on Kinsley Township or nearby areas. See his articles in the *Kansas Historical Quarterly:* "The Kinsley Boom of the Late Eighties," IV (Feb., May 1935), 23–49, 164–187, "The Turnover of Farm Population in Kansas," *ibid.,* IV (Nov. 1935), 339–372, and "J. A. Walker's Early History of Edwards County," IX (Aug. 1940), 259–284. See also "The Adaptation of the Agricultural System to Subhumid Environment. Illustrated by the . . . Wayne Township Farmers' Club of Edwards County, Kansas," *Agricultural History,* X (July 1936), 118–141.

[2] Kinsley *Mercury,* Jan. 8, 1887.

The bulk of the township is situated on a strip of flood plains and terraces extending from two to five miles west of the Arkansas. At a distance of some three or four miles from the river a gentle rise marks the limits of the "first bottoms." The soil here is of somewhat different character than that on the flood plains. Part of six sections lies to the east of the Arkansas in what are called "the sand hills." [3]

The soils on the flood plains are known locally as "deep, hard lands." Officially they are designated as "deep, friable, silty, to clayey soils," and are "characterized by friable, granular to crumblike, silty to slightly sandy surface soils which are eight to 10 inches thick and grade into somewhat heavier but friable . . . subsoils, 20 to 30 inches thick. In general they are fertile, easily tilled, absorb moisture at a moderate rate and have a high moisture storage capacity." [4] Drainage is generally adequate but the occasional saline spot or poorly drained area occurs.

The moderate slopes at the edge of the bottoms and along the drainage way in the northwest corner of the township are marked by a "friable or moderately friable, silty to clayey soil" which is similar to the "deep hard lands." [5] Soil conservation experts classified all lands in the township to the west of the Arkansas as fit for cultivation in 1940 when they surveyed Edwards County. The area of the township lying east of the river, however, was classified as fit only for grazing or woodland use and that with severe restrictions.

Precipitation in the county ranges on an average from twenty-four inches on the eastern edge to twenty-two inches on the western boundary. Some 75 per cent of the precipitation falls during the growing season, which, on the average, lasts 175 days. Both rainfall and growing season are, however, subject to wide variations from the mean. The average annual temperature stands between 55 and 56 degrees.

Yields in Edwards County are 88 per cent of the county average for the state and also fall somewhat below those of some of the neighboring counties. Today wheat is the dominant grain crop, although a significant acreage of sorghum is grown. But in the thirty crop years between 1911 and 1940, ten wheat crops failed, and only fair to poor crops were harvested in eleven other years. Drought which was suffi-

[3] An account of the physical characteristics of Edwards County may be found in United States Department of Agriculture, *et al., Physical Land Conditions Affecting Use, Conservation and Management of Land Resources: Edwards County, Kansas* (mimeographed; Manhattan, 1944).

[4] *Ibid.*, p. 5.

[5] *Ibid.*, p. 9.

cient to cause crop failure has occurred in as many as four consecutive years.

Kinsley Township fell within the boundaries of the land grant given to the Atchison, Topeka and Santa Fe Railroad in 1863. Land in the sections designated by odd numbers, therefore, became the property of that corporation to be sold in aid of the construction of its line. The land in sections bearing even numbers was eventually allocated directly to individuals by the federal government with the exception of sections 16 and 36, township 24, range 19, the state school lands.

The tract books of the United States land office identify the settlers who obtained title to government land.[6] The first such settler filed his application to homestead the northwest quarter of section 4, T25, R19 in June, 1873. He obtained his final certificate fifteen months later under the act of 1872, which allowed Union veterans to subtract the period of their war service from the five years of residence which were ordinarily necessary under the homestead act of 1862. The last settler to obtain government land in the township received his final certificate in 1903. Strictly speaking, title did not pass irrevocably until the patent to which the final certificate entitled a settler was issued, but for most purposes title was considered to vest in the claimant for government land as soon as he could show a final certificate.

In all, 91 individuals obtained title to 102 parcels of government land. Sixty-seven homesteads were granted; [7] 50 of these were 160-acre homesteads which were obtained under the provisions of the soldiers' and sailors' homestead act of 1872. Twenty individuals obtained tracts under the terms of the pre-emption act of 1841, while 4 homesteaders commuted their claims and purchased them for cash under the terms of the commutation clause of the homestead act of 1862. Finally, 11 settlers acquired title to timber claims.[8]

[6] Duplicate sets of land office tract books for the state of Kansas are held in the National Archives and in the Department of the Interior, Washington, D.C. Kinsley Township fell in the land district administered from Larned.

[7] The word "homestead" will be used throughout this chapter to refer to land either acquired by its owner under the terms of the various federal homestead acts or land in the process of being thus acquired. In the legal sense, of course, a homestead is a holding which its owner holds free from the claims of creditors under certain conditions.

[8] A comprehensive summary of the various acts under which title was transferred from the government in this township may be found in Thomas Donaldson, *The Public Domain* (Washington, 1884). The specialist, of course, will use the *U.S. Statutes at Large* as well.

But all of those who aspired to ownership of government land in Kinsley Township were not successful. Of the 196 entries filed between 1872 and 1898, 94, or 35 homesteads and 59 timber claims, were given up. In other words, 34 per cent of all homesteaders and 84 per cent of all those claiming land under the timber culture acts failed to obtain title.

Table 19. Disposal of government land in Kinsley Township.

	Successful entries	Unsuccessful entries	Final certificates		Successful entries	Unsuccessful entries	Final certificates
1872	—	3	—	1887	1	1	1
1873	14	9	—	1889	—	—	2
1874	10	9	1	1890	2	2	—
1875	5	10	6	1891	1	—	—
1876	10	12	6	1892	1	4	3
1877	6	9	11	1893	—	1	3
1878	19	9	8	1894	—	1	1
1879	12	5	18	1895	—	—	1
1880	3	3	7	1896	1	—	2
1881	3	3	4	1897	—	—	5
1882	1	1	5	1898	1	—	—
1883	4	5	2	1899	—	—	1
1884	1	4	8	1900	—	—	1
1885	5	2	1	1903	—	—	1
1886	2	1	4	Totals	102	94	102

The entry figures include some duplication. Of the 91 individuals who obtained title to 102 parcels of land, 24 had filed papers on a total of 25 other pieces of land which they eventually threw back into the public domain. Of those who failed to obtain any land whatsoever, 2 had sought both homestead and timber claims. The 94 canceled entries, therefore, represented the activities of only 67 individuals who did not obtain at least some land from the federal government. Altogether, 158 individuals laid claim to government land in Kinsley Township, of whom 41 per cent failed to obtain title to any land. Another 15 per cent obtained only part of the holdings which they claimed originally.

If such percentages appear startling, we should remember that all entrymen did not desire to obtain final title. Claims were sold despite the lack of final certificate or patent.[9] In only four of the ninety-four cases where the entrants threw up their claims did they abandon them outright. Instead, formal relinquishments were filed at the land office. Such formality could hardly have been accidental. Somewhat different were the cases of the four settlers who filed timber claims and relinquished them years later, only to homestead the same tracts. Whatever other advantages this practice involved, it undoubtedly postponed the day when a settler must pay taxes on his holdings.

In 1873 the Atchison, Topeka and Santa Fe Railway Company made its first sales of land in the administrative township of Kinsley.[10] Between 1873 and 1898, when the Santa Fe's title to several parcels of land was closed out by bankruptcy sale, the land department of the company sold land in the township to 110 individuals at prices varying from $1.25 to $10.00 per acre. In the order of the frequency with which they availed themselves of the terms, purchasers bought on eleven-year contract, on six-year contract, for cash, and on two-year contract. One contract provided for complete payment at the end of one year.[11]

Two-year contracts involved merely the division of the principal into three parts. One-third, plus a year's interest on the unpaid principal, was paid down, and the other installments, plus interest, were paid at the end of the first and second years. When purchasers used the six-year plan, they paid one-sixth of the principal down and interest on the remainder. The second payment was limited to interest on the principal and the final five payments were made up of one-sixth of the principal and interest on the principal outstanding. Similarly, combinations of interest and principal payments were arranged to extend over eleven years.

By 1879 the Santa Fe was advertising a discount of 33⅓ per cent

[9] See, for instance, Orange Judd's matter-of-fact references to the practice in "Who Shall Go West," pt. 1, *Prairie Farmer* (Oct. 24, 1885), p. 701; also Harold Hathaway Dunham, *Government Handout; A Study in the Administration of the Public Lands, 1875–1891* (Ann Arbor, 1941), pp. 144–164.

[10] The most useful published account of the early operations of this company is still Glenn D. Bradley, *The Story of the Santa Fe* (Boston, 1920). Administration of the land grant is discussed in Chapter 5. But see also L. L. Waters, *Steel Trails to Santa Fe* (Lawrence, 1950), ch. 5.

[11] The analysis of the land sales of the Santa Fe which follows is based on data taken from the tract book of the Santa Fe and from the volumes of the sales record held in the tax division of the Atchison, Topeka and Santa Fe Railroad Company, Topeka.

from list price, while two- and six-year contracts were to be scaled down by 20 and 30 per cent. On the two-year contracts interest on the unpaid principal was charged at the rate of 10 per cent, but on the longer contracts stood uniformly at 7 per cent. This latter rate should not, of course, be compared with the rate then charged on mortgage loans and cited as an illustration of the generosity of the railroad. The Santa Fe set both the rate of interest and the purchase price. An attractive rate of interest could be well compensated for in a higher list price.

Sales in the township by the Santa Fe were spread over twenty-two years, but by far the largest number were grouped in the three-year period between 1876 and 1878 and in the two years 1884 and 1885. Sales in 1873 were limited to three. One of these transferred sections 33, T24, R19 and 5, T24, R18 to the Arkansas Valley Town Company. Section 33 is the site of the town of Kinsley. A second sale transferred a quarter section to Edward Kinsley, an employee of the Santa Fe in Boston. The consideration was a nominal one of $1.00. The last sale in 1873 gave possession of the northwest quarter of section 7, T25, R19 to two local men.

Not until 1876 did the turnover of railroad land in the township become rapid. In that year 29 sales were made. An additional 27 followed during the next two years. Over the next five years only 10 sales were made, but in 1884 and 1885 the total number of sales recorded was 33.

Of the 56 sales transacted in 1876, 1877, and 1878, 39, or 70 per cent, were eventually canceled. Some of the blame for the cancellations may be placed specifically upon the weather.[12] In 1879 and 1880 drought severely damaged the crops in west central Kansas and thereby the hopeful plans of many settlers. The officials of the Santa Fe were not unaware of the settlers' problems. A correspondent of the Kinsley

[12] In his study of the turnover of farm population in selected townships throughout Kansas, Professor Malin has discounted the influence of physical phenomena in either raising or lowering the number of settlers that left pioneer communities. Rather, he emphasized group behavior, writing, "under any given set of general conditions, the farm operators in all parts of the state reacted in much the same manner, the variations of local physical environment exercising only a secondary or minor influence." "The Turnover of Farm Population in Kansas," *Kansas Historical Quarterly*, IV (Nov. 1935), 339–372. One can accept this qualification and still argue that years of drought played a significant role in producing cancellations since, according to Professor Malin, the inflow of population into pioneer areas fell off at such times. The outgoing settlers, therefore, who would have assigned or sold their contracts to newcomers, allowed them to lapse on their departure instead.

Graphic reported in August 1879 that the railway company had offered to furnish seed wheat to all farmers in Hodgeman, Pawnee, Ness, Edwards, and Ford Counties who had experienced crop failure.[13] The company offered to bear the transportation charges on the seed but the terms were to be "cash on delivery." The writer claimed that few settlers could meet these terms, since the stores of cash which they had brought with them into the region were exhausted.

Table 20. Santa Fe land sales: Kinsley Township.

	Total sales	Acres	Successful buyers		Total sales	Acres	Successful buyers
1873	3	1,600	2	1883	4	363	4
1874	6	880	2	1884	11	3,138	9
1875	1	80	1	1885	22	5,689	17
1876	29	5,150	10	1886	3	1,260	3
1877	14	1,860	3	1892	2	470	—
1878	13	1,220	4	1894	1	160	—
1879	2	240	2	1895	1	159	1
1880	1	40	—				
1882	3	690	3	Totals *	116		61

* Actually only 110 individuals purchased land and only 58 individuals or their assignees were successful in obtaining deeds. The totals in Table 20 stand at 116 and 61 because three buyers returned a second time to purchase land, two others similarly returned but failed to complete one of the transactions and one individual failed on two separate purchases. This table has been worked out in terms of the individual purchasers rather than in terms of contracts. All land contracts issued to the same buyer and bearing the same date have been treated as part of one sale.

Some months later the *Graphic* recorded that fifteen or twenty men had been sent west to work on the railroad on the previous morning and added that the railroad was pledged to furnish work for settlers who desired it.[14] Then, in 1880, after repeated references to exodus from the county, the *Edwards County Leader* reported: "The Railroad Company will furnish every farmer in the county with 25 bushels of wheat—money or no money—and take their note at 7 per cent interest. This is a good stand off, and we hope the boys wont be slow to take advantage of it." [15]

[13] Taylor Jackson in Kinsley *Graphic,* Aug. 9, 1879.
[14] Kinsley *Graphic,* Oct. 18, 1879.
[15] *Edwards County Leader,* Kinsley, Aug. 26, 1880.

Few who defaulted on their agreements in the late 1870's had a great financial stake in the land. On only seven of the twenty contract sales made in 1876 and eventually canceled was any principal paid. Of the eighteen sales made during the next two years and eventually canceled, however, a portion of the principal was paid on all but one.[16] But on only one of the twenty-four contracts of these years on which principal was paid did the Santa Fe receive more than one installment of the purchase price. During this period the company did not cancel contracts immediately upon default. In most cases contracts were canceled two or three years after the payments had been allowed to lapse.

With the return of more favorable seasons in 1881, central Kansas began to appear more attractive to prospective land buyers. By 1883 the Arkansas Valley was beginning to experience a real estate boom. As a result, the Santa Fe was able to dispose of all but a few parcels of its land in Kinsley Township during 1884 and 1885. Seventeen of the twenty-six cash sales made in the township were transacted in these two years, and the percentage of failure among purchasers stood at 21 per cent, in comparison to 69 per cent in the earlier period of heavy sales.

In all, 58, or 53 per cent of the 110 original purchasers of railroad land in Kinsley Township, saw land deeded either to themselves or to their assignees. Of the 58, 15, or 26 per cent, assigned their contracts to 18 assignees. The total number of individuals who received deeds from the Santa Fe, therefore, was 61.

The manner in which contracts were recorded and deeds issued makes it difficult to sort out all of the buyers who obtained holdings in several townships. But at least 7 of the original 58 were speculators, if we define such individuals as those who held their land for a rise in price with no intention of farming it themselves. Of these, Edward Kinsley obtained 160 acres; R. E. Edwards, merchant and banker of Kinsley, purchased 340 acres within the township and at least 100 acres outside its boundaries; Peter Chesrown of Ashland County, Ohio, bought 480 acres within the township; and Graham and Ellwood of Dekalb, Illinois held a section and a half. Two purchases formed part of much larger transfers outside the boundaries of the township. In this class fell a quarter section obtained by Alexander and Fred Forsha of Topeka in 1885 as part of a joint purchase which included ten and a quarter sections in adjacent townships and 1,100 acres in Kinsley Town-

[16] Three contracts whose terms are in doubt fell in this period.

ship, which a partnership, Ott and Tewkesbury of Topeka, purchased as part of a transfer of 5,200 acres. It is possible that other purchases should be classed as speculative. Of the 21 purchasers who bought more than 160 acres of railroad land, only 5 can be identified subsequently from the census rolls as rural residents in Kinsley Township, whereas a majority of those buying 160 acres or less appear in the returns of the census taker.[17]

In numbers, the small purchaser outweighed those who obtained relatively large units. Of the 58 original successful buyers, 40 bought a quarter section or less. The purchases of 15 fell between 160 and 640 acres. Three purchasers obtained more than a section. Three in the first class, however, and one in each of the other two size groups purchased additional land outside Kinsley Township. These 5 purchases ranged in total size from 400 to 6,000 acres.

In terms of acreage, the story is somewhat different. In round figures, the 40 purchasers of a quarter section or less bought 4,580 acres, while the remaining 18 buyers purchased 8,420 acres.

Although it has its limitations, a grouping by place of residence at the time of purchase gives some clue to the background of those who purchased railroad land. Of the 110 individuals whose names appear in the sales record of the railway, 42 gave their address as Kinsley, and 13 others resided elsewhere in Kansas. Thirty-two purchasers came from Illinois, 6 came from Iowa, 5 from Wisconsin, and 4 from Pennsylvania. Missouri and Massachusetts both contributed 2 buyers, while Minnesota, Connecticut, Delaware, and New Mexico were all represented by one purchaser.

Those who were successful in completing contracts issued prior to 1879 took, on the average, forty-nine months to meet their obligations to the railway company. Successful contractors from 1882 on paid out in forty-four months, on the average. The difference is not one from which significant conclusions can be drawn. The fact that funds were available more cheaply on mortgage security during the second period may have encouraged contractors to pay out more quickly.

There was no great overlapping among those who purchased railroad land and those who obtained land from the government. Fifty-eight of the original purchasers of railroad land and 18 assignees can be de-

[17] The manuscript census rolls of 1870 (federal), 1875 (state), 1880 (federal), 1885, 1895, and 1905 are held by the Kansas State Historical Society, Topeka.

scribed as successful in their dealings with the Santa Fe. Five of the original 58 succeeded in obtaining both government and railroad land. Five of the remaining 86 individuals who received patents on government land attempted railroad land contracts but failed to complete them.

Seventy-nine per cent of those who purchased railroad land elected to buy their land on credit. Twenty-one per cent paid cash.[18] Nine of the 23 who made up the group of cash purchasers obtained units of 320 acres or more. Two of these, the Forshas and Ott and Tewkesbury, received over 11,000 acres at a cost of $1.75 and $1.25 per acre. The prices paid by the seven other large purchasers ranged between $4.00 and $10.00 per acre.

Of the 87 individuals who sought to take the contract route to ownership, 52, or 60 per cent, failed either to obtain a deed or to assign their contracts to someone who did so. In contrast, 34 out of 100 settlers who attempted to homestead land in the township failed in their efforts. The record on timber claims, however, was worse than that made by the contractors with the Santa Fe. If we consider totals, 41 per cent of all individuals who sought land under the homestead, pre-emption, and timber culture acts were completely unsuccessful. In comparison, when cash sales of railroad land are considered along with contracts, 47 per cent of the purchasers or their assignees failed to obtain a deed. The percentages are surprisingly close.

If such percentages seem to indicate that price had little effect on the success or failure of those seeking title to land in Kinsley Township, the conclusion is modified by a comparison between the prices actually obtained by the Santa Fe in cash sales and on successful contracts and the prices specified in canceled contracts of the same years. In 1876, 1877, 1878, and 1885 a considerable number of both successful and abortive sales were transacted. In each of these years, the average price in cash sales and successful contracts fell below the average on the canceled contracts of the same year by amounts ranging from $1.25 to $2.60 per acre. The average price paid by successful purchasers on both cash sales and contracts in the four years was $4.90 per acre; the average price which unsuccessful purchasers agreed to pay was $6.70 per acre.

After this sketch of the way in which the land in Kinsley Township

[18] Actually twenty-five cash purchases were made, but two buyers returned to obtain additional land.

entered private ownership, let us examine its role as mortgage security in the pioneer days.[19]

Of the 91 settlers who were successful in obtaining title to government land, 41, or 45 per cent, did not mortgage their holdings. The remaining 50, or 55 per cent, did mortgage 53 tracts of land which they had acquired from the government. Thirty-eight homesteads, 8 pre-empted parcels, 5 timber claims, and 2 commuted homesteads were thus encumbered. In other words, 58 per cent of the homesteads in the township were eventually mortgaged by the homesteader who obtained title, while 50 per cent of the commuted homesteads, 40 per cent of the pre-emptions, and 41 per cent of the timber claims were similarly burdened.

The dates on which the settlers mortgaged their land are of some significance since they give a clue to the reasons underlying the decisions to encumber land. It is interesting also to discover whether the pattern of mortgaging differed radically on land which had been obtained under the terms of the homestead act and on land which had been obtained under other provisions of the land code.

Of the fifty-three parcels of government land which were eventually mortgaged by their owners, 51 per cent was mortgaged within six months after the settler had received his final certificate. Another 9 per cent was mortgaged during the second six months of ownership. A further 15 per cent was mortgaged in the second year, and only 2 per cent after five years had elapsed. There was little difference between the percentage of homesteaded and the percentage of pre-empted land which was mortgaged within the first year of ownership. All of the mortgages on pre-empted land were placed, however, by the end of the third year of titled possession, while 16 per cent of the homesteaded land was mortgaged after the third year of titled possession. The timber claims mortgaged were encumbered in the year after title was obtained. Only four out of seventy successful homesteaders, or 6 per cent, commuted their homesteads and paid for their land at the pre-emption rate of $1.25 per acre. Two of the four mortgaged their land, but only after two and five years had elapsed after the date when they acquired title. That the pre-emptors and those who commuted homesteads bought their land for cash seems to have had little effect upon the percentage of those who

[19] All mortgage statistics used hereafter are derived from an analysis of the Mortgage and Deed Registers of Edwards County in the office of the Register of Deeds at Kinsley.

mortgaged their holdings soon after obtaining title. Fifty per cent of the mortgagors among pre-emptors and "commuters" encumbered their land within a year of acquiring title; 57 per cent of the homesteaders who mortgaged did so during their first year of titled possession.

Table 21. Date of encumbering government land.

	Home-steads		Pre-emptions		Commu-tations		Timber claims		Combined totals	
	No.	%	No.	%	No.	%	No.	%	No.	%
Within 6 months after title	20	52	4	50	—	—	3	60	27	51
Between 6 months and 1 year after title	2	5	1	12½	—	—	2	40	5	9
Between 1 year and 2 years after title	6	16	2	25	—	—	—	—	8	15
Between 2 years and 3 years after title	4	11	1	12½	1	50	—	—	6	11½
Between 3 years and 5 years after title	5	13	—	—	1	50	—	—	6	11½
More than 5 years after title	1	3	—	—	—	—	—	—	1	2

Of the sixty-one individuals to whom the Santa Fe deeded land, nineteen, or 32 per cent, mortgaged all or part of their holdings. Ten of the nineteen mortgaged all or part of their holdings within six months after they had obtained title. One other purchaser mortgaged within a year after the Santa Fe had given him his deed, a second within two years and the remaining seven recorded mortgages on their land from two to thirteen years after acquiring their deeds from the railway. A smaller percentage of those who paid hard cash to the railroad for their land found it necessary to mortgage that land later than did those who homesteaded government land. As in the case of the government land which was mortgaged, however, more than 50 per cent of the railroad land encumbered by its first owner was mortgaged within six months after title had passed.

In total, the farmers of Kinsley Township recorded 343 first mortgages and 80 junior mortgages between March 15, 1876, and December 31, 1905. In only a few years, however, did second mortgages play a significant role in farm financing in the township.

Table 22. Mortgage debt in Kinsley Township.

Year	First mortgages			Second mortgages		Total	
	No.	*Amount*	*Acres*	*No.*	*Amount*	*No.*	*Amount*
1876	4	$ 1,299	640	—	—	4	$ 1,299
1877	9	3,711	1,353	—	—	9	3,711
1878	12	4,320	1,670	1	$ 100	13	4,420
1879	22	16,249	3,191	8	572	30	16,821
1880	14	8,003	1,598	8	1,387	22	9,391
1881	4	3,200	597	1	73	5	3,273
1882	2	1,600	241	1	1,000	3	2,600
1883	2	1,200	400	1	732	3	1,932
1884	5	2,850	1,043	1	1,000	6	3,850
1885	15	16,554	2,411	2	881	17	18,435
1886	37	55,462	5,991	15	7,076	52	62,538
1887	38	48,120	5,284	14	5,525	52	53,645
1888	13	40,300	2,611	14	11,358	27	51,658
1889	10	12,640	1,986	3	25,772	13	38,412
1890	4	5,050	929	2	2,625	6	7,675
1891	9	7,658	1,038	1	75	10	7,733
1892	12	14,200	1,630	1	1,500	13	15,700
1893	10	9,800	1,344	2	900	12	10,750
1894	10	9,270	1,928	—	—	10	9,270
1895	2	550	50	—	—	2	550
1896	1	375	160	—	—	1	375
1897	1	550	320	—	—	1	550
1898	2	650	400	—	—	2	650
1899	4	7,447	531	—	—	4	7,447
1900	10	4,780	1,791	1	140	11	4,920
1901	18	13,550	2,584	—	—	18	13,550
1902	11	17,300	296	1	4,800	12	22,100
1903	21	27,072	3,618	—	—	21	27,072
1904	17	29,596	4,220	1	400	18	29,996
1905	24	68,771	6,125	2	2,035	26	70,806

Four first mortgages were filed on the security of agricultural land in Kinsley Township during 1876. During the next thirty years, filings rose and fell in a cyclical pattern. Peaks were reached in 1879, 1886, and 1905. In 1879 thirty mortgages were recorded to the value of $16,821. In 1886 fifty-two mortgages represented loans of $62,538. The same number of mortgages was filed in 1887, but the amount of funds transferred under their terms dropped to $53,644. In 1905 twenty-six mortgages secured a total debt of $70,806. The lows occurred in 1883 when three mortgages totaling some $2,000 in value were filed, and in 1896 when one mortgage secured a loan of $375 (see Table 22).

The percentage of agricultural land under first mortgage behaved in the same fashion as did the number of loans outstanding and the value of the first mortgage debt. Slumping somewhat between 1880 and 1885, it reached a peak in 1890, when 42 per cent of the agricultural land in the township was under mortgage. By 1900 the percentage stood at 15 per cent, but the figure had risen to 25 per cent by 1905 (see Table 23).

Table 23. First mortgage debt at five-year intervals.

	No. of first mortgages	Value of first mortgages	Encumbered acres (agricultural)	Percentage of acres (agricultural)
Jan. 1, 1880	35	$ 20,093	4,766	17
Jan. 1, 1885	26	15,465	3,755	13
Jan. 1, 1890	76	109,478	11,851	42
Jan. 1, 1895	47	59,483	7,140	25
Jan. 1, 1900	25	30,183	4,225	15
Jan. 1, 1905	46	50,562	7,139	25

The first peak of mortgaging in the township coincided with the first large issue of titles by the federal government. In 1879 there were more final certificates issued than in any other year in the history of the township. The twenty-six settlers who obtained final certificates in 1878 and 1879 had, for the first time, real estate security which they could convert into funds. Accentuating the demand for equipment and supplies, which one suspects was normal in a pioneer area, was the drought which struck the counties of the ninety-ninth meridian in 1879. In April 1880 the *Edwards County Leader* relayed the rumor that the county commissioners had passed an order at their last meeting which forbade the township trustees to extend aid to parties who were able to work and had mortgagable property.[20] The editor stated that such an order should certainly be passed if it had not already been done.

In all, title to 57 tracts of government land was granted during the seven years 1874–1880. During the same period, title passed from the Santa Fe railway company on 24 parcels of land. Those same years saw 78 mortgages filed.

[20] *Edwards County Leader*, Apr. 22, 1880.

The majority of the mortgages which were recorded by the farmers of Kinsley Township before 1881 evidently represented an effort to obtain supplies and equipment. Of the 61 first mortgages filed in the five years 1876–1880, apparently 10 were negotiated to refinance mortgage loans which were coming due. Six represented part of the payment in real estate transactions, and 4 settlers evidently borrowed to pay out on their pre-emptions.[21] Five loans patently represented mercantile credit, since they were drawn for uneven sums payable at the store of R. E. Edwards. When these 25 loans are eliminated, 36 are left unexplained. Lumping the 5 mercantile credit loans with the 36 unexplained loans, 41 loans were unconnected with real estate transactions or the act of refinancing previous obligations. Presumably these 41 loans, or 67 per cent of the first mortgage loans obtained by Kinsley settlers in the early period of the township's history, were used to buy food, stock, and equipment, although a few doubtless financed the mortgagor's departure to other pastures.

During the real estate boom of the mid 1880's land sales and refinancing accounted for a much larger proportion of the first mortgages than during the 1870's. Of the 90 first mortgages recorded during 1885, 1886, and 1887, there were 58, or 64 per cent, which were obviously for refinancing or related to real estate transactions. By the years 1903, 1904, and 1905 this percentage had risen to 71 per cent.[22]

Some writers have pointed out that hard-pressed settlers often commuted their homesteads with borrowed funds. As soon as such settlers had evidence of title, they secured their loan with a mortgage and used any surplus in the loan above the land office price for family living. Such mortgages, it is inferred, were born of desperation or of the desire to obtain speculator's profits by a quick sale as soon as the settler had obtained title. Similarly, the pre-emption law was used to obtain title quickly.[23] Since none of the commuted homesteads in Kinsley Township was mortgaged within the first year after title had passed from the government, such use of the commutation clause of the homestead act was

[21] When a mortgage was recorded within six months after purchase of the property by the mortgagor, it was assumed that the indenture represented part of the purchase price. Undoubtedly the assumption leaves a margin of error.

[22] This total includes eight mortgages filed by six purchasers of railroad land within six months after the Santa Fe had issued the deeds.

[23] Charles Lowell Green, "The Administration of the Public Domain in South Dakota," *South Dakota Historical Collections*, XX (Pierre, 1940), 204–225, and Dunham, *Government Handout*, pp. 188–190. Basic material is contained in the

not illustrated there. However, 50 per cent of the pre-emptors who mortgaged their claims did so during the first six months of ownership. Presumably these settlers used a portion of their loans to purchase their land. But the percentage of pre-emptors who mortgaged within six months of obtaining absolute title was no greater than the percentage of homesteaders who mortgaged their holdings during the same time.

Of the nineteen purchasers who mortgaged railroad land, ten did so within six months after they had obtained their deeds. In every case, these men closed out contracts which still had several years to run. Presumably these buyers were mortgaging to obtain the funds with which to pay off the railroad. Since the prevailing interest rate on mortgage funds stood above the rate specified in the Santa Fe contracts at the time, they must have discerned some other advantage in obtaining full title to their land. Such advantage, perhaps, lay in the ability of those who had outright ownership to give a warranty deed promptly in case the opportunity to sell presented itself.

During 1876 and 1877, thirteen loans were made on first mortgages in Kinsley Township. Ten of the mortgagees were residents of Edwards County. Between 1878 and 1894 the borrowers of Kinsley Township obtained more than 50 per cent of the funds borrowed on first mortgage in all but two years from outside Kansas. Only six loans on first mortgages were recorded between 1895 and 1898, but they were all obtained within the county. Between 1899 and 1902 out-of-state capital was again the most important source of credit. Beginning with 1903, however, local lenders became more important than nonresident lenders, and this continued to be the case through 1904 and 1905.

The creditors of Kinsley farmers resided in most of the central and northeastern seaboard states, as well as in Missouri, Illinois, Indiana, and Ohio. A few loans may well have come from Great Britain. The first eastern investor to lend money in the township was William H. Hanson of Suffolk County, Massachusetts, who in 1876 lent $350 at 8 per cent per annum on the security of the southeast quarter of section 6, T25, R19. The next year, E. R. Robbins of Middlebury, Vermont, was in the field. With others of his family, he was to make numerous loans in the

---

Annual Reports of the General Land Office during the 1880's, and in Donaldson, *The Public Domain*. Kinsley Township was settled for the most part before the abuses of the commutation clause of the homestead act and the pre-emption act became most widespread.

township. In 1878 the National Loan and Trust Company of Topeka entered the district. Other companies followed the next year, which also saw the Travelers' Insurance Company of Hartford become the first of the Hartford insurance companies to lend funds in the township.[24]

Table 24. Percentage of nonresident capital loaned on first mortgages in Kinsley Township, 1876–1905.

Year	%	Year	%	Year	%
1876	27	1886	65	1896	—
1877	24	1887	76	1897	—
1878	66	1888	96	1898	—
1879	88	1889	88	1899	77
1880	99	1890	66	1900	90
1881	100	1891	82	1901	51
1882	—	1892	74	1902	83
1883	100	1893	52	1903	20
1884	47	1894	96	1904	48
1885	60	1895	—	1905	42

Many of the western mortgage agencies lent funds in Kinsley.[25] In only three years, between 1879 and 1888, did they handle less than 40 per cent of the funds loaned there on first mortgage. But after 1890 the loans negotiated by these companies were mainly secured by farms which they had acquired through foreclosure, or else the loans represented part of the sale price of such land. Most important of the agencies was the Watkins company, which negotiated 38 first mortgage loans in the township, totaling more than $30,000.[26]

During the heyday of the western mortgage companies in 1886–1887, the newspapers of Kinsley carried the advertisements of at least nine

[24] The *Annual Reports* of the Connecticut Insurance Commissioner contain much information on the lending activities of the Hartford companies. See particularly 1875 and 1876. The lending policy of the Travelers' Insurance Company is described in the 1891 *Report*, pt. 2, pp. xxx, xxxi.

[25] The *Annual Reports* of the Connecticut Bank Commissioners (1888–1895), of the Massachusetts Commissioner of Foreign Mortgage Companies (1890–1895), of the New York Superintendent of Banking relative to Foreign Mortgage, Loan, Investment and Trust Companies (1891–1896), and of the Vermont Inspector of Finance (1889–1893) provide the most satisfactory catalogue of the more important western mortgage companies of this period.

[26] See Chs. VI, VII, VIII, X, and XIV.

loan agents representing mortgage companies, three indigenous loan companies, and three local banks. Puffing the agent of the Watkins company, the editor of the Kinsley *Graphic* remarked, "L. W. Higgins is loaning money at rates so low, and on time so long that the borrower is liable to forget that he ever has it to pay." [27]

The commissions of the mortgage companies and of the local agents were often taken in the form of second mortgages. At least 50 per cent of the second mortgages filed from Kinsley Township were of this type. The notes backed by such mortgages seldom stipulated a rate of interest but merely specified that the principal should be paid in ten equal semi-annual installments.

The role of the local banks in the field of farm credit is worth mention. Two banks were started in Kinsley during the 1870's. The Edwards County Bank began operations as a private bank, and the Edwards Mercantile Bank grew out of the merchandising business of R. E. and W. C. Edwards. In 1882 the Edwards County Bank was organized as a state bank with a capital of $32,000. By August 1887 this capital had been increased to $100,000 and was supposedly paid up in full. In January 1885 the Kinsley *Graphic* listed among the things that it would like to see, "At least two more banks in Kinsley so that money could always be had whenever good security was furnished." [28] In March 1887 the Kinsley Exchange Bank was organized as a state bank with a capital of $50,000. The officers of this institution came from Iowa. During July of the same year the Edwards Mercantile Bank was reorganized as the First National Bank of Kinsley. Thus by the summer of 1887 there were three incorporated banks at the service of the community.

Before 1900 the three banks made only eight loans on real estate security in Kinsley Township, totaling $14,563. With the exception of three loans to the amount of $4,733, these loans were secured by second mortgages, which bore a higher rate of interest than did the first mortgages of the same years. If the $3,439 lent by R. E. Edwards in the same period and secured by six first mortgages and five second mortgages is added in, the total of $18,002 allocated by local credit agencies still falls far short of the $30,000 which the J. B. Watkins Land Mortgage Company provided. The local banks were more interested in short-term loans backed by chattel or personal security than in first mortgage farm loans.

[27] Kinsley *Graphic*, Mar. 12, 1886.

[28] *Ibid.*, Jan. 16, 1885.

But the local banks did perform a useful function in the long-term field by acting as local agents. The Bank of St. John, which was located in an adjoining county, the Edwards Mercantile Bank (later the First National Bank of Kinsley), the Kinsley Exchange Bank, and the Edwards County Bank all acted as local agents for either mortgage companies or individual eastern investors. If the local banking institutions and capitalists did not themselves lend heavily on first mortgage, they did perform the function of bringing lender and borrower together. In 1887 there was a tendency for this function to be shifted to a separate agency. The Kinsley Loan and Trust Company, which was organized in 1887, numbered R. E. Edwards of the Edwards Mercantile Bank among its directors, and the Edwards County Investment Company, organized at about the same time, listed L. G. Boies of the Edwards County Bank on its governing board. This development marked an attempt on the part of local men to enter the investment company field and to obtain all instead of merely a part of the middleman's fee or commission on funds which were sent from the east for investment.

The local banks shared in the financial misfortunes which struck down the nonresident investment and mortgage companies. The Edwards County Bank entered receivership in 1890. It was followed three years later by the Kinsley Exchange Bank. The First National managed to survive the year 1893 and reorganized under a state charter in 1894.[29]

As in Pebble Township, the provisions in the mortgages filed on land in Kinsley Township varied in their complexity. When the mortgagees were local men, the indentures were usually simple and short—a mere transfer of the security in case the terms of the note should be broken. The mortgages filed by eastern investors or their agents were much longer and filled with a greater variety of terms which were designed to safeguard the mortgagee.

In most of the forms used by eastern investors the failure of the mortgagor to pay taxes and the insurance on improvements promptly broke the contract. But in no case of foreclosure in the township did such grounds serve as the sole excuse for bringing suit. Generally a clause was included, "waiving all exemption, appraisal and redemption laws." Often the mortgagor authorized the levy of $25.00 for attorney fees, in case he allowed his loan to become delinquent. It was generally speci-

[29] For a comment upon the difficulties faced by a national bank in this area see the Kinsley *Graphic*, Feb. 16, 1894; also Malin, "The Kinsley Boom," p. 184.

fied that default would entitle the mortgagee to immediate possession of the premises and rents, issues, and profits. This clause had no validity in so far as actual possession upon default was concerned, but evidently did insure that the purchaser of the sheriff's deed was entitled to any crops growing on the security when the deed was issued. Most mortgages recorded by nonresident mortgagees named a place of payment in the eastern United States—a provision which insured that the mortgagor would pay the cost of exchange.

More unusual was the clause used by J. B. Watkins in 1879, which specified that payment should be made "in gold coin of the United States of America." This proviso reflected the fear of Watkins' conservative clients that the monetary supply of the county was about to be inflated by large infusions of greenbacks or silver.[30] In 1879 E. R. Robbins inserted a clause seldom found in the mortgages on the land in Kinsley Township when he bound several mortgagors to "break forty acres of prairie within a year."[31]

The average rate of interest on first mortgage loans stood in 1876 at 11 per cent. From this figure the trend was downward until 1889, when the rates of interest on nine mortgage loans averaged 7.4 per cent. Over the next ten years the annual average stood between 8 and 10 per cent, with the exception of 1892, when twelve loans called, on the average, for interest payments at the rate of 6.9 per cent per annum. The loans of this year were unusual in that five of them were drawn by the J. B. Watkins Land Mortgage Company and the Jarvis Conklin Mortgage Trust Company on holdings which they had foreclosed. Since the companies were themselves paying the interest on these loans, the rate was put at 6 per cent, which had little relation to the price of funds in Kinsley Township. After 1899 the average rate on loans recorded from Kinsley Township hovered around 7 per cent, with the twenty-two loans which were recorded in 1905, averaging 6.6 per cent.

The mortgagees of Edwards County consistently wrote a higher rate of interest into their contracts than did nonresident lenders. Invariably the papers negotiated by the western mortgage companies called for the lowest average rate of interest. In 1887, for example, six loans obtained in Edwards County averaged 9 per cent interest, the over-all average of the thirty-seven first mortgage loans recorded from the township

[30] Edwards County, Mortgage Register A, p. 300; J. B. Watkins to Edward Lewis, Philadelphia, Pa., Dec. 2, 1878.

[31] Edwards County, Mortgage Register A, p. 344.

stood at 7.5 per cent, the thirty mortgages held by nonresidents of Kansas averaged 7.3 per cent, and the twenty-two loans negotiated by the mortgage agencies called for an average rate of 6.9 per cent.

Table 25. Interest rates in Kinsley Township on first mortgage loans.

	No.	Rate—%		No.	Rate—%
1876	4	11	1891	6	8.3
1877	7	10.7	1892	12	6.9
1878	12	11.5	1893	9	8.2
1879	21	9.8	1894	10	8.3
1880	13	9	1895	2	10
1881	4	8.5	1896	1	10
1882	2	11	1897	1	8
1883	2	9	1898	2	10
1884	5	9.2	1899	4	8.4
1885	14	8.4	1900	9	6.9
1886	33	7.8	1901	18	6.9
1887	37	7.5	1902	10	6.5
1888	13	7.6	1903	21	7.3
1889	9	7.4	1904	17	7.2
1890	4	8	1905	22	6.6

Comparison of the resident and nonresident rate is complicated by the problem of the commission. The local resident who lent his own funds or accepted a mortgage as part payment in a real estate transaction probably did not take a commission from the mortgagor. Both the mortgage companies and their local agents received commissions. Often these commissions were paid by the mortgagor in addition to the rate of interest specified in the note and mortgage. But the companies might subtract their commission, and at times that of their local agents, from the interest payments called for by the note and mortgage. A 9-per-cent loan negotiated by the Watkins company in August 1887 was of this last type.[32] The note specified 9 per cent, and that was the actual cost to the borrower. Significantly, the average rate on the six loans obtained locally in that year was also 9 per cent. The local and nonresident level tended to equate at a common level. The local lender was neither more merciful nor more obdurate than the nonresident when specifying the interest which his debtor must pay.

[32] See letters of D. M. Sprankle to L. W. Higgins, Kinsley, June–Sept. 1887 in Watkins Papers.

In general, the loans of local lenders were for a shorter period of time than those of nonresidents. The early western mortgage companies almost invariably loaned for periods of three or five years. Such companies avoided repayment by installments because of the extra accounting involved. As competition among the companies stiffened, however, an increasing number of them gave "one year after the first interest payment the privilege of paying $100, or multiples thereof, on the principal upon sixty days notice" or some similar privilege. Such provisions became almost standard with major lending companies after 1900. Indentures specifically calling for repayment of the principal over a term of years also became very common after the turn of the century.

Of the 343 first mortgages analyzed in this study, judgment was rendered against the debtor on 52, or 15 per cent. Only 46 sheriff's deeds were issued, however, since a few mortgagors managed to buy the judgment before the judicial sale or compromise the case in some other way. One sheriff's deed represented the foreclosure of three first mortgages obtained by the same mortgagor on different portions of his property. Thirty-one first mortgages were terminated by the mortgagor deeding over his property to the mortgagee, his agent, or the holder of a second mortgage. Undoubtedly such deeding represented failure no less than did the issuance of a sheriff's deed. Seventy-nine first mortgages, or 23 per cent of those filed in Kinsley Township, ended, therefore, with the mortgagor giving up his land. Some half-dozen purchasers bought encumbered land and assumed payment of first mortgages while giving second mortgages of their own as part of the purchase price. Foreclosure of the first mortgage wiped out the equity of these individuals as well as that of the original mortgagors.

The mortgages negotiated in two groups of years were particularly ill fated. Of 36 first mortgages filed in 1879 and 1880, there were 18, or 50 per cent, which were closed out by foreclosure or deeding. Liquidation took place during 1880, 1881, and 1882, for the most part. Of the 88 first mortgages recorded in 1886, 1887, and 1888, there were 40, or 45 per cent, which terminated disastrously. These last contracts were liquidated between 1889 and 1893—the years when Populism was born and flourished in its greatest vigor.

In all, 67 individuals and one corporation contributed to the total of 79 mortgage contracts which ended in failure. They sacrificed 22 tracts which had been acquired under the provisions of the homestead acts.

Reduced to percentages, 33 per cent of the homesteaders who gained title in the township and 58 per cent of the homesteaders who attempted to raise funds by mortgaging failed to retain their homesteads because they could not repay their loans. Four out of the 8 pre-empted tracts which were mortgaged were surrendered, representing 20 per cent of all pre-emptions and 50 per cent of the pre-empted tracts placed under mortgage by their first owners. The 3 timber claims lost by mortgagors formed 27 per cent of all timber claims and 60 per cent of the timber claims which were mortgaged in Kinsley Township. Of 2 commuted homesteads, which were encumbered by their first owner, one was lost. Among the 61 individuals who obtained railroad land deeds, 10 lost all or part of their land by foreclosure. This figure represented 16 per cent of the successful purchasers of railroad land and 53 per cent of those who mortgaged their land after obtaining title from the Santa Fe. Four of the 10 were nonresidents. In total, 41 out of 79 securities were lost by the individuals who had obtained title to them from the federal government or the Santa Fe.

Thirty-eight securities, or 49 per cent of those lost by foreclosure, belonged to secondary buyers who had obtained title from the grantees of railroad and government. Since most of the mortgaging which ended disastrously was done by 1890, this last percentage illustrates the speed with which land in the township was transferred out of the hands of its original owners.

Of the 67 unsuccessful mortgagors, a significant percentage of individuals were not primarily farmers. Three mortgagors were women, of whom 2 were not residents of the county. At least 5 men were nonresidents at the time of mortgaging and so remained during the life of their mortgages. Three of this group were obviously speculators in railroad land. Two of the local mortgagors were bankers connected with the banks which failed in Kinsley. One local farmer died and the mortgage was foreclosed after his death. Another mortgagor was a tavern keeper attempting to make a living in a state bent on becoming dry. One had attempted to run an ice business in Kinsley. The corporation which negotiated an unsuccessful mortgage was the county fair association. Thus 14, or 21 per cent, of the unsuccessful mortgagors were not full-time farmers in the community. At least 5 others had sold out to a second party before suit was begun, but the assignees failed to meet the payments on the mortgages which they had assumed.

Among the 67 noncorporate individuals who surrendered land by foreclosure or deeding, 36 appear on the agricultural rolls of one or more of the censuses taken in 1875, 1880, 1885, and 1895. The acres reported in crop by these mortgagors were compared to those of the other farmers in the administrative township of Kinsley. The crop acres of all the operators at each census date were totaled and the farmers divided into upper, middle, and lower thirds. Hay acreage was not counted, since it represented prairie hay for the most part, while acreages in corn, wheat, sorghum, millet, flax, barley, and oats indicated that the settler had broken the prairie. In some cases such a technique would deal unfairly with stock farmers, but for the most part the farmers reporting large numbers of stock from Kinsley Township also reported large crop acreages.

Of the 36 unfortunate mortgagors who are listed in the returns of the agricultural censuses, 14 reported crop acreages in the upper third at the time of the census, immediately prior to their failures. Twelve fell in the middle third and 10 in the lower third. It is probably safe to assume that the crop acreages of most of the unsuccessful operators who were not caught by a census would fall in the middle or lower brackets, since their residence in the township was either of interrupted or short duration. But the 14 who reported a crop acreage in the upper third represented 21 per cent of all the mortgagors who failed. It was evidently not enough to have land broken and in crop. Misfortune could strike the large operator as well as the small one in an area where drought might bring crop failure in two or three successive years.

That a settler lost land by foreclosure or deeding did not necessarily mean that he failed as a farm operator in the community. Of the 67 who lost land, 8, or 12 per cent, survived the loss of their security and remained as farm operators in the township. One settler sacrificed 80 acres of railroad land but retained control of 240 acres which he obtained under the homestead and timber culture acts. In 1905 he reported a farm unit of 1,120 acres, of which 320 were in field crops.

M. E. Hetzel reported a farm of 160 acres in 1875, but not until 1878 did he enter eighty acres as a homestead and buy the other eighty acres under the terms of the pre-emption act. He mortgaged his pre-empted land immediately for $500 and raised $300 locally against his homestead, although he did not receive his final certificate until 1884. By 1885 he had acquired title to four quarter sections near his original holding. One of these he mortgaged for $360 in 1880. In 1884 the Kinsley *Graphic* reported that Hetzel had lost $3,000 worth of stock from the plague—presumably Texas fever.[33] In the same year his $500 mortgage went to judgment but he succeeded in purchasing it. During 1885 and 1886 Hetzel raised $4,500 on the security of first mortgages in the east and negotiated another $4,000 worth of second mortgages with local parties, including two of the banks. In 1886 and 1887 Hetzel deeded 640 acres of land to the Edwards County Bank. In 1892 Hetzel began to buy back this acreage, using a $4,800 mortgage as partial payment for the first 320 acres. By 1905 Hetzel could report a farm unit of 1,000 acres, of which 440 were in field crops, as well as a herd of 150 cattle.

Table 26. Crop acreages reported in Kinsley Township.

	Operators	Crop Acres		
Year		*Lower third*	*Middle third*	*Upper third*
1875	33	4–8	9–19	20–60
1880	134	5–25	26–53	54–645
1885	60	15–60	61–109	110–315
1895	81	4–74	75–153	154–672

Despite the exceptions, most of the mortgagors who lost their security disappeared from the records of the county thereafter. Many of them had left long before suit was brought against them. At least 80 per cent of the foreclosure cases in the township were extremely simple; the defendants neither demurred, answered, nor appeared. One settler, however, enlivened the court record with a show of patent bad faith when he mortgaged a quarter section adjacent to his own and later asserted that the indenture was a forgery.[34]

It is possible to exaggerate both the amount of land which was under mortgage at any one time and the amount of land which was foreclosed or deeded. On January 1, 1890, there was probably more land under mortgage in the township than at any other time during the thirty years of this study. Most of the mortgage debt of 1886 and 1887 which was to be liquidated in the early 1890's still stood untouched. Yet at this date only some 12,000 acres, or between 40 and 45 per cent of the agricultural land in Kinsley Township, was mortgaged. A veteran real estate

[33] Kinsley *Graphic*, Nov. 21, 1884.

[34] *McConaugh* vs. *Badger*, filed in District Court, Edwards County, Kansas, 1890.

agent of Kinsley estimated in his biography that in "1893 and 1894, at least two thirds of the land in the county . . . had been taken over and was owned by the loan companies and private investors all over the east."[35] The actual figures for Kinsley Township are hardly so generous. In all, the security surrendered by the sixty-seven individuals and one corporation over thirty years totaled some 11,200 acres, or 40 per cent of the agricultural land in the township.

Some attempt to correlate foreclosures and deeding with soil fertility in Kinsley Township may be made. North and west of the Arkansas River variations in soil and topography are not extreme enough to check against the statistics of foreclosure and deeding. The sand hills southeast of the Arkansas are infertile, and the fact was recognized locally at an early date. The editor of the Kinsley *Graphic* wrote in 1887, "Occasionally some eastern sucker gets salted upon a slice off the juicy side of the sand hills lying along the course of the Arkansas River. There are two things those hills are especially adapted to; one is to raise goats upon and the other is to be exchanged for eastern property belonging to parties who have never saw them."[36]

But mortgagees or their local agents paid too little attention to such local wisdom. Four sheriff's deeds were issued on some 600 acres of land in the sand hills. In addition, one mortgagor deeded a quarter section to his mortgagee, while the Interstate Galloway Cattle Company deeded 960 acres of land in the area to one of its creditors. Some 1,700 acres, therefore, out of 2,350, or 72 per cent of the sand hills area, changed hands by foreclosure or deeding in the thirty-year period.

By no means all of the foreclosed and deeded land was in the hands of the mortgagees at any one time, although the largest part of it was in their custody during the early 1890's. Until the market for real estate collapsed utterly in the early 1890's, the mortgage agencies and eastern investors sought to sell their foreclosed land as rapidly as possible. The mortgage companies at least were under considerable incentive to reconvert their operating capital to liquid form. When the land market disappeared, the investors and the receivers, or liquidating agencies of the mortgage companies, held until there was a market and then resold. By 1897 the local farmers were again interested in adding to their holdings. Their purchases before 1905 significantly

[35] G. E. Wilson, *Autobiography* (Kinsley, 1947), p. 27.
[36] Kinsley *Graphic*, Apr. 22, 1887.

altered the size of farm units in Kinsley Township. Where 52 per cent of the farmers reported a farm unit of 160 acres or less in 1895, ten years later only 23 per cent of the farmers reported such a unit, while 64 per cent listed farms of 241 acres or more, as compared with 39 per cent at the previous census date.

It is obvious that the liquidation in the 1890's was a painful one in Kinsley Township, although proportionately a smaller group of mortgagors failed than was the case in the early 1880's. The statistics of deeding and foreclosure cannot show the instances where proceedings were begun and dropped before a journal entry was made. Nor do they show the number of mortgagors whom one more poor crop would have placed in like case with their less fortunate fellows. On the other hand, the bald totals of mortgages and encumbered acres do not differentiate between the genuine settler who mortgaged to equip his farm or to tide himself over a poor year and the petty speculator who mortgaged merely to support himself until he could sell his holdings. When the schemes of the latter type went astray, he was quite willing to pull out and leave his creditor to realize upon the security.

Although willing enough to accept the services of the moneylender, the farmers of Edwards County were also willing to criticize him. By 1884 the leading capitalist of Kinsley had been dubbed "old three percent a month." [37] When L. G. Boies ran as Republican candidate for the state legislature in 1888, he was opposed because he was a banker.[38] In 1892 a local paper reprinted the accusation of the Mankato *Advocate* that the mortgage companies were foreclosing in an effort to obtain the land of the farmers of Kansas, although actually the foreclosures were to ruin the companies no less than the farmers.[39] Popular feeling against the moneylender contributed no little to the unrest which saw the local Farmers' Alliance men take over the county offices and newspaper during the early 1890's, and help to send Jerry Simpson to Congress from the seventh electoral district.[40]

[37] *Ibid.*, Dec. 5, 1884.

[38] Kinsley *Banner-Graphic*, Oct. 12, 1888; Kinsley *Mercury*, Nov. 15, 1888.

[39] Kinsley *Graphic*, Apr. 29, 1892.

[40] See Malin, "The Kinsley Boom," pp. 173–178.

A SUMMING UP

DURING the years between 1873 and 1895 an increasingly large proportion of the population of the plains states came to hold an agrarian interpretation of the moneylender.

The Populist and his predecessors considered the mortgage to be a sign of distress.[1] There were few among them who would suggest that a mortgage might fulfill a useful or productive function for the debtor. But if the mortgage indicated that the borrower was in distress, it represented profit for the moneylender. A memorial of the National Farmers' Alliance in 1889 pictured the growing indebtedness of the country, while in the meantime, "there are two classes of men who seem above the reach of adverse financial fortune, money-lenders and railroad owners. Of these the former are reaping a harvest of wealth unprecedented in the history of the world." [2]

[1] National Union Labor Platform given in *Kansas Farmer* (Topeka), July 19, 1888, p. 10. See also *ibid.*, Sept. 4, 1878, p. 310, Apr. 23, 1890, p. 8, July 2, 1890, p. 8; *Nebraska Farmer* (Lincoln), Sept. 20, 1888, p. 847 (quoting the *Country Gentleman*, Oct. 24, 1889, p. 736).

[2] *Alliance* (Lincoln), June 12, 1889.

Agrarian writers devoted much of their energy to proving that the interest rate was high.[3] Occasionally correspondents described rates of interest as high as 36, or even 50 per cent.[4] Generally they confined themselves to arguing that the use of money was bought too dearly. In extreme cases they asked why the security which was good for a loan at 10 or 12 per cent was not equally good for a loan bearing 5 or 6 per cent? [5]

The moneylenders were able to maintain high rates of interest because a highly organized money power had arisen in the United States after the termination of the Civil War.[6] The way in which this money power was organized and the tactics which its members followed made it virtually "a conspiracy against the people." [7] The association which the farmers regarded as synonomous with the organized money power was the American Bankers Association.[8] In hazy fashion the agrarians believed that the money power was composed of eastern capitalists who employed western agents as their tools. Occasionally a real estate agent or lawyer was admitted to be his own master, but the western bankers and moneylenders were regarded alike as proven agents of the money power. The price which the farmer paid for his borrowed money was a monopoly price.

When the representatives of an aroused people attempted to check the onslaught of the money power its agents rallied to corrupt the legislators. The will of the majority was perverted by the lobbying activities of the few. The editor of the *Kansas Farmer* wrote in 1889, "What was settled by the last Legislature was, that the combined forces

[3] *Nebraska Farmer,* Aug. 1877, p. 3, Jan. 15, 1891, p. 37, Jan. 22, 1891, p. 51; W. M. Taylor in *Farmers' Alliance* (Lincoln), Jan. 10, 1891; *Kansas Farmer,* July 12, 1888, p. 14, Dec. 6, 1888, p. 6, Dec. 27, 1888, p. 10, Oct. 2, 1889, p. 8, Oct. 16, 1889, p. 8.

[4] P. P. Fadely, in *Kansas Farmer,* Nov. 8, 1888, p. 6; W. M. Taylor in *Farmers' Alliance,* Jan. 10, 1891.

[5] *Kansas Farmer,* Nov. 6, 1889, p. 8, Aug. 16, 1888, p. 3, Sept. 20, 1888, p. 11.

[6] *Ibid.,* Apr. 12, 1888, p. 6, July 26, 1888, pp. 6–7, Apr. 23, 1890, p. 8.

[7] *Ibid.,* Mar. 12, 1890, p. 10, Feb. 16, 1888, p. 10; James A. Hammers in Anthony *Republican,* Mar. 13, 1891.

[8] *Kansas Farmer,* Nov. 6, 1889, p. 9. See the very significant case, *Watkins* vs. *Glenn, Kansas Reports,* LV, 417–451. "These defendants further allege that the plaintiff . . . is a member of the American Banking Association, a combination and association having for its object and purpose the controlling, regulating, and fixing the amount of money in actual circulation, and for the controlling, regulating and fixing the rate of interest" (p. 418).

of a corrupt lobby in the interests of money-lenders were able to override the representatives of the people and defeat the execution of the popular will."[9] Writing three years later, the correspondent of a Nebraska newspaper, the *Farmers' Alliance,* described the moneylenders' lobby as "the largest, best organized, and most shrewdly managed lobby that infested the capital the past session."[10]

As in many lands and at many times the moneylender was painted as an unlovely figure. He was a "hyena-faced Shylock" with a singularly unattractive personality.[11] He inveigled the innocent into borrowing money when they really had no need for funds.[12] In the process of making a loan the mortgage agent carried out an investigation of the farmer's personal life that was little short of a personal insult.[13] Once the loan was made, the moneylender busied himself in plotting the downfall of the debtor. In this he was merciless. As one editor put it, "A money-lender assuming the role of a philanthropist in his business transactions is about equal to a rum seller preaching temperance."[14] Shylock was eager to assume ownership of the security if at all possible since he obtained the land for a mere fraction of its value. He was, therefore, little better than a thief.[15] But not content with obtaining the farms of his debtors at well below their true value, Shylock often took a personal judgment against the unfortunates whom he had dispossessed.[16] The borrower might eventually lose much more than his farm.

Admittedly derived from a sampling of limited materials, the findings presented in this study have been less sensational than were these charges of the agrarian radicals.

The western mortgage was a recognized form of investment in the

[9] *Kansas Farmer,* Oct. 2, 1889, p. 8. See also *ibid.,* Nov. 6, 1889, p. 9.

[10] John Stebbins in *Farmers' Alliance,* May 7, 1891.

[11] Samuel Sinnett in *Kansas Farmer,* Mar. 5, 1879, p. 77; *Nebraska Farmer,* Jan. 30, 1890, p. 82.

[12] *Kansas Farmer,* Feb. 12, 1879, p. 56, Sept. 20, 1888, p. 11, Nov. 13, 1889, p. 4; Anthony *Republican,* Jan. 1, 1890, R. W. Drake in *ibid.,* Mar. 6, 1891.

[13] *Kansas Farmer,* June 5, 1878, p. 206.

[14] William Peffer in *Kansas Farmer,* Oct. 16, 1889, p. 8.

[15] *Nebraska Farmer,* Feb. 21, 1889, p. 125.

[16] James A. Hammers in Anthony *Republican,* Feb. 13, 1891; Anthony *Republican,* Feb. 19, 1892, quoting Topeka *Capital;* Article 10 of resolutions adopted by the Farmers' Alliance, Osborne, Kansas, Mar. 28, 1890, reported in *Kansas Farmer,* Apr. 16, 1890, p. 4. For the problem in Nebraska see A. E. Sheldon, "The Deficiency Judgment: A Story of the Nebraska Nineties, the Farmers' Alliance and the Supreme Court," *Nebraska History Magazine,* XIII (Oct.–Dec. 1932), 289–294.

eastern states during the 1850's. By the early 1870's large corporations like the life insurance companies of Hartford and private investors like the Davenports of Bath had sent millions of dollars west for investment. Smaller investors had made their contributions as well. The motives of such investors are easily explained. Money loaned on the security of agricultural land in the newly opened western states returned a handsome rate of interest. Moreover the security, if wisely selected, tended to appreciate in value, thereby guaranteeing that the lender would not experience loss if forced to assume ownership.

As the experience of the Davenports showed, however, the extra interest obtained was not all profit. To avoid loss the investor had to master the peculiarities of real estate law in the western states and refuse to accept land as security when the title was faulty or confused. Much hinged on the efficiency and caution of the agents whom eastern investors chose to gather loan applications and to administer the completed loans. These had to bear a safe relation to the total value of the security and, once negotiated, be kept under constant surveillance lest the borrower destroy the value of the security or fail to pay his taxes. The amount and type of control exercised over their agents by eastern lenders might well mean the difference between profitable returns and disastrous losses.

During some thirty years of lending operations in Illinois, Iowa, Kansas, and Nebraska, the Davenports used at least twenty agents for varying periods of time. No more than three gave complete satisfaction. Despite their close knowledge of conditions in the western states, the Davenports once discovered that they had entrusted funds to an ex-cattle rustler, while one agent left precipitately for California and another was incarcerated by the state of Kansas shortly after the termination of his service. He was a wise lender, therefore, who made frequent trips to the west and checked the work of his agents at first hand. Expenses incident to such supervision must be remembered in evaluating the return from western interest rates.

If eastern capitalists wished to lend funds to the more responsible members of western communities, they had to convince them that they were sincerely interested in the well-being of the borrower no less than in the interest rate. If some of the agents of the Davenports are to be believed, the New Yorkers were able to retain the respect of western borrowers while obtaining a return which stood above the legal interest rate. At times, moreover, they compounded the interest when calculating the debts of delinquent borrowers. Evidently some debtors at least were more interested in clement treatment during times of agricultural depression than in the lending rate. That the easterners obtained returns above the legal rate stands as an illustration of the ineffectiveness of usury laws in general.

Almost invariably moneylending involved traffic in land which had been acquired by foreclosure or deeded to the lenders by dispirited borrowers. The Davenports constantly informed both local agents and borrowers that they did not desire to obtain real estate. Since they also speculated in western land on a considerable scale, they possessed the knowledge to administer foreclosed farms as profitably as possible. But experience dictated their policy. The 106 farms, foreclosed in Illinois, Iowa, Nebraska, and Kansas, on which detailed cost and sale figures are available, returned profits which compared unfavorably on the average with the interest rate on mortgage security.

Because they controlled large funds of capital, investors like the Davenports found it profitable to recruit western agents with care and supervise them closely. Others hungered no less for the interest rates to be obtained in the west but lacked the capital which would make it worth while for them to visit the west frequently and allow them to command the undivided loyalty of western agents. Moving with increasing frequency in eastern business circles during the early 1870's were numbers of mortgage brokers, recruited in both east and west, who eagerly sought potential investors of this type. The activities of one such broker, J. B. Watkins, have been described in some detail. Located at Lawrence, Kansas, Watkins exploited the mortgage business to the full, as he sold over $12,000,000 worth of mortgages backed by western farms between 1873 and 1894.

Brokers of Watkins' type vastly increased the market for western mortgages, as they tapped the coffers of eastern educational and charitable institutions on the one hand and the small savings of professional folk on the other. Competition caused the mortgage salesmen to increase the services which they performed for investors. They offered to supervise loans completely so that investors need only deposit interest and principal payments as they arrived. To relieve further the minds of their clients some brokers gave their own guarantee that borrowers would meet their obligations. Where Watkins originally had accepted drafts for investment and then sought satisfactory mortgages to fill the order, rivals accumulated funds of capital and built up stocks of mortgages in their own names which they tendered to investors immediately on demand. To raise the capital for such business methods, many brokers, including Watkins, incorporated their businesses. The guarantee was transmuted by the mortgage companies when they issued their own debentures against a backing of farm mortgages deposited with a trustee. By the mid 1880's numerous companies were operating through the plains states of the American west; they played a significant role in financing the attempt to subdue the plains to the plow.

Many of the investors whom the mortgage companies enticed into their fold were captivated by western interest rates but completely ignorant of the problems of western farmers and the nature of the mortgage business. Unlike the Davenports—who weighed the merits of the western mortgage on the basis of years of hard-won experience—they believed that they had struck a mother lode among investments. Disillusion came in short order. Between 1888 and 1894 most of the mortgage companies failed. The causes were closely interrelated. The officers of the mortgage agencies had misunderstood the climatic vagaries of the plains country. They had competed vigorously to finance the settlement of the areas beyond the ninety-eighth meridian. Beginning in 1887 the plains country was struck by a series of disastrously dry years. The effects of drought and short crops are sometimes alleviated by high prices but in these years the prices of agricultural products were depressed. Many of the settlers along the middle border failed to meet their obligations. The real estate holdings of the companies grew to unmanageable size; operating capital was converted into land at a time when the bottom had dropped out of the land market.

Other factors had contributed to the disaster. The competition among the mortgage companies forced them to give considerable freedom of action to their local agents. Generally working on a commission basis, many of these individuals were overgenerous in approving loans. So rapid had been the rise of the companies that careless business practice and even fraud was common. As for Watkins, he had invested his ample profits in other enterprises, and the 1890's found him with insufficient liquid capital to meet current obligations. Although his judgment is open to question, it is impossible to charge him with either dishonesty or the intent to defraud.

Intensive research in individual townships allows us to place the various aspects of land credit in perspective. Between the two townships studied, there were significant variations in climate, soil, topography, location, and in the racial origins of the settlers. In both areas transportation facilities were excellent during the settlement period. Both lay within the bounds of railroad land grants, and most of the government land was settled under the terms of the homestead act of 1862 in each case. In Kinsley Township, lying between the ninety-ninth and one-hundredth meridians in Kansas, the 160-acre homestead was more important because of the large number of veterans among the original settlers. In Pebble Township, lying in the sixth range of townships from the eastern boundary of Nebraska, the eighty-acre homestead predominated.

In both townships mortgage filings showed a cyclical pattern. The first peak coincided with the first large issue of final certificates to settlers by the district land office. In both townships the second peak coincided with the real estate boom of the mid 1880's. After the liquidation of the boom, filings in Pebble Township tended to stabilize, whereas the number was rising sharply again in Kinsley in 1905. In general, mortgage filings, the amount of capital borrowed on agricultural land, and the percentage of agricultural land encumbered, all showed more violent cyclical swings in Kinsley Township than in Pebble Township. Taking the amount of encumbered agricultural land as an example, the figure stood at 42 per cent in Kinsley Township in 1890 and only 27 per cent in Pebble. So drastic was the liquidation in the western township that only 15 per cent of the agricultural land was encumbered in 1900, while the figure in Pebble Township had actually risen to 29 per cent.

Of the settlers who took up government land in Pebble Township, 47 per cent eventually mortgaged all or a portion of that land. In Kinsley 55 per cent of the original settlers on government land eventually mortgaged all or a part of their holdings. Of those who bought railroad land, 21 per cent of the purchasers paid cash in Kinsley Township, while only 4 per cent took advantage of cash terms in Pebble Township. In both townships the greatest number of those who failed to complete contracts were actual settlers. In Kinsley 32 per cent of those who purchased land from the railroad eventually mortgaged all or a portion of it. In the eastern township the equivalent percentage was 17 per cent. Individuals who purchased railroad land, therefore, had less recourse to mortgage credit after obtaining title than did those who obtained title directly from the government.

Apparently the settlers in both Kinsley and Pebble Townships had much the same reasons for mortgaging their land. More than 50 per cent of the settlers who mortgaged during the first peak of filings did so to finance the purchase of improvements, farming equipment, or supplies. Within a few years, however, the mortgages negotiated to refinance other obligations or as part of the purchase price of land together totaled more than 50 per cent of all the indentures recorded. Little support can be found in either township for the theory that homesteads were frequently commuted to pre-emptions by borrowing on mortgage, thereby allowing hard-pressed settlers to obtain title as a prelude to a quick sale. The percentage of commuted homesteads mortgaged immediately upon receipt of title was no greater than the percentage of homesteads so encumbered.

Nonresident capital made a significant contribution in the financial history of both townships. When any considerable number of mortgages were filed in the years before 1900, more than 50 per cent of them were financed by nonresidents of the state. Even in 1905 nonresident capital still provided more than 30 per cent of the land credit in both townships. The significance of the nonresident lender was reflected during the 1880's in the large number of mortgage companies whose names appear in the mortgage records of both counties in which the sample townships were located.

Local banks loaned little of their own capital on the security of agricultural land in either township. Bank funds were used instead in the more profitable chattel and personal fields. In both townships, however, the banks did provide land credit, since they acted as local agents for mortgage companies and other nonresident lenders. Bankers from the county seat in both cases helped to organize mortgage companies which transacted business within the sample townships.

Interest rates in both townships followed similar patterns. In the early years the rate stood at, or very close to, the legal maximum allowed by the usury laws of Kansas and Nebraska. Had the commissions of mortgage agents been added to the interest rate in these years the mortgagors would be shown to have paid more for their money than the law allowed. By 1905 rates had been cut approximately in half in both townships. Despite the difference in location, there was little variation in the rates charged in the two townships until the liquidation of the late 1880's. Subsequently rates were somewhat higher in Kinsley than in Pebble Township. In 1905 the average rate in the western township stood at 6.6 per cent, while the average rate in the Nebraska township was 4.9 per cent. Undoubtedly the difference in the two rates was a reflection of the comparative risks of lending in the two townships.

If we except the first few years in both townships and the occasional year in which a small number of mortgages were filed, the rates charged by nonresident investors and those obtained by resident mortgagees bore a constant relationship to each other. The rate charged by residents stood above the rate charged by nonresidents by the amount of the commission paid to the mortgage agent.

The greatest contrast between the credit history of Pebble Township and that of Kinsley Township is found when one compares the relative success and failure among the mortgagors. During thirty years some 23 per cent of the farmers who borrowed on first mortgage in Kinsley Township lost their security. During a thirty-seven-year period in Pebble Township only 3 per cent of the borrowers on first mortgage failed to retain their security. The deviation from the long-run average was by far the most spectacular in the western township. Fifty per cent of the first mortgages which were negotiated during 1876 and 1877 were closed out by foreclosure or deeding. Of the first mortgages filed during 1886 and 1887, 45 per cent ended in the failure of the mortgagor. The mortgagors of only one year were particularly unfortunate in Pebble Township. Of the first-mortgage debts recorded in 1876, the borrowers failed to repay 17 per cent. But significantly, in both townships a higher rate of failure was found among mortgagors in the very early years of settlement than in the fractious days of Populism.

Taking the homesteaders as an example of those who obtained government land, 33 per cent of those who successfully completed their homestead duties in Kinsley Township subsequently failed to redeem all or a part of it from the claims of mortgagees. By contrast only 4 per cent of the homesteaders fared so unfortunately in Pebble. Yet the statistics of failure in Kinsley Township hardly reflect a mass exodus. Undoubtedly Wilson's estimate that two-thirds of the land in Edwards County was held by mortgagees in 1892 represents an interpretation common among the local historians of the plains country. But in Kinsley Township at least, the ownership of no more than 40 per cent of the agricultural land was transferred to mortgagees during the whole period of study. Since the amount of land found to be encumbered in Kinsley Township was almost identical with the percentage of land encumbered in the county as a whole according to the census of 1890, the foreclosure figure for the township may be closer to the actual truth in the county as a whole than Wilson's estimate. Nor did a foreclosure always signify that a settler had failed. Almost 30 per cent of the unsuccessful mortgagors in Kinsley were nonfarmers or nonresidents or else were local men who saved part of their real estate.

Did the western settler borrow because he was in dire distress? The motives of mortgagors are difficult to discover. In the township studies certain classes of mortgages were distinguished. Mortgages negotiated as part of the purchase price of land and those floated to finance existing obligations could be identified without great difficulty. But in the early years of settlement especially, a substantial number of mortgages did not fall into these categories. Undoubtedly some of them financed the purchase of improvements, equipment, and supplies. Others were possibly negotiated to support the settlers after a disastrous crop year or other catastrophe. Unfortunately, these distress mortgages cannot be segregated from those designed to finance improvements or the purchase of equipment by a mere examination of the county records.

During the census of 1890 an intensive study was made of the mortgage debt in 102 counties of the United States where investigators sought to learn at first hand the motives of those who mortgaged their property. One of these sample areas, Pawnee County, Kansas, lay adjacent to Edwards County on the north. If truthful answers were obtained, no more than 9 per cent of the mortgages in effect in 1890 in that county could have been negotiated to relieve conditions of acute financial distress. More than 90 per cent of the first mortgages had been negotiated for purposes which were ostensibly productive.[17] Presumably much the same situation held true in other counties of the middle border country.

Strikingly apparent in both Kinsley Township and Pawnee County was the high percentage of mortgages which were obviously negotiated to finance the purchase of real estate. During the boom years of

[17] United States Census Office, *Report on Real Estate Mortgages in the United States at the Eleventh Census: 1890* (Washington, 1895), pp. 286–287.

1885, 1886, and 1887, almost one-half of the mortgages from Kinsley Township were of this type. The mortgages of these years were the ones which the Populists were to cite as proof that the farmer was sinking into peasantry; their liquidation sparked the agrarian effort to amend the credit code. Eventually, it is true, many of these mortgages were a monument to shattered hopes, but they were not an indication of distress in the beginning.

The agrarians argued that interest rates were high. As we have seen, J. B. Watkins obtained returns which at their maximum approached 16 or 17 per cent in the mid 1870's—this rate to be split of course between the mortgage agency and the eastern investor. In all probability the total rate stood between 10 and 12 per cent in western Kansas during the late 1880's. Meanwhile rates had dropped in central Kansas, where money could be obtained on the security of good land at a total cost of between 8 and 9 per cent. Such rates appear high by modern standards but low in comparison to the rates of 36 per cent and more which prevailed in eastern Kansas and Nebraska during the 1850's. Rates in Kinsley and Pebble Townships in 1905 were about one-half what they had been in the early years of settlement. That the interest rate lagged in its decline behind falling agricultural prices is probable, but rates were never stable at a high level over any period of time in the plains states during the time span of this study.

Certainly the mortgage brokers believed that the interest rate was tumbling in precipitate fashion. Their effort to hold a uniform rate in Kansas during the early 1880's was an outgrowth of such thinking. The attempt, however, was a failure. The supply of funds was too large and the agencies of credit too varied to allow a monopoly rate. Conversely the western state legislatures had little success in establishing a legal maximum when that rate stood below the market rate. Of the four states studied in some detail in this investigation, only in Nebraska did the usury law perhaps have some effect in holding interest rates down.

No evidence has been uncovered to show that the eastern investor was any more avaricious than local lenders. Local rates usually ran above nonresident rates by an amount approximately equivalent to the amount of the commission obtained by the eastern investor's agent.

Evidence has been presented to prove that the mortgage agents did seek to influence the course of legislation. Yet the funds subscribed by major mortgage agencies for that purpose were of small amount, and it is doubtful if the "timely *douceur*" had as much influence as did the simple argument that strict collection laws would draw nonresident capital into the state. Moreover, most lawyers and bankers profited from the mortgage business through the fees which they derived for legal services or from commissions earned as local agents. Legislators from these professions hardly needed bribes to guard the interests of the mortgage trade. Nor, in the final analysis, is lobbying proof positive of either corruption or predatory motives.

Undoubtedly the mortgage agents did advertise their wares vigorously during the years when funds were available in large amounts. J. B. Watkins, for example, scanned the assessment rolls for potential borrowers. But never was a loan made knowingly when the borrower's ability to repay was in doubt.

The agrarian was on particularly shaky ground when he charged that the nonresident investor or the mortgage agent desired his land. The business experience of the Davenports shows that foreclosed land was actually a less profitable investment than the sound mortgage which was repaid when due, while foreclosures on a large scale could bring bankruptcy to an agency such as that operated by Watkins. Nor was the nonresident investor as likely to covet the borrower's security as the local lender; the latter had no problem of absentee administration to solve.

As for the use of the personal judgment, the borrower who was hopelessly in arrears was usually allowed to deed his land to the lender. In return for the deed such borrowers sometimes received a small consideration which was roughly equivalent to the cost of foreclosure. On the other hand, J. B. Watkins once used the threat of the personal judgment to force borrowers to stay on their land and to make an attempt to pay out. In so far as this writer could find, the personal or deficiency judgment was followed up only where it was thought that the borrower had sought deliberately to defraud the lender. Yet there were brokers who dealt in judgments; the use of the judgment is a subject which demands further study.

Although evidence has been presented to show that the mortgage foreclosures of the late 1880's and early 1890's probably fell with less severity on actual farmers than the Populists claimed, a substantial proportion of settlers did lose their security to mortgage holders. Approximately one-third of those who obtained title to government land in Kinsley Township lost it to lenders. But no one villain can be blamed for this high turn-over.

The fundamental motives of the settlers must bear closer scrutiny than most historians have bothered to give them. Undoubtedly some of the settlers were petty speculators who hoped to obtain title to tracts of land with a minimum of work and investment, only to sell their holdings when the pressure of settlement had caused land values to rise in their communities. Mention of such petty speculation occurs frequently in the frontier press. Settler speculators used the mortgage to assist them in surviving until a purchaser appeared. However, they would hardly admit their true intent when asking for a mortgage loan. The mortgage agencies desired to lend to settlers who wished to sink in their roots and who could be expected to remain on their land despite periods of economic adversity. The petty speculator therefore mortgaged ostensibly to obtain funds for the purchase of equipment or improvements. But if dry years halted the flow of settlers into his area or if his funds ran out before he found a purchaser, he had little compunction about selling his land to the mortgage agency which had financed him. We cannot estimate the exact percentage of such borrowers along the middle border during the early period of settlement, but their activities swelled the foreclosure totals which the agrarians used so tellingly. One official of the J. B. Watkins Land Mortgage Company blamed the exodus of borrowers from western Kansas during the late 1880's and the early 1890's almost entirely on "the character of the settlers."

Other settlers failed because they had miscalculated the ease with which farms could be carved from the tough sod of the plains country. Despite the terms of the homestead law of 1862, the settler still needed capital before his land could be brought into production. Nor could this need for capital be minimized in the plains country by a system of subsistence farming. The subsistence farmer had little place in the plains states. The range of crops was limited. The settler had to grow maximum amounts of the crops best adapted to the climate, sell the harvest, and purchase his other needs with the proceeds. Not only was he now exposed to the full play of the business cycle, but also he had little guidance in selecting the crops which were most suitable for the area. During the 1870's and 1880's these crops were the subject of hot argument, and once these were selected the cultural practices best adapted to a subhumid environment again provided food for discussion. It is understandable that a settler could in all honesty play a losing gamble with borrowed chips.

Perhaps only in exceptional circumstances could a settler obtain an economic unit for farming in the plains environment unless he added to his original claim or claims by purchase. The land laws were geared to the subhumid agriculture of the Mississippi Valley; more acres were needed west of ninety-eight. Out of the liquidation of the 1880's and 1890's came larger farming units but at no little cost to the pioneers.

It was only logical that those who failed should vent their spleen on the mortgage agencies and nonresident lenders. Many of the settlers of American origin had been reared in a subsistence agricultural economy where the antibanking traditions of Jacksonian democracy were still strong. Such men found the business methods of commercial farming irksome. One of the less advertised functions of the mortgage companies was to assist in teaching business methods to reluctant farmers. The efforts to enforce prompt payment and other business procedures appeared to be no more than petty tyranny to many borrowers. If they failed, the foreclosure proceedings merely confirmed their hostility toward the mortgage broker and the investor.

Yet, if the mortgage agencies have perhaps received too much blame for the debacle of the 1880's and 1890's, they cannot be completely exonerated of guilt. Their local agents functioned with too little supervision and gouged commissions from the settlers which they did not report to the companies. Company officials like Watkins subscribed to the belief that rainfall rose with the increase in cultivated acreage in an area. In this they were innocent of intent to deceive, for the view was widely held, but the result was disastrous. Today the banker assures himself that the borrower will use his loan in a fashion that will give a reasonable chance of success. The mortgage companies made no real effort to do so, although the occasional investor did suggest that settlers should be supervised in the uses to which they put the proceeds of their loans.

Finally, the eastern investor deserves consideration. During the 1880's the eastern lender was often ignorant of western economic life—content merely that his mortgages returned a fine rate of interest. In the veritable craze for western mortgages which developed in the mid

1880's, the financial responsibility of the mortgage companies went at first unchecked. Charlatan companies were allowed to survive and by their competition force sounder companies into reckless practices. When depression revealed the excesses of the business, enthusiasm was replaced by panic. Mortgage companies found themselves in a hopeless position between borrowers who could not pay or had abandoned their farms and investors who would not wait for their money. Leniency was well nigh impossible. But undoubtedly in the debacle of the 1880's and 1890's there was much more of misunderstanding than malice or avarice, more of ignorance and undue optimism than calculated fraud and, as always on the frontier, much more of suffering than the bountiful resources of the United States might seem to demand.

BIBLIOGRAPHY

Primary Sources

MANUSCRIPT COLLECTIONS

William W. Backus Papers. Library, Yale University, New Haven, Conn. Several hundred letters between agents of the Showalter Mortgage Company and Backus written in the years 1887–1891. This collection well illustrates the impact which the failure of the western mortgage companies had upon eastern investors.

Douglas Boardman Papers. Collection of Regional History, Cornell University, Ithaca, N.Y. Six boxes of correspondence which includes letters from agents on the Wisconsin frontier concerning moneylending, 1850–1855, and from loan agents in Iowa and Kansas, 1884–1890. Letters of 1890 include a few from E. L. Williams, the treasurer of Cornell University, describing mortgage investments of Cornell University.

Cousens Papers. Manuscript Division, Baker Library, Cambridge, Mass. Some 100 letters of Enoch and F. H. Cousens, Kennebunkport, Me., relating to mortgage investments in Colorado, Minnesota, and Dakota, 1885–1904.

Davenport Collection. Collection of Regional History, Cornell University,

Ithaca, N.Y. Thirty-three letterpress books, letter books, ledgers, etc., and over 6,000 deeds, land contracts, etc., related to the landholding and moneylending activities of John and Ira Davenport of Bath, N.Y. A smaller collection of similar material was examined at the office of the Davenport Estate, Bath, N.Y., and several hundred letters were made available to the writer at the office of Richards and Keene, Fremont, Neb.

Thomas Ewing, Jr., Papers. Kansas State Historical Society, Topeka, Kans. Nine hundred and nineteen letters written by the members of the law firm of Sherman, Ewing and McCook of Leavenworth, Kans., 1857–1861, containing some references to the land warrant business and territorial conditions generally.

Gates-Moore Papers. Collection of Regional History, Cornell University, Ithaca, N.Y. Nine boxes of the correspondence of a Savona, N.Y. family, including letters from loan agents in North Dakota and Michigan, 1891–1900.

Nathaniel Gordon Papers. Manuscript Division, Baker Library, Cambridge, Mass. Several hundred letters to Nathaniel Gordon of Exeter, N.H., relating to land speculation and moneylending in Iowa, Minnesota, and Nebraska. Useful mainly for the years 1852–1857.

S. N. Hawkes Papers. Kansas State Historical Society, Topeka, Kans. Fourteen letterpress books showing the growth of an eastern brokerage business, 1872–1888.

Carter Kingsley Papers. Collection of Regional History, Cornell University, Ithaca, N.Y. Ninety-eight manuscript boxes and thirty large boxes of correspondence and other material relating to the business of three lawyers of Bath, N.Y., Charles F. Kingsley, his son Carter Kingsley, and Reuben Robie, as well as some forty letterpress books of outgoing letters. From the mid 1870's to 1920 this material contains considerable information on the western mortgage investments which all three lawyers made on behalf of themselves or their clients.

H. Miles Moore Papers. Kansas State Historical Society, Topeka, Kans. Letter Book from Office of Van Doren and Havens, Leavenworth attorneys. References to real estate and mortgage law and moneylending during the 1860's.

R. E. Moore Collection. Nebraska State Historical Society, Lincoln, Neb. Between 300 and 400 volumes of examiner's reports, ledgers, etc., belonging to the Security Investment Company, organized in the 1870's by R. E. Moore at Lincoln. A few hundred pieces of correspondence were examined at the home of W. H. H. Moore, Martel, Neb.

C. H. Van Wyck Papers. Library, University of Kansas, Lawrence, Kans. Seven boxes of papers formerly held by Van Wyck's executor. A few letters deal with Van Wyck's early moneylending activities on the Nebraska frontier.

J. B. Watkins Papers. Library, University of Kansas, Lawrence, Kans. Some 500 letterpress books, ledgers, etc., along with 480 boxes of the incoming correspondence of one of the largest of the western mortgage companies.

CORPORATION RECORDS

Aetna Life Insurance Company, Hartford, Conn. Mortgage registers, 1867–1900; also real estate record, vols. I and II.

Atchison, Topeka and Santa Fe Railroad Company, Topeka, Kans. Land grant tract book and volumes of sales records held in the tax division.

City Bank Farmers' Trust Company, New York, N.Y. This corporation is successor to the Farmers' Loan and Trust Company and as such made available its files relating to the J. B. Watkins Land Mortgage Company.

Connecticut Mutual Benefit Life Insurance Company, Hartford, Conn. Bond and mortgage loan ledgers, 1867–1900; also a historical file containing several hundred pieces relating to the development of farm mortgage lending by the company.

Phoenix Mutual Life Insurance Company, Hartford, Conn. Mortgage investment registers, 1861–1900; also assorted books of applications, real estate accounts, etc.

Union Pacific Railroad Company, Omaha, Neb. Tract books of the Union Pacific land grant in Nebraska.

MORTGAGE COMPANY ADVERTISING LITERATURE

Corbin Banking Company, New York and Boston.

Ten Per Cent Mortgages. 1874. Baker Library, Cambridge, Mass.

Testimonials. 1885. Baker Library.

Globe Investment Company, Boston.

Annual Report, 1887. Baker Library.

Jarvis, Conklin and Company (later Jarvis Conklin Mortgage Trust Company of New York and Kansas City).

Alfred Fryer. *The Great Loan Land.* 1887. Library of Congress, Washington, D.C.

Lombard Investment Company, Wichita and Kansas City. Three *Annual Reports* and nine assorted advertising brochures are held at the Baker Library. Of special interest is a *Report to Stockholders and Security Holders of the Lombard Investment Company Resident in Philadelphia and Vicinity Held at the Merchants' Exchange on Thursday May 5, 1892.* Irregularities in the administration of the company were alleged.

New England Loan and Trust Company, Des Moines.

How We Make Loans and How We Take Care of Loans. 1883. Also two similar brochures of 1884 and 1887. Baker Library.

Mr. Edward Atkinson Explodes Some Popular Errors. 1894. Cornell University Library.

Showalter Mortgage Company, Wellington, Kans., and Boston. Testimonial pamphlets, one of 1885 and one undated. Baker Library.

J. B. Watkins Land Mortgage Company, Lawrence, Kans.

Perkins vs. *Watkins in Magistrates Court; The President of the Western Farm Mortgage Co. F. M. PERKINS* vs. *J. B. WATKINS, Libel Suit for $10,000 Damages.* Lawrence, Kans.: The Company, 1887. University of Kansas Library.

Testimonials. 1892. University of Kansas Library.

Homes in Kansas. 1898. University of Kansas Library.

UNITED STATES DOCUMENTS

Bureau of the Census. *U.S. Census of Agriculture, 1950.* Vol. I. "Counties and State Economic Areas." Pt. 12. Washington, 1952.

Census Office. *Report on Real Estate Mortgages in the United States at the Eleventh Census:* and *Report on Farms and Homes at the Eleventh Census: 1890.* Washington, 1895.

Department of Agriculture *et al. Physical Land Conditions Affecting Use, Conservation and Management of Land Resources: Edwards County, Kansas.* Manhattan, 1944.

Department of Agriculture *et al. Dodge County Soil Conservation Guide.* Undated.

Department of Agriculture *et al. Soil Survey of Dodge County, Nebraska.* Washington, 1918.

Kansas census rolls, 1860, 1870, 1880. Held by the Kansas State Historical Society, Topeka, Kans.

Land office tract books for State of Nebraska. Held by the Nebraska State Historical Society, Lincoln, Neb.

Land office tract books for State of Kansas. Held in the National Archives and the Department of the Interior, Washington, D.C.

Senate Executive Document No. 61, 47th Congress, 2d Session, vol. III, (1882–1883), 41–49. "Report of Special Agent William W. Burke to the Commissioner of the General Land Office."

STATE DOCUMENTS

Connecticut.

Annual Report of the Bank Commissioners (1888–1895).

Annual Report of the Insurance Commissioner (1871–1895).
General Statutes, 1888.

Illinois.
Public Laws, 1867, 1879.

Kansas.
Biennial Report of the Banking Commissioner (1892, 1894).
Census rolls, 1865, 1875, 1885, 1895, 1905. Held at the Kansas State Historical Society, Topeka, Kans.
Journal of House of Representatives, 1855[–1900].
Laws and Revised Statutes, 1855[–1900].

Massachusetts.
Acts, 1889.
Annual Report of the Commissioner of Foreign Mortgage Companies (1890–1895).

Nebraska.
Journal of House of Representatives, 1855[–1905].
Laws and Revised Statutes, 1855[–1905].
Nebraska Department of Agriculture and Inspection *et al. Nebraska Agricultural Statistics, Annual Report, 1951.* Lincoln, 1953.
Nebraska Legislative Reference Bureau. *Nebraska Blue Book.* Lincoln, 1938.

New York.
Annual Report of the Superintendent of Banking relative to Foreign Mortgage, Loan, Investment and Trust Companies (1891–1896).
Laws, 1890.

Texas.
General Laws, 1881, 1889, 1891, and *1892.*
Revised Statutes, 1879.

Vermont.
Annual Report of the Inspector of Finance (1889–1893).
Public Acts, 1888.

COUNTY RECORDS

Dodge County, Nebraska. Mortgage Registers, Deed Record, and Miscellaneous Records held in office of Register of Deeds, Fremont, Neb., covering period 1869–1905 for Pebble Township. Foreclosure cases were read in the office of the Clerk of the District Court.

Edwards County, Kansas. Mortgage Registers, Deed Record, and Miscellaneous Records held in office of Register of Deeds, Kinsley, Kans., covering period 1872–1905 for Kinsley Township. Foreclosure cases were consulted in the office of the Clerk of the District Court.

Franklin County, Kansas. Mortgage Registers, Deed Record, and Miscellaneous Records held in the office of the Register of Deeds, Ottawa, Kans., covering period 1857–1900 for Pottawatomie Township. Foreclosure cases were consulted in the office of the Clerk of the District Court.

Steuben County, New York. At the Surrogate Court, Bath, N.Y. Record of Wills, X, 262–264 and Folder 2767, Will of Ira Davenport, Sr. Record of Wills, XXXII, 267–268 and Packet A. 2789, continued to F. 29 and F. 29a, Will of Ira Davenport, Jr. Record of Wills, XVIII, 362–366, Packet A. 2781, Will of John Davenport.

COURT CASES

Beverly vs. *Barnitz, Kansas Reports,* LV, 451.

Bixby vs. *Bailey, Kansas Reports,* XI, 359.

Board of Supervisors of Tazewell County et al. vs. *John Davenport, Illinois Reports,* XL, 197.

Bowen vs. *Elder and Walruff,* Case 1359, filed in District Court, Franklin County, Kansas, 1874.

Burhaus vs. *Hutcheson, Kansas Reports,* XXV, 625.

Cheney vs. *White, Nebraska Reports,* V, 261.

Cheney vs. *Woodruff, Nebraska Reports,* VI, 151.

Dudley vs. *Reynolds, Kansas Reports,* I, 285.

First National Bank of Kansas City, Missouri vs. *Elder and Walruff,* Case 1321, filed in District Court, Franklin County, Kansas, 1874.

Girard Life Insurance, Annuity and Trust Company vs. *J. B. Watkins Land Mortgage Company,* Cases 7083 and 7370, filed in United States Circuit Court, District of Kansas, First Division, 1894 and 1896.

Lombard Company vs. *Anglo-American Land Company, Federal Reporter,* CXXXII, 721.

McConaugh vs. *Badger,* filed in District Court, Edwards County, Kansas, 1890.

Myers vs. *Wheelock, Kansas Reports,* LX, 747.

National Bank of Lawrence vs. *Elder and Walruff,* cases 2306 and 2385, filed in District Court, Douglas County, Kansas, 1872.

Ogden vs. *Walters, Kansas Reports,* XII, 283.

Philo vs. *Butterfield, Nebraska Reports,* III, 256.

Rector vs. *Rolton and Rolton, Nebraska Reports,* III, 171.

Risdon vs. *Davenport, South Dakota Reports,* IV, 555.

United States vs. *Cameron, Northwestern Reporter,* XIII, 561.

Watkins vs. *Glenn, Kansas Reports,* LV, 417.

Watkins vs. *National Bank of Lawrence,* case 6100, filed in District Court, Douglas County, Kansas, 1887.

NEWSPAPERS AND AGRICULTURAL JOURNALS (WEEKLY UNLESS OTHERWISE NOTED)

Illinois.

Champaign *County Gazette,* Mar. 5, May 14, Sept. 3, Oct. 13, 1873; Apr. 5, 1876.

Chicago: *Prairie Farmer,* Jan. 9, 1869–July 14, 1888.

Kansas.

Anthony *Republican,* Jan. 3, 1890–Jan. 18, 1895.

Atchison *Squatter Sovereign,* Feb. 3–Dec. 25, 1855.

Beloit *Gazette,* Mar. 21–Oct. 29, 1881.

Junction City *Union* (began as *Smoky Hill and Republican Union*), Sept. 12, 1861–Apr. 14, 1866.

Kingman *County Citizen,* May 7–Sept. 10, 1880.

Kinsley: *Graphic* (began as *Valley Republican*), Nov. 3, 1887–Dec. 21, 1894. *Mercury,* Aug. 18, 1883–Nov. 15, 1888. *Edwards County Leader,* Mar. 29, 1877–June 3, 1880.

Larned: *Chronoscope,* Dec. 11, 1878–July 30, 1886. *Pawnee County Herald,* May 5, 1877–Aug. 6, 1878.

Lawrence: *Republican,* May 28, 1857–May 8, 1862. *Kansas State Journal,* Feb. 21, 1861–Apr. 3, 1868. *Kansas Tribune,* Dec. 27, 1866–Aug. 27, 1874, *Journal* (daily), May 29, 1880–Apr. 6, 1894. *Journal,* Jan. 12–Aug. 16, 1888. *Journal World* (daily), Feb. 5, 1921. *Tribune* (daily), Dec. 21, 1880–Jan. 3, 1881.

Leavenworth: *Kansas Herald,* Sept. 15, 1854–Mar. 26, 1859. *Herald,* Mar. 10–July 28, 1860.

Lecompton *Union,* Apr. 28–Nov. 20, 1856.

Ottawa *Republican,* July 1, 1880–Oct. 16, 1890.

Olathe *Mirror Gazette,* Apr. 3–May 22, 1884.

Paola *Miami Republican,* Aug. 19, 1871–Aug. 2, 1873.

Topeka: *Kansas Farmer,* May 1863–Aug. 1899 (broken file of monthly and semimonthly until 1874, thereafter a weekly). *Kansas Commonwealth* (daily), Feb. 8, 1872–Feb. 11, 1879, *State Journal* (daily), Jan. 6, 1881. *Capital* (daily), Aug. 8, 1888, Jan. 13, 1893, Jan. 24, 1895.

Nebraska.

Brownville: *Nebraska Advertiser,* Aug. 15, 1856–Jan. 10, 1863. *Nebraska Farmer* (monthly), Oct. 1859–May 1862.

Fremont *Tribune,* July 24, 1868–Dec. 31, 1892 (occasional year missing).

Nebraska City *News,* Feb. 28, 1857–Sept. 29, 1860.

Neligh *Advocate,* Aug. 6, 1881–Nov. 30, 1890.

Omaha *Bee* (daily), Jan.–Mar., 1871, 1873, 1875, 1877, 1879.

Lincoln: *Nebraska Farmer,* Jan., 1877–Jan. 14, 1897 (a monthly until 1880's). *Alliance, Farmers' Alliance and Nebraska Independent, Alliance Independent,* May 24, 1890–Apr. 6, 1893.

Miscellaneous.

New York *Times* (daily), Nov. 11, 1877, Dec. 27, 1887, Jan. 23, Feb. 6, Feb. 11, 1888. Yankton *Press and Dakotan* (daily), Oct. 30, 31, 1882.

Financial journals.

Boston, *United States Investor,* May 19, 1894–Feb. 29, 1896, May 14, 1914.

Chicago, *Spectator,* vol. XX (Mar. 1878), monthly.

ARTICLES IN CONTEMPORARY PERIODICALS

Allen, William V. "Western Feeling towards the East," *North American Review,* CLXII (May 1896), 588–593.

Bemis, Edward W. "The Discontent of the Farmer," *Journal of Political Economy,* I (Mar. 1893), 193–213.

Dunn, J. P., Jr. "The Mortgage Evil," *Political Science Quarterly,* V (Mar. 1890), 65–83.

Frederiksen, D. M. "Mortgage Banking in America," *Journal of Political Economy,* II (Mar. 1894), 203–234.

Gladden, Washington. "The Embattled Farmers," *Forum,* X (Nov. 1890), 315–322.

Gleed, Charles S. "The True Significance of Western Unrest," *Forum,* XVI (Oct. 1893), 251–260.

Harger, Charles M. "The Farm Mortgage of To-Day," *Review of Reviews,* XXXIII (May 1906), 572–575.

Mappin, W. F. "Farm Mortgages and the Small Farmer," *Political Science Quarterly,* IV (Sept. 1889), 433–451.

Peffer, William A. "The Farmers' Defensive Movement," *Forum,* VIII (Dec. 1889), 464–473.

Welch, Rodney. "Horace Greeley's Cure for Poverty," *Forum,* VIII (Jan. 1890), 586–593.

Secondary Works

BOOKS AND PAMPHLETS

Adams, T. S. *Mortgage Statistics and Taxation in Wisconsin and Neighboring States.* Madison, 1907. A report submitted to the Wisconsin Tax Commission. Taken from the 3rd Biennial Report of the Wisconsin Tax Commission.

Andreas, A. T. *History of the State of Kansas Containing a Full Account of Its Growth from an Uninhabited Territory to a Wealthy and Important State.* Chicago, 1883.

Bentley, Arthur F. *The Condition of the Western Farmer as Illustrated by the Economic History of a Nebraska Township.* (Johns Hopkins University Studies in Historical and Political Science, 11th ser., nos. vii–viii.) Baltimore, 1893.

Blanchard, Leola H. *Conquest of Southwest Kansas.* Wichita, 1931.

Boyle, James Ernest. *The Financial History of Kansas.* (University of Wisconsin Economics and Political Science Series, vol. V, no. 1.) Madison, 1908.

Bradley, Glenn D. *The Story of the Santa Fe.* Boston, 1920.

Briggs, Harold E. *Frontiers of the Northwest; A History of the Upper Missouri Valley.* New York, 1940.

Buss, William H., and Osterman, Thomas T. *History of Dodge and Washington Counties, Nebraska, and Their People.* Chicago, 1921.

Campbell, R. A. *Mortgage Taxation.* (University of Wisconsin, Comparative Legislation Bulletin, no. 17.) Madison, 1908.

Cather, Willa. *My Antonia.* Boston, 1946.

Connelley, William E. *A Standard History of Kansas and Kansans.* 5 vols. Chicago, 1918.

Curley, E. A. *Nebraska; Its Advantages, Resources and Drawbacks.* London, 1875.

Darrow, E. N. *A Treatise on Mortgage Investments.* Minneapolis, 1892.

Diller, Robert. *Farm Ownership, Tenancy, and Land Use in a Nebraska Community.* Chicago, 1941.

Dunham, Harold Hathaway. *Government Handout; A Study in the Administration of the Public Lands, 1875–1891.* Ann Arbor, 1941.

Eliot, Clara. *The Farmer's Campaign for Credit.* New York, 1927.

Garey, L. F. *Factors Determining Type-of-Farming Areas in Nebraska.* (University of Nebraska College of Agriculture Experiment Station, Bulletin 299.) Lincoln, 1936.

——. *Systems of Farming and Possible Alternates in Nebraska.* (University of Nebraska College of Agriculture Experiment Station, Bulletin 309.) Lincoln, 1937.

Garland, Hamlin. *Main Travelled Roads.* London, 1892.

Gates, Paul W. *Fifty Million Acres.* Ithaca, 1954.

George, Arthur F. *Annual Farm Business Report, 1951, Eastern Nebraska, 38 Farms.* (Extension Service, University of Nebraska College of Agriculture *et al.*) Mimeographed. Lincoln, 1952.

Green, Charles Lowell. *The Administration of the Public Domain in South*

Dakota. (South Dakota Historical Collections, vol. XX.) Pierre. 1940.

Herrick, Myron T., and Ingalls, R. *How to Finance the Farmer, Private Enterprise—Not State Aid.* Cleveland, 1915.

Hicks, John D. *The Populist Revolt; A History of the Farmers' Alliance and the People's Party.* Minneapolis, 1931.

Hinman, Eleanor H., and Rankin, J. O. *Farm Mortgage History of Eleven Southeastern Nebraska Townships, 1870–1932.* (University of Nebraska, Agricultural Experiment Station, Research Bulletin, no. 67.) Lincoln, 1933.

Holmes, George K. *A Decade of Mortgages.* (The American Academy of Political and Social Science Annals, vol. IV, no. 6, publication no. 120.) Philadelphia, 1894.

Humphrey, Seth K. *Following the Prairie Frontier.* Minneapolis, 1931.

Inter-State Publishing Company. *History of Logan County, Illinois.* Chicago, 1886.

Ise, John. *Sod and Stubble; The Story of a Kansas Homestead.* New York, 1936.

Johnson, Harrison. *Johnson's History of Nebraska.* Omaha, 1880.

Jones, Leonard A. *A Treatise on the Law of Mortgages of Real Property.* Eighth edition. Indianapolis, 1928.

Judd, Orange, and Company (publishers). *Mortgage Lifters: How They Paid Off the Farm Mortgage.* Chicago, 1896.

Kellogg, Edward. *Labor and Capital; A New Monetary System.* Revised edition. Edited by Mary Kellogg Putnam. New York, 1883.

McNeal, T. A. *When Kansas Was Young.* Topeka, 1934.

Malin, James C. *The Grassland of North America; Prolegomena to Its History.* Lawrence, 1947.

Malin, James C. *Winter Wheat in the Golden Belt of Kansas.* Lawrence, 1944.

Mott, T. Bentley. *Myron T. Herrick, Friend of France; An Autobiographical Biography.* New York, 1929.

Murray, William G. *Agricultural Finance; Principles and Practice of Farm Credit.* Second edition. Ames, 1947.

Murray, William G. *An Economic Analysis of Farm Mortgages in Story County, Iowa, from 1854 to 1930.* (Iowa State College of Agricultural and Mechanic Arts, Agricultural Experiment Station, Research Bulletin no. 156.) Ames, 1933.

Reed, Homer. *The Science of Real Estate and Mortgage Investment.* Kansas City, 1899.

Roberts, Millard F. *Historical Gazetteer of Steuben County, New York.* Syracuse, 1891.

Rochester, Anna. *The Populist Movement in the United States.* New York, 1944.

Ruede, Howard. *Sod-house Days; Letters from a Kansas Homesteader, 1877–78.* Edited by John Ise. New York, 1937.

Sandoz, Mari. *Capital City.* Boston, 1939.

Shannon, Fred A. *The Farmer's Last Frontier; Agriculture, 1860–1897.* (*The Economic History of the United States,* vol. V.) New York, 1945.

Trottman, Nelson. *History of the Union Pacific: A Financial and Economic Survey.* New York, 1923.

Waters, L. L. *Steel Trails to Santa Fe.* Lawrence, 1950.

Weaver, Martha. *Nebraska Farm Mortgages.* (Nebraska Studies in Business, no. 30.) Lincoln, 1932.

Webb, Walter P. *The Great Plains.* New York, 1931.

Western Historical Company. *The History of Linn County, Iowa.* Chicago, 1878.

Wilson, G. E. *Autobiography.* Kinsley, 1947.

Winn, Henry. *Mortgage Exemption and Taxation of Real Estate Only.* Boston, 1889.

Woodruff, Archibald M. *Farm Mortgage Loans of Life Insurance Companies.* New Haven, 1937.

Wright, Ivan. *Farm Mortgage Financing.* New York, 1923.

Zartman, Lester W. *The Investments of Life Insurance Companies.* New York, 1906.

UNPUBLISHED MONOGRAPHS

Beezley, E. L. "A History of Webster County, Nebraska." M.A. thesis, University of Nebraska, 1937.

Farmer, F. M. "Land Boom of Southwest Nebraska: 1880–1890." M.A. thesis, University of Nebraska, 1936.

Hollingshead, A. DeB. "Trends in Community Development: A Study of Ecological and Institutional Processes in Thirty-Four Southeastern Nebraska Communities." Doctoral dissertation, University of Nebraska, 1935.

Kellogg, R. S. "Riley County Real Estate Mortgages." M.A. thesis, Kansas State Agricultural College, 1899.

Miller, R. C. "The Populist Party in Kansas." Doctoral dissertation, University of Chicago, 1928.

Neu, Irene. "Land Credit in Frontier Wisconsin." M.A. thesis, Cornell University, 1945.

Raymond, B. M. "A Study of Political and Economic Conditions in Nebraska in the Early Nineties." M.A. thesis, University of Nebraska, 1923.

ARTICLES

Abel, Annie Heloise. "Indian Reservations in Kansas and the Extinguishment of Their Title," *Kansas Historical Collections,* VIII (1903–1904), 72–109.

Barnhart, John D. "Rainfall and the Populist Party in Nebraska," *American Political Science Review,* XIX (Aug. 1925), 527–540.

Danhof, Clarence H. "Farm-Making Costs and the 'Safety Valve': 1850–1860," *Journal of Political Economy,* XLIX (June 1941), 317–359.

Destler, Chester McA. "The Influence of Edward Kellogg upon American Radicalism, 1865–96," *ibid.,* XL (June 1932), 338–365.

Hayter, Earl W. "The Western Farmers and the Drivewell Patent Controversy," *Agricultural History,* XVI (Jan. 1942), 16–28.

Farmer, Hallie. "The Economic Background of Frontier Populism," *Mississippi Valley Historical Review,* X (Mar. 1924), 406–427.

Gates, Paul Wallace. "The Homestead Law in an Incongruous Land System," *American Historical Review,* XLI (July 1936), 652–681.

Malin, James C. "The Kinsley Boom of the Late Eighties," *Kansas Historical Quarterly,* IV (Feb.–May 1935), 23–49, 164–187.

Malin, James C. "The Turnover of Farm Population in Kansas," *ibid.,* IV (Nov. 1935), 339–372.

Malin, James C. (ed.). "J. A. Walker's Early History of Edwards County," *ibid.,* IX (Aug. 1940), 259–284.

Miller, Raymond C. "The Background of Populism in Kansas," *Mississippi Valley Historical Review,* XI (Mar. 1925), 469–489.

Murray, William G. "Problems in Using County Records in Farm Mortgage Research," *Journal of Farm Economics,* XIV (Oct. 1932), 681–682.

Preger, Dave. "Junior Lienholders and Mortgage Foreclosures," *Journal of the Bar Association of the State of Kansas,* X (May 1942), 413–419.

Ricketts, Eugene. "The Operation of the Kansas Recording Acts," *Journal of the Bar Association of the State of Kansas,* IX (May 1941), 399–404.

Rozman, David. "Land Credit in the Town of Newton, Manitowoc County, Wisconsin, 1848–1926," *Journal of Land and Public Utility Economics,* III (Nov. 1927), 371–384.

Saloutas, Theodore. "The Spring Wheat Farmer in a Maturing Economy, 1870–1920," *Journal of Economic History,* VI (Nov. 1946), 173–190.

Sheldon, Addison E. "The Deficiency Judgment; a Story of the Nebraska Nineties, the Farmers' Alliance and the Supreme Court," *Nebraska History Magazine,* XIII (Oct.–Dec. 1932), 289–294.

Ward, Charles M., and Stewart, John D. "Mortgage Assignment and the Payment Statutes," *Journal of the Bar Association of the State of Kansas,* VIII (May 1940), 488–501.

INDEX